Inside America's
Fastest Growing
Companies

# Inside America's Fastest Growing Companies

M. John Storey

**WILEY**

**JOHN WILEY & SONS**

New York • Chichester • Brisbane • Toronto • Singapore

**Library of Congress Cataloging-in-Publication Data:**

Storey, M. John, 1943–
   Inside America's fastest growing companies / M. John Storey.
      p. cm.
   Bibliography: p.
   Includes index.
   ISBN 0-471-60249-3
   1. Corporations—United States—Growth—Case studies.
2. Entrepreneurship—United States—Case studies.    3. Success in
business—United States—Case studies.    I. Title.
HD2746.S76   1989                                              88-15520
650.1—dc19                                                        CIP

Printed in the United States of America

10  9  8  7  6  5  4  3  2  1

*To Martha M. Storey*
*Friend, Wife, Partner*
*May we stay in love and*
*in business forever.*

# Preface

**W**hen I began this project, I said to my brother-in-law, Jim Edgar, whose San Francisco-based firm Edgar, Dunn, Conover is the fastest growing independently owned general consulting business on the West Coast, "Tell me about the really dramatic growth breakthroughs that your clients have experienced." He responded with a question: "Why the hell are you messing around with writing a book like this anyway? Make several million dollars in your own business and *then* write the book!"

That was a couple of years, and many interviews ago. The truth of the matter is that when I began reading other people's "post-millionaire" business success biographies, I found them, for the most part, self-serving. Many who have achieved great business success have a tendency to build paper-and-ink monuments to themselves. No such problem here. Since I still have a long way to go on the success curve, I promise that this will not be a monument to mine.

On the other hand, there has been precious little helpful analysis or insight into the entrepreneurs who are behind America's fastest growing companies. While it's true that you can read the *Inc.* 500 America's Fastest Growing Companies list annually, the *Fortune* 500 list, the *Business Week* 100 Fastest Growing list, and the *Inc.* 100 Fastest Growing Small Public Companies list, and follow Dun and Bradstreet reports till your eyes bulge, what you have in the end is an enormous mound of undigested growth data. I kept asking myself *after* reading these annual compilations, "Why?" What was the critical breakthrough that Steven Jobs experienced with his Apple concept? What was the biggest disappointment that Tom Monaghan had to overcome in launching Domino's Pizza? How prepared was Fred Smith to respond to the federal legislation that held the key to unbridled growth for his novel Federal Express service concept? The data was interesting, but the answers just weren't there.

Thus, when my friend and editor Mike Hamilton at John Wiley & Sons suggested that we do this book, I was anxious to proceed. My own credentials are modest: 10 years of publishing experience in the 1960s at Time Incorporated, a *Fortune* 500 company, and then at Hearst, at the time the world's largest private publishing corporation. Following the launch of my own first entrepreneurial effort, a newsletter, I joined one of the 1970s' fastest growing private entrepreneurial companies, Garden Way Incorporated, a manufacturer and marketer of garden products, but now, for the past five years I have been busily creating and growing my own business, Storey Communications, in Vermont. As the author of two previous books (*The Insider Buyout* and *Starting Your Own Business: No Money Down*), I've been fortunate to have received and been enriched by the literally hundreds of phone calls and the thousands of conversations I've had with people not unlike myself—entrepreneurs anxious to connect by phone, if only for a few minutes, with another lonely entrepreneur, just to compare notes. "What's working for you? How did you overcome that problem? What are you going to do next?"

These conversations have led to my own personal growth and to a much deeper understanding of the nature of entrepreneurship and business growth in America. They have also led to a rather fundamental conclusion: that virtually all growth in our United States economy is a result of those entrepreneurs. I hope this book will be helpful to: (1) entrepreneurs such as myself, seeking ideas for growth breakthroughs; (2) small business operators seeking fresh inspiration; and (3) corporate managers seeking techniques that fast-growth entrepreneurs have successfully utilized to grow their own businesses. It's about smallish businesses that are getting bigger at dramatic rates of speed. It's about big companies that enjoy recollecting what it was like when they were smaller. It's about people who know their craft pretty well. And it's about adding real value, from your own ideas, to your organization as you grow.

Every single one of the fast-growth entrepreneurs with whom we have spoken has one thing in common: Each is passionate and persistent. Passionate about their dreams and about their prospects. Persistent, particularly in adversity. You'll meet them, and hopefully make some new friends in the process. Perhaps reading about them will stimulate your own dream. What is that dream? A low-tech garden product such as Lyman Wood's Troy Bilt Rototiller? A revolutionary computer such as Steven Jobs' Apple? Creative advertising services of the type that Jim Kobs offers? You'll meet these entrepreneurs and hundreds of others in the saga that follows. By the end, I believe you'll have more new and usable ideas than you thought possible.

M. *John Storey*

*Williamstown, Massachusetts*
*September 1988*

# Acknowledgments

This undertaking was a significant one for all of us and could not have been completed without the good will and good humor of many people: To Jennifer Sara Storey for outstanding research during the summer of 1987 that took her to some of the fast-growth "hotspots" of America—from Cambridge, Massachusetts, to Boulder, Colorado, to San Francisco and the Silicon Valley and back again—in our quest for the fastest of the fast-growth companies; to Jessica Storey for a wonderful job of word processing and gentle editing along the way; to Martha Storey for her insights and help in keeping moods mellow and laser printers running; and, of course, to Matthew Storey who personally demonstrated fast growth by putting on five inches while I was writing this; to Cyndi Garrison for her spectacular text-processing skills and unfailing sense of humor even when things weren't very funny. Additionally, my thanks to Roger Crafts, Jr. of Main Street Marketing for his ability to computer access the names and addresses of so many of the fast-growth entrepreneurs that we wanted to meet; to Tom Neely, whose insights on fast-growth private companies that are thinking about going public were helpful; and to Don Dubendorf, friend and attorney, who, as always, provided valuable insights into the way people think, grow, change, and behave.

All of these skills, which these people brought to bear on this project, made the job of author a considerably easier one. For this I am grateful.

M.J.S.

# Contents

# Inside America's Fastest Growing Companies

# Introduction

**A** word about methodology. I've been reading *Inc.* magazine since its first issue. For perhaps five years, I've been fascinated by their "Fast Growth 500," and impressed by the job they did in ever so briefly profiling these private, entrepreneurial, fast-growth companies. We approached them on the possibility of cooperating with us so we could get greater in-depth stories on those people who had made the fast-growth list during the past several years.

But they're in the magazine business, and preoccupied with other things, including their *own* spectacular growth, so I quickly realized that I had to find another way to get directly to the chief executives of these kinds of corporations myself. Slightly disappointed by *Inc.*'s tepid response, I found myself sitting at my desk in Pownal, Vermont, looking out at a hillside and scratching my head, wondering how I was going to avoid hundreds of hours of thankless research digging into "standard" directories of advertisers to get chief executives' names, addresses, and five-digit zip codes and calling North Salt Lake, Utah, "information" to track down an obscure phone number. The answer came in my Saturday morning mail—a letter from a bright young entrepreneur in Scituate Harbor, Massachusetts, Roger Crafts, Jr., inviting me to "get directly to the chief executives of the fastest growth companies in America by using our data base."

Although I was initially stunned by the fortuitous circumstance, part of me really wasn't surprised at all. One of the sharpest and fastest growing segments of the publishing and direct marketing industry within the past five years has been the mailing list and service support end of it. I knew you could rent narrow, even exotic list segments (Anyone for left-handed woodworking enthusiasts, or over-80 gardeners?). In fact, when I asked Lou Robinson, a 30-year consulting veteran of the marketing field, whom he thought the best candidates were for fast-growth profiling, he said, "Take a look at the list segmentation specialists, the Compu-Names, the Smart Names, the Life Style Selectors. These are people who are not just making money but adding real value to the marketing process."

So I picked up the phone, immediately called Roger Crafts, Jr. at Main Street Marketing, and said, "Roger, let's get together." After he decided I wasn't crazy for calling him on a Saturday morning, he was happy to provide me with incredible pinpoint marketing possibilities. His company has labored over the past several years to computerize data from several sources on America's fastest growing companies. He now has a reusable asset, his own data base, which he updates annually, and which will lead inevitably to his own fast growth. His asset, renewable and rentable to me and thousands of other researchers, writers, and marketers is worth over and over again a minimum of $150 per thousand names.

Roger's Main Street Marketing simplified my research greatly. I was able to reach 600 of these companies, and about half responded to my inquiries for specific information on how their growth occurred. I followed up on the most interesting, unusual, and reflective of those and produced enough research to fill five volumes like this.

My problem now is what to leave out. If you're anything like me, time is a precious commodity, and with that in mind, I've had to be selective. So with apologies to those who responded but did not make the final list, I believe you'll find that the profiles that are included are unusually interesting and helpful.

Our approach has been journalistic, not scientific. The question I asked over and over again of these fast-growth entrepreneurs was, how, specifically, did you do it? At what point did you sense a critical marketing breakthrough? What was your toughest crisis, and how did you weather it? What products, customer, and employee approaches have worked for you?

Each of their stories is quite different. In the end, a picture of great diversity, a patchwork quilt, of Iowans, Italians, Indians, and Iranians emerged. Each entrepreneur I met was colorful (no corporate blandness here), as likely to wear jeans and loafers as gray flannels and wing tips. They were people with products having names as exotic as "royal silk" and as plain as "gummy bears," people who have made a fortune producing shiny floors. They were older people, like Cecil Hoge, who at the age of 75 flew to Milan, Italy, and cornered the market on "stomach eliminators"; young people like Kirk Cottrell of Deerfield Beach, Florida, whose "Crazy Shirts," appealing to several generations of surfers and "surf groupies," have made him a millionaire many times over while he's still in his twenties.

Our findings explode some myths, such as "If you're not entrepreneuring before you're 40, you'll never do it!" A middle-aged guy like Ray Kroc, who developed his first McDonald's franchise at the age of 51, wouldn't have even responded to that! Or "Make sure you have a good organization chart." Bill Gore developed Gore-Tex without any semblance of traditional organization.

All of these people have very deep-seated beliefs that distinguish them—people like Paul Hawken of Smith and Hawken, in Mill Valley, California, who has introduced millions of Americans to higher quality gardening tools, and achieved sales of $25 million in the process. Or like Dick Considine of Lincoln Logs Ltd., who moved from Brentwood, Long Island, to Chestertown, New York, in order to pursue his dream of building quality log homes at an affordable price for Americans who had only read of log homes in their history books. Dick's company will do $20 million in sales this year, and is now publicly traded.

Most of these people operate on instinct, feel, gut. Few are calculating, "strategic" planners. Few have studied what industries are going to be hot in the 1990s or where the jobs will be in the new century. They are people, entrepreneurs all, who through instinct and street smarts have built their dreams into small businesses—small businesses that are getting bigger and, in the process, creating virtually all of the new job growth in the American economy.

You'll be meeting winners like Jerry Hardy whose idea for selling books by subscription allowed a major corporation, which was only dabbling in books, to create a new $400 million profit center. Time-Life Books remains today, 27 years later, the dominant force in mail order book selling in this country.

And Pierre de Beaumont, whose "hard-to-find tools" idea became the Brookstone Catalog, a company that grew from a fledgling startup to $27 million in just over a decade before Quaker Oats paid handsomely for the opportunity to try to run it (which it never did as well as Pierre and his wife Deland).

You'll also meet some "losers," people whose dreams were close to being fulfilled but who have had those dreams snatched away because of inadequate control or too great a belief in people around them. And you'll see how those people resiliently start over again. You'll meet some might-have-beens, corporations that grew quickly like Radio Shack but that failed to achieve profitable growth consistently through misreading consumer signs and not fully understanding their customers' desires.

The picture you'll have by the end of the book will be one of "real folks" of average education (virtually no MBAs!), average people with good ideas who are willing to be persistent, willing to pursue their own dream. They're people who don't speak in fancy words, people with average IQs and lousy handwriting (take it from your bug-eyed author!).

This is a book that is partly authorized and partly unauthorized, but dedicated to uncovering not the "what happened?" which is available in the daily business press, so much as the "why did it happen?" Why were these people able to break through? How did they achieve success? And how can their lessons become useful for our own dreams, yours and mine? Let's go.

# How Big,
# How Fast?

I had to learn something about the gardening business when, as a green publishing trainee, the series that I was assigned at Time-Life Books was failing. The series concept had come to us from Jim Crockett, who eventually started the enormously popular "Crockett's Victory Garden," but who, at the time, was just another gardening author with a big manuscript.

He brought it to Time-Life in the hope that it could be produced as a large, single-volume gardening encyclopedia. Time-Life, which had mastered the art of continuity book selling, about which we'll hear more later, *never* saw things as single volumes. They envisioned at least 10 volumes and perhaps as many as 20. So, coming up with the seemingly generous, indeed unbelievable, sum of $100,000, Time bought all rights to Crockett's gardening manuscript with no future royalty payments, as has long been their practice.

I was a young product manager and had a chance to test my wings on this very high potential new "how-to" series, a relatively new direction for Time-Life. We would "test" in 1969, and "launch" in 1970. Now, virtually all Time-Life launches soar like eagles. *Gardening* flapped and sputtered like a turkey. Our results were dismal.

What happened? What went wrong? What had we forgotten? We were just coming off the most sensational launch in our history, *Foods of the World*, which had added not the 250,000 subscribers expected but 500,000. I had to retrace my steps, and quickly.

This included actually having to learn something about the avocation—which has now become a national obsession in America—of gardening. I hastily planted three tomato plants in the unencouraging soil of my split level "homestead" in northern New Jersey and each day watched, childlike, with apprehension and excitement as the tomato plants grew. One shot forward, creating lots and lots of buds; the second did modestly; and the third withered and faded within a very short period of time. Again I was surprised. The growing conditions were identical. The soil was the same. I had paid the same attention to them all. And yet one had shot forward and the others had not.

I began, unconsciously, to dig deeper into the nature of tomato growth. What was going on here? Having checked all possible reference sources, I went to the best gardener I knew, my father-in-law, Aulton Mullendore, who lived a few houses up the street. Now you should understand that Aulton comes from a Texas farm upbringing and has answers for just about everything. I showed him my struggling tomato patch and he looked at them soberly and then pronounced, "Well, here you have blossom end rot," pointing to some brown and black spots on the bottom of my tomato. "You can probably save it if you throw a little calcium on it. Over here you've got some cut worms. They hide during the day but come out at night and like to chop your plants right off at the surface. And this third one looks fine, growing good healthy buds, good plants, you'll be in good shape with this one but I'd remove the other two."

On Aulton's advice, out they came and the one plant left managed to produce enough for all of the pasta sauce that our young family needed for the summer and beyond. But I didn't soon forget that incident. In fact I frequently remember it when wondering why some products or businesses grow well and some do poorly. Why some grow quickly and some slowly. Why certain conditions lead to quality growth, and others to decay.

# The Unpredictability of Growth ▰▰▰▰▰

In doing research for one of the books that we recently published at Storey Communications, where we concentrate on books for country living, I learned from *The Guinness Book of World*

*Records* that "the slowest flowering of all plants is the rare Puya raimondii, the largest of all herbs, discovered in Bolivia in 1870. The panicle emerges after about 150 years of the plant's life. It then dies." On the other hand, the text goes on, "the fastest growing probably of all plant species is bamboo, which has been known to reach growth rates of as much as a yard a day, or .00002 miles per hour, and can reach a height of 100 feet in less than three months."[1]

Growth in businesses, as well as in herb and bamboo plant life, is unpredictable. I've discovered, after reading about thousands of companies and having had hundreds of conversations with business leaders, that no three companies—any more than any three tomato plants—grow the same way. Virtually all companies *want* growth. (The exception is what one economist has identified aptly as "income substitution" businesses. These are frequently "mom and pop" type stores or enterprises that are geared strictly to the production of income to cover expenses.) Some are obsessed by it. But each must develop its own growth cycle and growth curve, which, like a fingerprint, will never repeat itself anywhere else on earth.

I remember being asked to help organize a meeting at Time-Life Books in 1969 (where we eventually got rid of the "blossom end rot" affecting the Crockett series) on the subject of growth. Joan Manley, Jerry Hardy's first employee at Time-Life Books after he started it in 1961, handed me a sheet with suggested topics to cover; at the top she had scribbled, "How big, how fast?"

"What do you mean by that, exactly?" I asked.

"Well," said Joan patiently, "we're trying to get people to think in terms of where we're going but also how we want to grow. How big do we *want* to be, and how *fast* can we achieve it?"

Now one of the things I quickly learned was that a company like Time, Inc., which at the time was doing half a billion dollars annually in sales, can *will* growth. And a modest 10% in growth represents another $50 million in revenues. One of the ways it does this is by mobilizing capital resources behind good new ideas. The results, as in the case of Time-Life Books, can be spectacular. This division grew from concept in 1961 to a half billion dollars of its own by the late 1970s.

The results of such "willing" can also be disastrous, of course. The story of Time's entry into the publication of *TV-Cable Week*, called "What Happened When the Media Empire of Time-

**9**

Life Leaped Without Looking into the Age of High Tech," is the story of how at least $50 million can be invested with no return on investment but with a lot of egg left on a lot of faces.[2]

But in those days little could go wrong at Time-Life Books. We had grown from a start-up operation founded by Jerry Hardy, who had come over from Doubleday and introduced the concept, a fresh one to American publishing, of "series" publishing. Although "part works," also called "fascicles," already existed in Europe, the concept of subscribing to a series of books, sight unseen, had not been commercially proven on any large scale in the United States. Hardy had a vision, believed in it, and showed Time, Inc. and then the world how it could work—and work spectacularly.

Of course the Time-Life aegis gave the fledgling books operation instant credibility and, more importantly, instant access to millions of subscriber names, primarily from *Life Magazine*. All of the early series were called Life Libraries, and they were built around predictable, if somewhat unspectacular, concepts: The World Library, The Nature Library, The Science Library, and so on. By 1967, six years later, the business had grown to about $50 million a year and serious forward planning was being tried for the first time.

For Joan's meeting, I was asked to go back and take a look at where the business had actually come from. It was fascinating to discover that in the earliest days, before Jerry's arrival from Doubleday, those first books, *Great Religions of the World, The Epic of Man, Life on Earth, World War II,* and *The Second World War,* were no more than articles bound together from *Life Magazine*. It was hardly a dynamic, or original, publishing program. But when Jerry came aboard and began talking about product uniqueness, combined with a unique selling proposition—automatic shipment to "subscribed" customers—the business took off. The Life Nature Library, Science Library and World Library made it clear that a wholly new publishing concept had emerged.

And the biggest surprise was yet to come. By 1968 we had been publishing primarily family-oriented reference series. Nothing particularly "upscale" or specialized had been attempted. Enter *Foods of the World,* a new idea based on America's discovery of international cuisine and gourmet cooking. This culinary revolution had pushed Time-Life Books into testing the series of cookbooks, a series with novel how-to information. *Foods* was tested successfully, and off we went with a launch that produced, as I mentioned before, twice the number of subscribers we had budgeted for. There wasn't any single publishing intellect behind this series idea, and we weren't seeking Pulitzer prizes. In fact, editorial decisions were being made by management committees. Time-Life Books was even referred to by some as the "McDonald's of Publishing" because of the packaged goods appearance of our product. The literati sipping port at the Algonquin were not talking about the latest from Time-Life Books!

But *Foods of the World* showed that a strong series idea, attractively assembled, nicely packaged, and going into a new market that was more than a little curious about exotic methods of cooking could fuel enormous growth. Twenty-eight volumes were eventually produced,* and sales at Time-Life Books jumped to around $90 million in 1971. By 1977 sales had reached $200 million. By the early 1980s it was approximately $500 million.

All of this increased everyone's confidence, and we began to test a dozen new series concepts at a time.

Some series were great successes, like *Foods of the World*; others, like *Sewing,* which was launched in 1972, were real disappointments. In this latter case we were delivering books that did not match up editorially with the expectations of the hundreds of thousands of subscribers the marketers had brought on board. Others, like *Gardening,* were initially failures but became successes over time. By the end of two years, for example, *Gardening* had attained tremendous growth as a result of the explosion of national interest in gardening, together with a new lead book, *Foliage House Plants,* which beat *Annuals and Perennials* hands down. A very healthy new series was launched that eventually went to 20 books.

In the early 1970s at Time-Life Books we believed in growth. We believed absolutely that every new year would bring a new series success. In addition, we were becoming international.

---

*I had the unenviable task of having to inform the editorial department that the marketing department wanted at least 12 more titles than the original editorial prospectus called for. "All right," bellowed Managing Editor Jerry Korn without a touch of humor at one point, "if you guys want the 'Cooking of Staten Island and the South Bronx,' it's OK with us!"

11

## HOW BIG, HOW FAST?

Nearly half of our business was being done in other parts of the world, notably Japan, Latin America, and, particularly, Mexico. We also believed that growth would come from testing new business ventures ranging from audio to travel clubs.

However, our optimism was a bit premature. Costs grew to the point where industry observers could not believe their ears: "You spent $400,000 to develop, editorially, a single volume in a series?" It was unfortunately true.

Growth became uneven. Some years were successes and other years weren't. Furthermore, overseas operations were incredibly volatile and didn't become as large a part of the business as they eventually became at Time-Life Books in the late 1970s. Both because of dramatic differences in consumer taste as well as the challenge of repatriating foreign profit dollars, Time-Life Books was in for some nasty surprises in the mid-1970s. In one year alone the company went from a $40 million profit to a $20 million loss! Finally, successfully launching new ventures such as audio and travel clubs, which had little to do with publishing, proved always to be difficult. With the exception of Time-Life Music,* not a single, successful, parallel business was ever launched at Time-Life Books.

But the people at Time-Life Books were people who intelligently, and cheerfully, learned their lessons. Time-Life Books goes on today thriving, prospecting for new series hits, regaining its growth trajectory, concentrating far more on profits than revenues. It owes much of this growth spurt to the atmosphere that has prevailed since the earliest days, when a single good idea from entrepreneur Jerome S. Hardy was nurtured into a $500 million a year business.

Last October, in New Orleans, when Jerry was accepting the Direct Marketing Association's Hall of Fame Award (one of 31 ever awarded), he said simply, "Companies could learn a lot by allowing their good people with fresh ideas to experiment. They should let those people try to deliver new products that they believe the consumer wants." Jerry Hardy, now approaching 70, remains as fresh an entrepreneur as many 30-year-olds. Any corporation would be damned lucky to find a Jerry Hardy in their midst in the 1990s.

*Time-Life Music, a failure in the 1960s and 1970s has, under Paul Stewart, a true corporate entrepreneur, become a highly profitable segment within the Time-Life Books structure.

# Measures of Growth ■■■■■■■■■■■■■

How should we best define growth? How big is good? How fast is bad? What are we really talking about when we discuss it? The *Inc.* 500 has steadfastly depended on sales as an indicator of fast growth. This can be dangerous. As David L. Birch points out in his remarkable study of business growth, *Job Creation in America*, fast-growth companies are extremely volatile. His figures, based on facts compiled on 12 *million* companies in his MIT data base, indicate that although about 500,000 companies (7% of the total 7 million in the United States) grow more than 20% per year and 80,000 businesses (1% of all companies) grow at 50% per year, the average for 1987 *Inc.* Fast Growth 500 companies has been 90% a year since 1982.[3]

This volatility can lead to fast decline, decay, and even death. As Birch points out, of the 500 fastest growing companies from *Inc.*'s 1982 list, 16 have closed and he was unable to find by phone or mail another 61 of the businesses. This is a 15% "disappearance" rate—a seemingly high percentage for a group of companies that were supposed to be growth leaders.[4]

The *Inc.* approach *is* helpful in tracking the relative growth rates of the private companies in America that are contributing most of the power, fueling most of the growth in the U.S. economy. Birch's study of job creation has determined that "of the 7,000,000 U.S. companies, close to 90% employ fewer than 20 workers." This group has created far more jobs than the *Fortune* 500, which are publicly traded, large-capitalization companies. They also grow considerably more rapidly, run much greater chances of failure, and show far more adaptability than slower growth companies.[5]

Another way of analyzing fast growth is to take a look at *Inc.*'s publicly held "100" list, which also tracks sales but has one advantage over the 500 privately held fast-growth companies. That is, because net income figures are available for these public companies, we can track operating *profits* as well. It's instructive to note that some companies on the Public 100 list have performed beautifully on both the sales and earnings front. Lotus, for instance, the software development company out of Cambridge, Massachusetts, had a five-year compounded sales growth rate of 535%, putting it in the number 2 position on the list, and was able to improve its profitability from a loss of $1,145,000 in 1982 to a profit of $48.3 million in 1986.

On the other hand, the number 8 "fast-growth" company on the Public 100 list, Price Communications, a New York City–based operator of radio and TV stations, grew at a 271% sales rate but increased its losses from $242,000 in 1982 to $24,594,000 in 1986. Shareholders probably have strong opinions about how valuable that type of fast growth has been. Tracking profits in most cases is a better measure of quality growth than sales. As another business analyst, Mack Hanan, president of the Wellspring Group, a consulting corporation, puts it, "If sales growth is mistaken for true growth, as long as the sales curve is rising it will be assumed that growth is still taking place and that maturity is being deferred. But when a proper indicator of growth is used as the criterion, the presence of maturity is surprisingly revealed even as volume and share points continue to rise and market leadership becomes more firmly entrenched."[6]

Others measure growth in terms of return on investment or return on beginning equity. Every year *Fortune* does its annual "500" issue and slices assets, earnings, sales, profits, and employees into a dozen or more different performance ratios, right down to profits per employee and return on beginning equity by company. Putting this kind of data under a microscope is revealing. Also revealing is the fact that companies rarely hold their positions in the multivaried analyses from one year to the next.

Perhaps a better measure of company growth, however, is the factor of value added . . . how much more *valuable* is the company as a result of its growth. Jim Kobs, chairman of Kobs and Brady, a leading national advertising agency, speaks about the development of marketing strategies for maximum growth. "By emphasizing tactics of creative execution, direct response marketers have often neglected *marketing strategies*."[7] The author suggests seven valid questions that should be asked. When he approaches clients, Jim tries to get a sense of their fundamental growth objectives. He asks basic marketing questions of his clients, such as:

- Is it more important to build sales or profits?
- How heavily do you want to invest in new customer acquisition?

- Can present customers be profitably contacted more often with existing products or services?
- Should you try to increase the size of your product category or mine it more deeply?
- How do you position and price your product or service?
- Can your media or distribution channels be expanded?
- Should you try to add new products, launch new businesses, or develop new markets?

He concludes that the real growth companies of America, the ones that are going to be around for years to come, are those that are working to increase their customer base. Ironically, most traditional sources of venture money, of debt and equity, refuse to this day to recognize a fast-growing customer list as an asset worthy of being listed on a company's balance sheet, and under no circumstances will a bank lend any money on it. We'll look into this later in more detail in our chapter on customers.[8]

Growth is sometimes measured by how fast companies move. One of my most helpful mentors, Cecil Hoge, who built his business, Huber Hoge Associates in Long Island, by identifying products that could be brought to the American consumer quickly through space and television advertising said to me recently, "It's a foot race! Once you've identified a product that will sell, you're going to have 15 competitors on your heels. This will cause immediate, cut-throat competition, bringing the price of the product down from say, $24.95 initially to $2.95. So you'd better move quickly."

He's right. In my experience when you finally do get something hot, the imitators will be right behind. So the question on a product breakthrough becomes how quickly can you get from home plate all the way around the bases. In our own case, one of our most successful cookbook titles, *The Zucchini Cookbook*, launched in 1983, was "the original." It was based on the simple, but powerful premise that gardeners had too much zucchini in the months of August and September and didn't know what to do with it all. We felt a cookbook on this admittedly unglamorous subject could work, and after a false start, where we had given it the dull name of *Squash Cookbook*, it did spectacularly well, selling more than 400,000 copies. Today there are 10 zucchini cookbooks on the market, but ours still sells a steady 10,000–15,000 copies annually.

Other consultants look for a more qualitative measure of growth: excellence. Thomas J. Peters and Robert H. Waterman, Jr., in writing *In Search of Excellence*, created a growth business within Harper & Row, the fortunate publisher. Harper had taken a look at the property, saw "another business book," and finally decided to produce 12,000 copies in their first printing, which author Tom Peters himself thought was excessive. "I thought of who would buy the book . . . , my family and friends but after that it got murky. I thought perhaps we could sell 300–400 copies. Anything beyond that would be a surprise."[9]

What happened reflects the essence of fast growth. The hard-hitting book found an eager management audience, and a quick million copies were sold at $19.95 each. Then another million was sold, giving the U.S. economy a $40,000,000 injection at the retail level. Harper, now sensing a great opportunity, offered Warner Books (to whom they had already sold paperback rights) $1 million *to put off* the paperback publication for a year! Warner happily did, and made as much or more than they had anticipated, starting a year later. (One Warner executive said, "I haven't run into this good a deal since I heard the government was paying Kansas farmers not to produce!")

Peters and Waterman point out in the book that excellent companies also tend to be growth companies, and that innovative companies have the following characteristics:

- A bias for action
- Closeness to the customer
- Autonomy and entrepreneurship
- Productivity through people
- A hands-on, value-driven ethic
- Sticking to their knitting
- Simple form and lean staff
- Simultaneous loose and tight properties

The authors also point out that, "Every industry was once a growth industry. They start believing growth is assured and that's when their decline begins. Advances rarely come from the major companies of the industry."[10]

Laurence Shames, looking at Harvard Business School's "most successful class and how it has shaped America" in his book *Big Time*, put it this way, "The word on everybody's list was growth. Growth dictated the strategy by which business deployed its talents."[11]

Many of the companies Shames describes were looking for rapidly growing or quickly expanding industries, where many companies and many new products had a better than even chance of making it. As those industries declined, however, the losses were great. As Mack Hanan points out, even IBM was subject to this change. "Over the 1970 to 1979 period, IBM's annual rate of earnings growth was 13.5%. In 1979 it showed its first decline in 30 years. Maturity of their industry had set in, growth had been overtaken by decay."[12]

When an industry begins to shrink you clearly need a new growth strategy, unless you've taken a dominant position within that industry. Some have. For instance, in 1973 and 1978, when the wood energy business was going crazy, Vermont Castings and Consolidated Dutchwest took strong leadership positions in the industry. When the industry declined, and the number of manufacturers fell from 500 to about 5, Vermont Castings and Consolidated Dutchwest was still there, producing their high-quality product. And when IBM fell on softer times, as it did in 1985, it reduced its work force from 405,000 to 389,000 people (a decision that went against its entire history and ethic of maintaining full employment), and as a result of this overhead reduction and increase in margins, it began to increase its earnings.

# Growth in
# Nontraditional Areas ━━━━━━━━━━

New pressures for growth have recently turned people away from manufacturing and marketing and toward what Laurence Shames calls "paper entrepreneuralism."[13] "Companies used to turn a profit by the sale of products and services. Now they try to beat the game by the buying, selling, and occasional dismantling of other companies." Corporate raiding has been very much "in" during the early to mid-1980s and Hollywood's rendering of corporate greed in the recent movie *Wall Street* showed just how far some people will go to show apparent growth. The growth is only apparent, not real, because in truth no value is being added during these corporate raids. There may be one exception: corporate treasurers, 49% of whom, according to one report, fear that they're becoming very real targets of takeovers based on their company's increase in apparent growth.[14]

On the other hand, growth in the service industry has been not only real, it's been staggeringly successful. As David Birch in his research on small businesses indicates, the United States "is running a deficit in foreign trade for visible things such as machine tools and autos. We have a sizable export trade, however, some $144 billion in 1985 in what usually are called services." "The fastest growing area of world trade is invisible," said Henry Eason of the U.S. Chamber of Commerce. "You can't load it on a ship or stack it on a display shelf. We call it services and it's the area in which the United States leads the world."[15]

In my own industry, direct marketing, 21 companies made *Inc.*'s Fast Growth 500 list this year. Typical of these are companies like PC Connection of Marlow, New Hampshire, ranked number 2 in growth percentage among the 500, and Early Cloud of Newport, Rhode Island, number 28 on the list. These companies are providing valuable mailing list services to a fast-growing industry, direct marketing.[16]

Many of these direct marketing entrepreneurs are contrarian, people who prefer to go against the grain, people who commute out of the city in the morning rather than into the city. They're not unlike salmon swimming upriver, trying to avoid the pools and eddies as well as the hooks and traps. As I commuted out of New York with one of my entrepreneurial friends one morning at 7 A.M., we talked about fighting off the corporate fish (many of them sharks) coming the other way and my friend said to me, "You know, 50 million people come into Manhattan every day to call each other on the telephone."

# Planning for Growth ▬▬▬▬▬▬▬▬▬▬

Frequently businesses will call for strategic planning sessions to think about how they're going to grow. But such sessions are rarely successful in creating growth because they're based on the fallacy that new strategies cause growth! Says fast-growth consultant Hanan on this subject: "We will never reach it by traditional management strategies that deal with businesses whose rates of growth certify them as being at rest. A business at rest tends to remain at rest. A business in a growth mode tends to grow. The best way—perhaps the only way—to grow is to start the process of growth. There is no substitute for doing something. To plan growth and do nothing more simply grows the planning process. The only way to grow a business is to grow the business."[17]

I remember vividly Bob Thomson of WGBH's "Victory Garden" television program explaining to me how bulbs grow. "You can speed up the germination process of a bulb by making perfect growing conditions, artificially resulting in early blossoms indoors," said Bob. "This is great for an early surprise, but in so doing you lose the longevity of the bulb. Forced bulbs, for the most part, only bloom once. Let them grow naturally and they'll blossom year after year."

I have thought more than a little about what Bob said to me. In growing our business we don't want to try to "force it," but rather do it naturally. We started Storey Communications in Vermont in 1983, and we're going to do about $5 million in sales in 1988. Sometimes that seems like a lot, other times it seems a bit too slow. But to grow too quickly, to outrun our logistical support would be a real mistake. Quality would suffer. Customers might be abused. Our talented people would burn out.

We've had a taste of this. One of the most memorable setbacks we had came, ironically, from our first real success on our mail order catalog, "Books for Country Living." We'd been struggling for about two years with a catalog that just wasn't pulling adequately, when suddenly we hit the right formula. We went to a simple 8½ × 11-inch format, and from a one-page to a four-page ad on our best product line, a series of 100 books called "Country Wisdom Bulletins." The orders poured in. Instead of our normal two boxes of mail on Monday we got nine. We were backed up, and it got worse on Tuesday and Wednesday. It took us more than a month to get out of the hole, and unfortunately we lost many customers due to our slow turnaround on order processing and shipping. But it was a good early lesson for us. We vowed *never* to let that happen again.

And to make sure it didn't we sat down and sharpened our objectives, which came out very simply as follows:

- Quality editorial product
- High levels of customer satisfaction
- Employee fulfillment, and
- Positive cash flow

Each company defines its growth objectives differently. Lee Iacocca at Chrysler would talk about maximizing shareholder value. IBM might talk about market share and maintenance of their full employment policy, the envy of America for many years. L. L. Bean, one of the true legends of entrepreneurial America, might discuss product expertise. Privately held and approaching $500 million a year, Bean was built on a *single* quality product. That's worth pausing over for a moment.

In 1911, when he was 39 years old, L. L. Bean created the leather top, rubber bottom Maine hunting shoe.[18] In 1912 he founded his company, and if you pick up today's Bean catalog you can read his own words on his company's success: "No doubt a chief reason for the success of this business is the fact that I tried on the trail practically every article I handled. If I tell you a knife is good for cleaning trout it is because I found it so. If I tell you a wading boot is worth having, very likely you might have seen me testing it out at Merry Meeting Bay."[19] Believable, trustworthy advertising copy. Knowledgeable product expertise. Compare this to your most recent shopping experience at the local mall, and you'll see why Bean's growth isn't surprising.

But Bean's company *didn't* "take off." In fact, from 1946 through his death in 1967, gross sales moved only from $1 million to $3 million.[20] In the 1960s, when Leon Gorman, Bean's son-in-law, came in sales increased simply by everyone's working the old system harder. Gorman managed to increase sales from

$3.8 million to $20.4 million in 1974, with net profit increasing from $85,000 in 1966 to $1.3 million in 1974.[21] Nice growth, but not uncommon.

Bean's incredible growth occurred between 1975 and 1980, a period that took Bean from $30 million to $120 million and then on to $225 million in 1983.[22] To be sure, the product was unique and the Bean service was excellent, but there had to be more to explain it.

The explanation is based on a combination of external events and able entrepreneurship. The U.S. Postal Service installed the first five-digit zip code and an entirely new opportunity developed for pinpoint market segmentation. Bean took advantage of both these events under the able management of Bill End and Bill Henry in the 1970s. With enlightened management using the most precise marketing tools available, the company tested mailing list after mailing list and simply did more of what worked and less of what didn't. The company grew from its modest $30 million to nearly $500 million today.

One more aspect of the growth picture needs to be mentioned: How fast is too fast? On top of their phenomenal success, the people at Bean have been asking that question. "There is enormous pressure on us," one Bean manager said. "We are caught between making the company grow and managing the growth so that we don't strangle on it. Everyone who came up here for the good life is gone."[23]

Some companies have to consciously decide to slow their growth at some point for digestive purposes. Bean did so in 1984, when it projected a leisurely 5% growth rate.[24] Unless companies are willing to do this, the logistical props can fall out from under them. Orders can overtake capacity to process, warehouses will get stocked with products that don't match customer orders, shipments will be delayed, complaints will increase, the Federal Trade Commission will get involved, and management will have nightmares every night. Joe Sugarman, of JS & A Products, Northbrook, Illinois, made this painful discovery in the mid-1970s, when his marketing brilliance outstripped his fulfillment capacity. Customer service consultant Stan Fenvessy has become the "business healer" for many companies with sputtering fulfillment functions, or even those with 48-hour flu, such as Bean has occasionally experienced.

## HOW BIG, HOW FAST?

So we're underway with our journey into the world of fast business growth. It's clear already that there are many types and styles of growth. Some faster, some slower. Growth in sales, growth in profits, growth in ROI (return on investment), growth in ROBE (return on beginning equity), growth in customer value and satisfaction. Some of these can be translated into very positive growth for companies, some into painful growth. In the next chapters we'll see in considerably greater detail how growth unfolded at companies ranging from Book-of-the-Month Club, Domino's Pizza, Doubleday, Royal Silk, Garden Way, Hume Financial Services, and many, many others. Stay with us.

# Entrepreneurs

2

# The Nature of
# an Entrepreneur

Show me an entrepreneur and I'll show you a growth company.

Understanding the nature of an entrepreneur, what makes him or her tick, is fundamental to understanding growth in today's American economy. As we have already learned from David Birch's pioneering work, virtually all job creation in the economy is coming from firms that have fewer than 100 employees. These are not necessarily "mom and pop" donut shops that want to stay forever at 20 employees. On the contrary, these are people who are pursuing their own dreams and in the process creating opportunity, jobs, and wealth not only for many of the people around them, but for the U.S. economy as well.

This spirit is not new, or foreign, to U.S. business. Robert Dalzell, chairman of the American Studies Department at Williams College in Williamstown, Massachusetts, describes in his landmark book, *The Enterprising Elite*, an early entrepreneurial group, the Boston Associates. He writes that "between 1815 and 1861 in the U.S. there was a network of interrelated business enterprises that in many ways functioned as an economist's dream of rational organization." Behind this network were marketing, manufacturing, and financial entrepreneurs completely committed to the development of enterprise based on their own entrepreneurial behavior.[1]

**25**

## ENTREPRENEURS

We know, without even delving very deeply into 19th-century industrial history that virtually every one of today's *Fortune* 500 corporations was started by a man or woman with a singular vision. Many of these large-capitalization corporations have long since ceased to demonstrate the kind of entrepreneurial behavior that allowed them to grow rapidly in the early days under their founder's vision. But let's not forget that Time Incorporated, the Hearst publishing empire, IBM, Pan Am, General Motors, Polaroid, and many, many more corporations were, in fact, all started by a high-energy entrepreneur with an "itch."

Many of these original entrepreneurs were laughed at. The Wright Brothers were greeted with derision when they tried to fly their first airplane. Henry Ford met the same kind of skepticism with his automobile; so did Chester Carlson with his copy machine. According to Mack Hanan, all of this was "simply a continuation of the process by which human minds in business replicate the act of denying growth by 'laughing at Fulton.'"[2] Bell Telephone, strapped for cash in its earliest days, offered all of its telephone rights to the Western Union Company for $100,000. After a short consideration the offer was turned down by Western Union management, who thought the product was nothing more than "an electrical toy." Thomas Edison himself rejected talking pictures in 1926.[3]

One might conclude that the entrepreneurial process of launching a new business is inherently embarrassing. Failure is frequent. Adjustments and mid-course correction steady. Having to start all over again routine. But nearly a million Americans will try to do this very thing in the next year alone. In fact, entrepreneuring, or starting growth businesses, has become almost a national pastime. The nation's entrepreneurs are venturing as never before.

There are many reasons for all this activity. David C. Allais, president of Intermec Corporation, provides one: "Adapting new technologies to market niches is what the entrepreneur in his garage does best. He can put together a solution faster than a larger sluggish company that is not so focused."[4] Perhaps it's simply the abundance of garages in America that helps to explain our entrepreneurial bent!

In any event, the trend has even been hailed by President Reagan. In an address to young people, he asks, "Why not set out with your friends on the path to adventure and start your own business? You too can become leaders in this great new era of progress—the age of the entrepreneur."[5] Said Kevin Farrell of *Venture* magazine in the earliest days of this decade, "By almost any measure the 1980s are shaping up as the most entrepreneurial decade in U.S. history."[6] He was something of a seer.

From time to time I've been asked to lead roundtable discussions on entrepreneurial spirit for professional affiliates at the Direct Marketing Idea Exchange (DMIX) in New York City. The DMIX, founded by Nat Ross nearly 15 years ago, attracts about 100 senior-level New York direct marketing pros to its bimonthly luncheon.

We found that 85% of our roundtable group of direct marketing practitioners had formed their own companies or purchased them through an insider or leveraged buyout. Most admitted to making the move into their own businesses after years of frustration and dissatisfaction as managers or officers of larger corporations.

The consensus of the group was that the motivation to become an entrepreneur came from three sources: (1) a desire to get greater control over your own future, (2) the hope of integrating your personal life and work to a greater degree, and (3) the wish to put your personal style and touch on your own business activities. Rewards and growth of personal assets were also expected to come faster, but money and "getting rich quick" were not primary motivators.

This bias was echoed at a similar gathering in Washington, D.C., in the spring of 1988. "People aren't doing it for money," said Bill Black, partner in the McNamee Consulting Group of New York. "They're doing it for personal fulfillment." Two informal statistics supported this view: (1) Participation in the 1988 roundtable was 25% higher than it was in 1987, and (2) entrepreneurs at the gathering outnumbered corporate managers by three to one.

One roundtable group agreed that the climate for entrepreneurial startups and buyouts during the 1980s had been encouraged by three major economic trends:

1. A greater willingness by managers and investors to take personal risk than in previous decades
2. More divestitures by large corporations of small divisions

3. More available capital from traditional and nontraditional financing sources

These three major trends—entrepreneurship, deconglomeration, and available capital—are logically parallel and related. They represent the buyers, sellers, and money that are fueling much of the fast-growth boom in the United States.

# The Effect of
# Outside Events

As conglomeration reverts to deconglomeration, new opportunities have arisen and big rewards are possible for skilled and dedicated businesspeople who understand and are responsive to these opportunities and entrepreneurial trends. Such an environment should sustain the entrepreneurial boom into the 1990s and beyond.

Certainly external business conditions, business cycles, and other outside forces have a major impact on the growth, success, and failure rates of new companies. But without the entrepreneur, the agent of business change, there would be no business. As Mack Hanan put it, "The entrepreneur provides the driver for growth whose objective is profit, whose time frame is tight, and whose market sensitivity is ultra sharp."[7] Lyman Wood put it more succinctly when he asked a non-creative accountant in a corporate board of directors' meeting, "Where were you when the page was blank?"

It is a safe conclusion that some outside factors coincide with growth, some are actually responsible for it, and some simply coexist with it—but without the entrepreneur nothing would happen.[8]

Why then, do corporations, as they get larger, fail to be able to encourage the same kind of growth that new entrepreneurial ventures can? Hanan says, "When major corporations try to grow internally they fail far more often than they succeed. They fail to advocate growth. They decline its sponsorship. They fail to reward growth. They underestimate the ignition point of business growers. They fail even to buy good growth, typically acquiring businesses so closely related to their own that they are also mature or will soon become so . . . even when growth comes knocking at their door, they turn away from it."[9]

This entrepreneurial/corporate divide has never been more dramatically evidenced than in the story of Royal Silk Limited and CBS. When Pak Melwani, founder of Royal Silk Limited, launched his first space advertisement for a "Royal Silk" blouse in *Cosmopolitan* magazine back in 1978, he succeeded far beyond his expectations. "We needed about one order out of 2000 Cosmo readers to break even," said Melwani when I spoke to him. "When we got one of 666, I knew it was hot." Nonetheless, he yielded to the temptation to accept a supply/distribution agreement with corporate giant CBS, which was desperately seeking fresh product ideas. Through an intermediary, a media barter specialist named Mike Shapiro, the entrepreneur Melwani and the mega-corporation CBS were put together. The agreement called for CBS to test market Royal Silk products in major print media and Melwani to be the supplier.

But according to Melwani, "Nothing happened." There was no effort, no understanding, no launch, and no follow-up of test results. A very good idea was suddenly "withering on the vine."

Following his entrepreneurial instincts, Melwani, who was not about to let a good test result languish, created a new product, a safari-style blouse, and prepared to launch it on his own without CBS. But the lawyers from CBS got wind of the ad and immediately put him on notice that he couldn't do it.

Melwani negotiated his way out of the supply agreement, which would have led to a shifting, captive relationship, and relaunched his entrepreneurial business, which is now a $40 million plus per year *Inc.* Fast Growth 500 story. Royal Silk, located in Clifton, New Jersey, operates its catalogs and retail stores throughout the United States, and will open four new stores in 1988.

# Characteristics of the Entrepreneur ▬▬▬▬▬▬

In 1985, Stanford University's Business School sponsored a Conference on Entrepreneurship. Their findings were important.

## ENTREPRENEURS

They concluded that a "dedication to excellence and performance" is central to entrepreneurial success. Perhaps this is obvious. Not so obvious were some of the additional characteristics of entrepreneurs, including: "frequently ego-driven, impatient, reluctant to delegate, very high energy-level, thrives on stress, works and plays hard, unusually demanding of subordinates, has a sense of the core of a problem, often has a mentor, and often had an uncomfortable or not particularly well adjusted childhood or home life."[10]

Despite this lengthy list, however, no group, not even Stanford, will ever be able to completely catalog what makes for successful entrepreneurs. A. David Silver, in his book *The Entrepreneurial Life*, goes to incredible lengths to find connections between entrepreneurship and personal traits. (According to Silver, entrepreneurs are shorter, and speak faster than their corporate peers!)[11] One might just as easily ask what exactly makes for successful book titles. (Is it type face, color of jacket, title?) Only a few out of the 50,000 published each year become best sellers.

To get a better understanding of your own entrepreneurial mentality, get a sheet of paper and ask yourself the following questions. Try to be as specific as you can in answering them:

1. What functions (not titles) have you been doing for the past 5, 10, 20 years? Are they relevant to your own fast-growth business?
2. Are you active—a doer, an initiator? Or more of an administrator?
3. Are you able to deal with adversity? Able to fail and start over?
4. What are your hobbies, your passions? Can they be turned into a growth business?
5. Are you direct?
6. Are you aggressive?
7. Can you be flexible in the face of unforeseen circumstances? Do you roll with the punches?
8. Are you analytical? Are you able to get to the root of a problem? Then solve it?
9. Are you a salesperson? Have you *ever actually sold anything* before? Are you willing to go door-to-door to try?

(Two entrepreneurs, Ariane Daguin and George Faison, believed so firmly in their foie gras and imported New Zealand venison that they put $15,000 into a cart full of products, which they rolled door-to-door to get their first accounts in 1984. Now, they have above $500,000 in sales!)

10. Are you willing to make personal sacrifices for the sake of your new firm? (Almost certainly there will come a week when you will not be able to meet the payroll. This is not the worst thing in the world. It just means you may have to grit your teeth and pull your last $1000 from an already modest bank account to cover it so you can open the doors again on Monday.)

11. Are you creative? An idea person? Can you spot niches? (Norman W. Edmund did, when as an amateur photographer, he needed a special lens that stores didn't carry. He had to buy a whole set from the manufacturer in order to get the one he needed. Now his "Edmund Scientific Catalog" offers specialty lenses and thousands of other products and does $12 million annually. Son Robert Edmund told me recently, "We've just begun to explore our potential!")

12. Are you willing to do any task that comes along? (You'd better be. The advantage is that you'll learn more about your own business. But can you get beyond the ego and mental block of always having had someone else do it for you? Tom Davidson, president of Cambridge Tile Manufacturing in Cincinnati, put it this way: "At Procter & Gamble, you have a myriad of resources that you can call on for everything from a new ad to a sales letter. At a small company you don't have that. You are doing a lot more of the things you once had done for you.")

13. How do you handle failure? Not just setbacks, but real failure? Can you convert it into your next marketing success? (Recently we were asked by WBZ-TV in Boston to do a 12-minute stint on a new hot-selling book title, *The Cat Lover's Cookbook*. We went out and spent $75 on aprons and chef's hats, thinking this would be a cute way to get people's attention. The day before the presentation, the executive producer called and said we were

off. Bumped! But rather than licking our wounds, we looked at the beautiful aprons with silk-screened cats that we had created for the TV show, and decided we had a unique merchandise item. It's now one of our stronger sellers. Are you prepared to look for silver linings in black clouds?)

14. Finally, are you persistent? Do you keep coming back again and again? (My friend Harold Schwartz, direct marketing entrepreneur, once called me a "palooka bag." "Remember the old blow-up punching bags that we got when we were kids?" asked Harold. "You'd knock them down only to have them pop back at you! That's you," he went on. Do you have that kind of resilience?)[12]

The dictionary says the word *entrepreneur* comes from the French *entreprendre*, meaning to undertake. Certainly a major characteristic of entrepreneurs is their need to constantly initiate.

One of my corporate friends, a marketing manager at General Foods, told me recently, "The difference between you and me is you have to initiate everything." He's right. Nothing in small business flows in "over the transom." One business analyst has described the entrepreneur as "coach, providing motivation and pep talks. He is his own self-starter who handles his own uncertainty and depression at work and indicates that those who must look to others constantly for support are heading their own small businesses into trouble."[13]

Even the Small Businesses Administration (SBA) got into the "what's an entrepreneur" act recently by defining what, in their experience, are the five most important characteristics of an entrepreneur that correlate with success in business ventures. According to the SBA, these are (1) drive, (2) thinking ability, (3) human relations ability, (4) communications ability, and (5) technical knowledge.[14]

Americans have been fascinated with entrepreneurs since colonial days. Benjamin Franklin took a bit of paper, printing ink, and a press, and became one of Philadelphia's earliest entrepreneurs with a product called *Poor Richard's Almanac*. More recently, the rags to riches story of Lee Iacocca has captured our national imagination. Here was corporate giant Chrysler, teetering on the edge of bankruptcy, saved by the brashness and entrepreneurial qualities of a man who grew up in a tough Italian neighborhood, and who, along the way, learned the right questions to ask and what to do about the answers.

Or Steven Jobs. Starting out in a garage together with technical genius Steve Wozniak he built Apple Computer from literally nothing to a billion dollar corporation in just a matter of years. His was an overnight success, unheard of at the highest levels of competition in American business life. Why? How? As David Birch puts it, "America permits its entrepreneurs to hold onto the rewards that flow from their efforts."[15] And that's one of the reasons, certainly, why America attracts such entrepreneurs.

"We encourage striving for success and tolerate failure more than other countries do," says Birch.[16]

When I asked one of our fast-growth entrepreneurs what his description of an entrepreneur was, he amazed me by sending me a 15-page letter listing 45 different characteristics. My favorite among them was this one: "When the ball is on the two-yard line, don't risk a fumble; carry it in yourself."

Richard Considine, of Lincoln Logs Ltd. follows his own advice well. "You have to make it happen yourself," he told me recently. "Most people want to deal with the number one man . . . there are times when you must maintain personal presence and control."[17] Considine built his own log home business from scratch in 1978 and turned it into a $20 million business that's now publicly traded over-the-counter.

Many of the entrepreneurs we studied have a contrarian quality about them—they tend to struggle upstream when everything else is floating downstream. Bernard Baruch, when asked how he had become so successful and wealthy, said, "It's easy: Buy when everybody is selling, and sell when everybody is buying."[18] Entrepreneurs work when others sleep, travel when others are having dinner, plan when others entertain. They fail to notice the difference between Saturday night and Tuesday afternoon.

We certainly see this contrarian trend in our publishing business. We are serious about our "country living" publishing line. We've published gardening, cooking, building, and practical books on country living for a long time, in a slow and steady fashion. This year, with Americans showing renewed interest in all forms of gardening, most of the major New York publishers have produced their own gardening lines *and* asked us to create gardening lines for them. As gardening cools, as it does from year to year, they'll ditch those lines as though they were yesterday's newspaper, and move on to the newest, hottest thing around (the occult? new age?). Other companies, like our own, will continue to steadily mine the veins we've found for ourselves.

We still have a line of energy books (*The Wood Burners' Encyclopedia, Solid Fuels, Heat Pumps*, and others) that are sitting in our warehouse gathering dust. While Americans enjoy what Professor James MacGregor Burns calls "the champagne era," no American publisher in his or her right mind is publishing such books. Given one more good oil crisis, though (the "brut" era according to Burns), and we'll dust our "classic" titles off and trot them back out to market, where they'll find a whole new audience of readers. This technique has taken us from $1 million in 1983 sales to an expected $5 million in 1988 sales.

Another common characteristic of fast-growth entrepreneurs is persistence. In fact, this may be *the* priceless entrepreneurial ingredient. One of our fast-growth companies, Action Equipment Company, Inc. of Londonderry, New Hampshire, is headed by Francis P. Rich, Jr. His company, which retails and leases construction equipment, did $11 million in 1985 sales. Says Rich, "We simply did not know that it couldn't be done. It was a matter of attitude. Going out each day, making sure that our philosophies about the equipment rental sales and service business were being communicated properly. Even in 1980, a recession year, many customers, employees, and vendors were willing to take risks with us because of the economy. Customers were willing to buy from someone new with creative ideas. Employees were willing to share responsibility for the promise of wealth, and vendors needed product sold from inventory."

Perhaps the unwillingness to recognize just how great the risks might actually be has helped a company like Action Equipment achieve fast-growth status (number 18 on *Inc.*'s 1985 list). Apparently, relatively few people want to take on the physical exhaustion that the 20-hour daily routine of an entrepreneur regularly requires. "Add all of the normal business factors, meetings, hiring, firing, travel, hotel rooms, airports, to the need to initiate everything and an absence of staff support, and the potential personal cost of being wrong, you essentially double the load on one person," said analyst Steven Brandt.[19]

These kinds of obligations, which frequently arise in the face of adversity, cause many to drop out of the entrepreneurial fast-growth race. It certainly tests the mettle and the character of anyone who tries. Richard B. DeWolfe, president of DeWolfe New England, a firm that provides real estate and financial services, puts it this way: "Our determination to survive in the 1980–1981 housing market and to continue to pursue growth, led us to an acquisition which doubled our size and tripled our sales. That gave us new momentum and credibility with our banks and with our clients. Frequently, the greatest success will come at the time of the darkest cloud cover." DeWolfe did $12 million in 1985 sales.

Entrepreneurs are rarely bashful. When Ray Kroc, a "Multi/Mixer" soda equipment salesman before he hit the jackpot with his McDonald's fast food hamburger empire, sat down with the McDonald brothers in California, he talked with them about the two restaurants they had created in their native California. The conversation eventually came around to the possibility of this great mini success being franchised all over the country. At that point, the McDonald brothers sat back and wondered out loud, "Who would possibly want to take on such an enterprise?" "What about me?" said Kroc, unabashedly.[20]

Kroc's "caution to the winds" approach set McDonald's on the track to becoming America's most successful ever franchise operation. Today based in Oak Brook, Illinois, the company grew from nothing in 1957 to $14.3 billion in sales today. Kroc described this when he was addressing a group of graduate students at Dartmouth College in March of 1976, "You're not going to get it free, . . . and you have to take risks. I don't mean be a daredevil, that's crazy. But you have to take risks, and in some cases you must go for broke. If you believe in something, you've got to be in it to the ends of your toes. Taking reasonable risks is part of the challenge. It's the fun."[21]

# Money Isn't the Answer

As we've noted before, money does not appear to be the primary motivating factor in the entrepreneurial psyche. As David Birch puts it: "Income appears not to be their primary motivation. They are driven by a desire to create an innovative force in the corporate world."[22]

Most entrepreneurs are prepared to take considerably less than they've been used to getting in corporate environments. Jim Edgar, president of Edgar, Dunn, Conover Consultants, was a top producer for Touche Ross, one of the "Big Eight" CPA firms, in their Detroit and San Francisco offices, eventually coming to run their entire West Coast operation. When he launched his own venture, he took a third of his previous salary. Prescott Kelly, who had worked for Glendinning Associates in Connecticut, and for Playtex International in New York, bought a correspondence course business, The Institute of Children's Literature in Redding, Connecticut, taking a fraction of his previous corporate income. (Kelly's operation now does close to $11 million annually.) "We're still conservative," Kelly told me recently. "We've eliminated our long-term debt, and are building cash reserves."

Following his lead, I took half of what I had been making in the corporate world when I started Storey Communications. It turned out to be too much (!) for the new business, and I wound up taking a third! I learned what lean and hungry meant!

Many entrepreneurs will go for the first two to three years in a new venture without taking any money out of it at all. They simply get by from day to day and week to week fueled by their mission. Martin Greif and Larry Groh, both of whom came from the New York corporate publishing world, launched their Main Street Press in Clinton, New Jersey, a dozen years ago and ran "on fumes" for the first three years they were in operation. "We worked long hours and put everything back into the business," said Greif. "We researched, authored, edited, and prepared everything ourselves. We always substituted our time for money." Main Street has recently hit a major best-seller, *Dogue* (a spoof on *Vogue* magazine), and is now growing rapidly; its cofounders are now happily taking compensation.

Money isn't a primary motivator for Paul Hawken either. Hawken, whose Smith and Hawken Company in Mill Valley, California, is approaching $25 million in annual sales, eloquently states: "To see the reward of commerce as money and the risk of commerce as failure is to see nothing at all. The bottom line is down where it belongs—at the bottom. Way above it in importance are the infinite number of events that produce the profit or loss."[23]

Occasionally, an unusual pair of entrepreneurs will come along that have virtually *no* interest in becoming wealthy, and no particular vision of building a large corporation. A case in point is Vermont's own Ben Cohen and Jerry Greenfield who launched an ice cream business in 1977 in the unlikeliest of spots—a Burlington, Vermont, run-down gas station. They decided to produce the highest quality ice cream available, and drew attention to it with an old-fashioned ice cream maker in their store window. They had no intention to take on the major forces in this $2 billion a year industry, but, in fact, they've grown at such a rate that they've made the *Inc.* Fast Growth 500 list consistently. Their desire was only "for some interesting, engaging work that would tide them over."[24] Ben and Jerry's will do about $30 million this year in sales, staying nicely ahead of inflation. Their current objectives? To open a Ben and Jerry's operation in Moscow. In a recent radio interview, Cohen said, "We're taking over 45 pounds to serve as samples, including some White Russian."* Don't bet against them!

# The Desire to Succeed ▬▬▬▬▬▬▬▬▬▬

Desire goes a long way. Fast Growth 500 entrepreneur Gerard J. Schaefer, president of Moss Telecommunications Services in Grand Rapids, Michigan, put it very simply: "The single factor that was most critical to our growth was simply desiring to grow. We looked for opportunities, we took some chances, but the fundamental reason was that we wanted to grow." Moss, which provides telephone and data cable systems, did $1.3 million in 1985 sales.

Some entrepreneurs have had a larger itch than others. Tom Monaghan, president and founder of Domino's Pizza, Inc., is probably one of those. Said observer Duane Newcomb, "Monaghan had been raised in an orphanage, worked as a laborer on a number of northern Michigan farms until he was 17, then joined

*National Public Radio, March 1988.

the Marines to get his life started. Discharged from the service a few years later and flat broke, he was determined to make it big."[25]

Newcomb, who wrote a mini-biography of Monaghan, went on, "Armed with a plan and hidden managerial abilities that had never been tapped, Thomas Monaghan and his brother borrowed $500 as a down payment and opened a small pizzeria near a midwest college campus. Although handicapped by the lack of a phone, the pizza delivery business still took in $99 the first week."[26] Monaghan's real breakthrough came when he looked at his competition and developed a strategy that would help his business grow from a one-shop "peanut" to a mega-corporation ranked as the fastest growth franchise across America by *Venture* magazine in their Franchise 100 list (November 1987). This strategy included setting up outlets close to the source of greatest demand—college campuses and military bases—and operating only between the hours of 4:30 and 12:30 P.M., thus cutting on labor costs and insuring greater supervision.[27]

The plan worked. Monaghan's pizza delivery service now operates more than 300 stores in 28 states across the country. He'll do over $1 billion in sales this year. But he also leaves no stone unturned. According to Newcomb, he now "makes sure all pizzas are delivered fresh within 30 minutes by installing car delivery warming ovens, and by developing a heavy-duty corrugated box to keep the pizza hot during delivery."[28] He's underway, loaded with money, but aiming to continue his quest to dominate every pizza nook and cranny in America.

An entrepreneur who started at the other end of the American economic spectrum was Fred Smith. While a junior at Yale, Smith wrote his now famous term paper, outlining what has become the billion-dollar-a-year Federal Express business. Although the paper received only a C grade, it described the development of an overnight delivery service operating out of Memphis, Tennessee, based on a hub concept. He incorporated, raised $50–$100 million, and set up Federal Express in 1971.

The early history of the company has been widely reported. David Birch says, "Operations began on April 17, 1973 with services to 22 cities. From the first it was obvious Smith faced enormous problems, not the least of which being that few potential customers knew anything about the company. Large sums went into advertising but after a while, word of mouth produced equally good results. Business customers soon learned that Smith was as good as his word, and Federal's rapid growth prodded the other private companies to greater efforts, while attracting newcomers to the field."[29]

But Birch and most others missed the real story. According to Pete Willmott, former president and chief executive officer of Federal Express, with whom I spoke directly, Federal Express would have been a good but small growth company had Jimmy Carter not signed the Air Cargo Deregulation Act of 1977. Following the signing of that act, Smith and Willmott were able to upgrade their small aircraft fleet to jumbo jets because they no longer had to fly the mini-jets they needed under the old, stricter regulations. It was a major investment, but one that led to considerably greater efficiency and increased their ability to meet the demand their new, highly successful advertising was now generating.

This is a case where an incredible amount of research, analysis, business planning, funding, and entrepreneurial push was matched on the outside by an outside event, in this case a government deregulation, that put the company into the fast-growth mode. By 1984 Federal Express had become a $1.5 billion corporation. For the 6 months ending November 30, 1987, the company achieved $1.9 billion in sales.

Birch describes Smith this way. "He's a prime example of a reshuffler who is engaged in wedding an old concept (the mail) to a new technology (sophisticated telecommunications). One might imagine he has gone just as far as one might, given the nature of his technology."[30]

## Mastering the Fundamentals ▰▰▰▰▰▰

Once underway, the entrepreneur must attend to the details and master the fundamentals. Unlike the large corporation, where much gets delegated, the new entrepreneurial manager finds himself or herself making high-level contacts *and* emptying the garbage. Dick Considine puts it this way: "In the beginning I had to do everything for my Lincoln log home business. I designed the houses, did the sketching and blueprints, wrote the contracts, did the collections, supervised the shipments, went up and found the logs in the woods. There is no substitute at the earliest stage of your business for doing absolutely everything yourself. How can you possibly instruct an employee in how to do things if you haven't done it yourself?" Considine's attention to detail has paid off. He's now sitting on top of one of the fastest growing log home businesses in the country, based in his Adirondack, New York, dreamland.

Victor Kiam, who relaunched the Remington Razor business into growth and profitability, put it this way: "You've got to face the fact that 'the buck stops here.' The manager in a large corporation can bluff and bluff," Kiam said in an interview. "But when he runs his own ship and it is his decision, the confidence he gained by presenting his ideas to a corporate group who then made the decision is shaken because he doesn't have that corporate group to go to anymore. He sits in a little mental cubby hole of his own and he has to come up with a solution. Maybe he had some good people around him who will suggest what has to be done. But ultimately it is his decision."

Kiam suggested the loneliness of being both boss and owner, the difficulty of a corporate manager making the transformation from a player in the middle to the star at the top. "Sometimes you cannot come up with a decision based on your intellect, you have to come up with a decision based on your feelings, on emotion. Your gut is what's going to tell you what's right or wrong." Since Kiam bought Remington in the spring of 1979 for $25 million, he has doubled the work force, tripled the sales, increased productivity, and lowered prices. Kiam's Bridgeport, Connecticut–based Remington surpassed $160 million in 1987 sales.

Steve Frisbie, president of Calibrake Inc., of Independence, Missouri, one of *Inc.'s* Fast Growth 500, put it this way: "Making the transition from entrepreneur to businessman has to be the biggest single challenge that we've had. It's my belief that the quality it takes to put a company on the fast track is not always the qualities it takes to keep it there . . . usually the person that starts the growth possesses unusual strengths or insight but to keep it growing profitably you must develop your strengths and strategies beyond that. When companies fail to achieve desired growth rates, it can usually be traced to a lack of talent or adequate planning in the areas of marketing, finance, accounting, personnel, management, or engineering manufacturing."

Frisbie's firm, which remanufactures auto components, did $1.7 million in 1985.

## The Problems of Growth ▬▬▬▬▬▬▬▬▬▬

In virtually every conversation I had with fast-growth entrepreneurs, I found that their early, original difficulty came in hiring others to do most of the jobs that they had been doing by themselves for a long time. Certainly in our own case, our early hiring success of mid- to senior-level players was not great. We hirerd a chief financial officer and a top editor, both of whom had hopes and expectations from the business that were not matched by our business realities in the early years. They moved on, as did we.

One fast-growth chief executive, Judith Kaplan, of Action Packets, Incorporated, of Ocala, Florida, has noted: "The biggest single difficulty we had was moving from an entrepreneurial to a professional company and in the process, upgrading our personnel. We found that we needed to be firm but fair to all while keeping in mind the needs of the corporation." Kaplan took her firm, which was founded in 1976, to 1979 sales of $125,000 and 1983 sales of $2.1 million.

Analyst William Delaney, writing for the American Management Association, suggests that entrepreneurial managers are the antithesis of business managers in that "entrepreneurial managers love to work in an unstructured environment where rapid changes are occurring all the time. Routine, sameness, predictability, and order do not fit into the entrepreneurial manager's environment."[31]

Another problem cited candidly by several of our fast-growth executives was that they were the original entrepreneur in their venture, making any subsequent entrepreneurial manager's role very challenging. The founders will say, "It wouldn't have succeeded without my entrepreneurship" but having more than one entrepreneur almost always results in new difficulties. "It's the old case of too many cooks spoiling the broth."[32]

I remember one of my own earliest problems as an entrepreneur. I had a constant fixation about our inventory that was impeding our growth badly. Out of the blue came a phone call from Cecil Hoge, a 75-year-old friend and mentor who said, "Why are you always worried about that? Tell me what's *working* for you?" He caused me to focus on the one thing that was working for me at the time, an advertisement offering our Country Wisdom Bulletins. He said, "Focus on that. Forget about the inventory. You'll make more money on your winners than you'll lose on your losers." It was damned good advice.

Steven Brandt echoes this thought. "Don't concentrate too heavily on what you have to sell, but rather on what needs to be bought. Think about what your customers might buy from your new company, who might be making the buying decisions, and why might various types of buyers buy the product?"[33]

Entrepreneurs can also face an awful lot of distractions in the early days. "There's a lot of fun things like choosing an office or a letterhead. Also, it's easy to use up a lot of your time doing what you do best. But the interesting challenges must be faced also. Producing quality products, getting new customers, calling venture capitalists, keeping your objectives clear helps you to use your time most efficiently."[34] After a period of time, and as growth occurs, many entrepreneurs have had to decide whether to manage more and do less (William Gates, Microsoft) or to start a new company and innovate all over again (Steven Jobs, Apple).

At Garden Way Incorporated, the garden equipment manufacturer which had gone from a single advertisement in 1966 to $135 million a year by 1982, it became virtually impossible to hire outside professional managers. These "hired hands" were never really given significant responsibility for decision making and implementation, and as a result, incalculable waste and great duplication occurred, as everyone tried to satisfy his or her own ego. This ultimately led to a wide "San Andreas Fault" within the corporation that shifted with great force and resulted in Lyman Wood, the founder, and eventually all of his senior management, being ousted. Had he been able to recognize and accept the need for responsible management at a point when the company had gotten to be considerably bigger than his original entrepreneurial idea, it would have grown to many times the size it was when Lyman departed in 1982.

There is a need for fresh leadership after things get going. As Paul Hawken points out, "Good management can be real good.

Good management is the art of making the problems so interesting and their solutions so constructive that everyone wants to get to work and deal with them. These problems are like a box of Cracker Jack, containing an extra little charm inside. Bad management involves presenting problems in such a way that people seek to avoid them, put them into memo form, delegate, or toss them into the circular file underneath the desk. Good problems energize. Bad problems enervate."[35]

Many fast-growth executives find that their largest problem is delegating. Said Marty Halpern, president of M. W. Halpern and Company, a general contracting business based in Garland, Texas, "My personal involvement has been curtailed to a great extent, but to grow as we're doing I must rely more and more on other people. Therefore the biggest challenge is my ability to hire quality people and my greater satisfaction is in seeing the fruits of their efforts." Apparently Halpern's efforts have paid off, as he achieved $5 million in 1986 sales, and fast-growth status.

Another chief executive, Ronald O. Himberg, president of ADD Electronics Corporation, echoed this feeling, indicating, "The biggest challenge I had was going from a size which could be controlled by myself to the size company which requires control decentralized to a management team." ADD Electronics, based in East Syracuse, New York, distributes electrical components and grossed more than $10 million in 1985.

Eric Berg, president of Technicomp, Inc., suggested that "Transforming the organization from the entrepreneur's original vision to a culture that arises from the employees is a big task. In the process, adding senior managers that were not present at the start of the company and bringing these people in was a major time-consuming task. But to date it has worked." Technicomp, which provides technical training assistance and services, did $1.4 million in 1985.

William Delaney, in his study done for the American Management Association makes the following seven points: "(1) Failure to build a management team can be disastrous leading to a situation where only one person can act or the company stays small, (2) employees will wait their turn from the boss to get their verbal orders, (3) the leader gets so bogged down with details that he can't handle big problems or new business, (4) his family or home life may suffer, (5) personal friendships become neglected, (6) the boss gets ill and no one can step in, (7) no second level management for expansion or growth has ever been developed."[36] Delaney suggests, "Conduct the orchestra, don't play the instruments. If you need a violinist go hire a trained one, but don't rush off the podium, grab a violin and start playing. If you do, the concert will sound like a chorus of alleycats—even if you're playing the violin beautifully."[37]

So while Stage 1 of a company's growth may require pure entrepreneurial involvement, entrepreneurs have to be able to and willing to delegate during later stages of growth.

"Stage 2 may require a little more delegation and responsibility in a broadening of management talent," says Steven Brandt.[38] "In the second stage the entrepreneur must start getting results from and through others as opposed to only through his own effort. Many entrepreneurs find this a tough stage to go through."[39]

Many fast-growth entrepreneurs confess to this. "Stage 3 growth . . . means that at least one additional level of general management has been added to the organization . . . profit centers are formed around a single product line, piece of geography or type of customer." But as Brandt points out, "The actions of independent profit centers also bring the next stage of crisis—control."[40]

Finally, most entrepreneurs find that in their focus, loneliness can develop and they simply need help from others. This is where a Cecil Hoge can pull you up from the "black hole," the unproductive depths of your concerns, your wallowing in the details of your business, and suggest helpful new directions. Every entrepreneur we interviewed had a mentor of some sort. You're lucky if you can find one as helpful as Cecil Hoge.

Today, America continues to experience an absolute explosion of entrepreneurship which is noted around the world. When, in the summer of 1986, Mitch Kapor decided to leave Lotus Development, the startlingly successful company he'd started in 1982 and shepherded into a $225 million company in four years, the British newspaper *Economist* wrote, "Lotus Development is one of those business successes that seem peculiar to America."[41] We'll learn more about this peculiarly American phenomenon in the pages ahead.

# What Others Say

Observations from dozens of phone conversations on entrepreneurial characteristics:

## ENTREPRENEURS

- Have a vision, or dream, which they pursue daily
- Believe, passionately, in their product or service
- Are trying to build something
- Are innovators
- Are impatient. Have tight time frames
- Believe in adding value to the process
- Are persistent
- Have a profit objective
- Assure success. Plan to be around for years
- Understand better than anyone their own strengths and weaknesses
- Are not afraid of starting over again
- Are not primarily motivated by money
- Do it all themselves
- Are not necessarily brilliant
- Understand subtle changes and their impact on the business
- Are confident, secure in their direction
- Want to grow
- Understand the primacy of the customer
- Do not think that they are taking major risks
- Know how to spend pennies, and to bootstrap
- Understand that problems are predictable
- Are practical
- Ask for what they want
- Are market-sensitive

**45**

## ENTREPRENEURS

- Are difficult to intimidate
- Are used to loneliness
- Sense the arrival of a parade in time to get in front of it
- Are willing to be embarrassed
- Don't do strategic plans or MBOs
- Are willing to share
- Are contrary

# Markets

3

In 1967 we found ourselves in Bologna, Italy, for a year of study at Johns Hopkins School of Advanced International Studies. We were trying, in our first few days, to furnish a small apartment that gave us very little to work with. We also had no money, so my wife Martha (now business partner as well) and I decided to try our hand at the flea market, held every Saturday morning in the largest public square, a piazza that dates back to the 11th century.

It was quite a scene. The piazza had been transformed from an empty place where a few tourists looked at statues on a Friday afternoon into the most incredible marketplace you'd ever imagine. There was absolutely nothing that could not be found in that market. As we worked our way up and down the aisles, street-sharp Italian merchants shouted their wares at us; we got the feeling that it was highly unlikely we would leave the place empty-handed.

"Cosa vuole?" (what do you want?) asked one merchant. "We're looking for a rug for our apartment," we responded in laughable Italian. A large smile covered the merchant's face, and immediately feverish activity began in his stall. We were suddenly surrounded by not only the proprietor but his three brothers and two sisters. "What size, what shape, what color, what texture?" These and a dozen other key questions were asked in rapid fire,

**49**

staccato fashion. We tried to answer each and he said finally, "I have just the thing for you."

Martha and I looked into the small, sparsely stocked stall, but there was certainly nothing there that met our description. Emerging, miraculously, within minutes, were two of the younger brothers—with the exact carpet we had in mind. Of course there was nothing to say except, "How much?" We paid our 20,000 lire after a half-hearted attempt at negotiating, and went happily on our way—genuinely satisfied customers.

That morning I learned something I've never forgotten: The smart Italian merchants wanted to sell us what we wanted to buy, not simply what they had in their store. In truth, the two brothers were sent running down to a competitor's stall, where they took a quick option on the piece that we were looking for, brought it back, slipped it in behind the curtain, and suddenly the merchant, to our astonishment, had what we were looking for.

## What Do the Customers Want?

People frequently press to sell what they have. Markets are made by people providing goods and services that people want, not by selling what they happen to have produced.

Again, I won't forget the powerful advice of mentor Hoge, who suggested that I was overly preoccupied with what I had produced—my slow-moving inventory rather than what people wanted.

Management guru Peter Drucker puts it this way: "Business enterprise has two basic functions, marketing and innovation. The purpose of business is to create a customer. True marketing asks—these are the satisfactions the customer looks for to fill his values and needs."[1] Drucker points out what is becoming increasingly obvious to all businesspeople: It's not how you produce, it's how you create your customers. Let's focus on the techniques for creating both customers and channels of marketing distribution that have contributed to the success of America's fastest growing companies.

# Creating Customers ▰▰▰▰▰▰▰▰▰▰▰

Lyman Wood sat at a Ping-Pong table, which we called a conference table, in the log cabin on Lake Champlain that was the headquarters for a burgeoning $130 million garden products business, Garden Way Incorporated. One of the financial types, relatively new to the organization, was spelling out all of the people, offices, desks, computers, and logistical support that was going to be required for a new venture that we were discussing. While down deep I knew he was following an orderly, logical approach, I chuckled to myself when Lyman exploded in the meeting saying, "What you folks in accounting just don't understand is that nothing happens until something is sold!"

Too often new or growing businessses become preoccupied with the *structuring* of extensive logistical support systems *before* sales materialize. And just as frequently, the sales *don't* materialize, or else they're made in a way that is inconsistent with the way in which the logistical support has been (prematurely) designed. This leads to incongruity, excessive overheads, and the inability of the company to react quickly to what the customer is really seeking.

Jim Kobs, chairman of Kobs and Brady, the fast-growing Chicago direct response agency and one of the sharpest advertising minds in the country puts it simply: "Marketing is the offense for corporate growth." Jim pointed out to me that companies should focus on the fundamental objectives of marketing: either acquiring new customers or maximizing the value of existing customers.[2]

Our fast-growth-company list shows an extraordinarily wide variety of marketing methods and techniques (direct-to-consumer, dealer-distributor, party plans as made famous by Tupperware) as well as a wide variety of distribution channels. Creating new markets has never been accomplished by simply following tradition. More often than not, making markets is a matter of putting a unique twist on a particular advertising, promotional, or sales technique, or looking at a distribution channel and saying, How could we position, package, and sell this product better?

One of the reasons for the slow growth of the Garden Way Publishing Company before we acquired it in 1983 was that a basically editorial group was trying to supply a traditional channel of distribution (the "Book Trade") with a product that sometimes the "Trade" liked and sometimes it didn't. The trade practice of bookstores sending back books, called "returns"— books that in most cases they haven't tried very hard to market— leads to uncertainty for publishers. It makes it difficult to project financial results, and can even lead to disaster when returns are considerably heavier than anticipated, reserved against, or budgeted. It also creates an unhealthy treadmill that the poor, haggard publisher keeps pumping for fear that more returns will come back than new books will get out—that is, "negative sales." This can actually happen to people who encourage returns. One month at Time Inc's shaky Book Find/7 Arts Society Books Clubs, we received more returns of a $25 book that we had shipped two months earlier than we had new sales on our $10 book-of-that-month.

As we looked at ways to try to break out of this unappetizing box of traditional marketing we decided, as a tactic, to go after additional channels that would bring us more directly in touch with the customer, thus eliminating as much of the middle contact, the bookstore, as possible. These included advertising in magazines, mail order catalog selling, and special outlets, where returns are simply not the practice.

We also began asking major accounts such as the Eckerd Drug Store chain what kind of publication they would really *like* to have, and what would they think about having *their* name on such a publication (e.g., "Eckerd's Easy Guide to Lawn and Garden Success"). Actually, many of them liked the idea quite a lot, and this innovation, which we call "custom publishing," has led us into extraordinary arrangements with considerably higher return on investment, and considerably less risk as the goods become non-returnable.

If we had listened to the wisdom of the trade we would probably still be limping along with relatively low sales and relatively high numbers of returns. Instead we listened intently to the daily beat of the market, talking to thousands of customers. We began to publish what they wanted to read, not what our authors and editors wanted to write. Sales in the new channels quickly out-shipped sales from the trade.

# Today the Marketers

Too many executives in corporate divisions or in companies experiencing relatively slow growth become bogged down with the routine, the infrastructure—what they perceive as the "meat and potatoes" of the business. Eliot Janeway wrote recently, in *Low Marks For Executive Group Think*, "The historical trends in management over the last 50 years shift the emphasis from production experts to those with marketing and financial skills."[3]

Today's fast-growth business "action" lies in the hands of the marketers. If we look at the backgrounds of the chief executives of the *Fortune* 500, we see an increasing number with marketing background and experience. The same is true of the leaders of companies on the *Inc.* Fast Growth 500 list. They're either born leaders or have learned how in a hurry.

An analysis of the *Inc.* honor roll companies (five years on the Fast Growth list) by business analyst Curtis Hartman has shown that those companies with at least 60% growth each year were driven by marketing. "The doing of business begins with the getting of business,"[4] according to Hartman, who has analyzed hundreds of fast growth companies. Again, nothing happens until something is sold.

One of the major challenges that many of the fast-growth company chief executives have had to face is moving from their initial background in finance, research and development, engineering, or production, and becoming proficient with the marketing of their product. One case in point is Clouis "Duke" Duclos, chief executive officer of Slotline Golf Company, a fast-growth company located in Huntington Beach, California. Duclos developed a line of "high tech golf clubs" that promised to make duffers happy by getting those uncooperative golf balls to go straighter. It worked. His young company doubled its sales from $4 million to $8 million in 1986 and is looking at twice that in 1987.

Said Duclos, "Perhaps because of my background in engineering, my biggest challenge was to become good at marketing." But which came first—the chicken or the egg? "Our growth is due to better marketing as well as better engineering," Duclos has learned quickly. A former McDonnell Douglas engineer, he "mortgaged the ranch" literally, by taking out a $30,000 second mortgage on his home and got the business going in 1982.[5] His biggest breakthrough came in the form of a newspaper advertisement that said "Putt 2½ times better."

Slotline even got *Time* Magazine's attention: "Slotline has sold more than 400,000 putters. Last year the company introduced heel and toe weighted irons and sold 12,000 sets in 15 months; 6,000 sets of its new metal woods were sold in 7 months."[6] Duclos is learning quickly about advertising, sales, marketing, and promotion, and has lined up both Arnold Palmer and Billy Casper to endorse the clubs. The company has made a niche for itself in the golf club market and should continue growing rapidly.

Many of the executives with whom we spoke admit to thinking strategically about their business but not thinking strategically about their marketing. This is where an advertising professional like Jim Kobs of the Kobs and Brady advertising agency comes in. Jim has his own strategies for maximizing the growth of companies through marketing techniques. By introducing executives to creative advertising, and promotional techniques, he's been able to help dozens of companies. Jim makes the world of marketing understandable. He speaks clearly, with no "mumbo jumbo." He suggests tactics to marketing and chief executives that can be easily and readily tested. For example, Will an offer with a premium pull the greatest number of orders? Did two different headlines for an advertisement or for a direct mail letter produce greater response when tested? Should you use a two-page letter or a four-page letter? Large companies such as Florsheim, Alberto Culver, Cincinnati Microwave, Home Box Office, DHL, The Mayo Clinic, Quill, Ace Pecan, Ameritech Mobile Communications, and others listen, and implement Kobs' fast-growth advice.

In looking at DHL, a smaller competitor to Federal Express, Jim suggested this: "Let's take the air express business as an example. The U.S. market for overnight delivery is about $4 billion a year. And it's a category that's still growing rapidly—roughly 20% a year. Federal Express dominates the market in the U.S. with more than 90,000,000 shipments a year, and a 45% market share. Smaller competitors, like DHL or Emery, should let Federal grow the category and then fight for a larger share of it.

Federal, on the other hand, would try to grow the market partly with new products and services like Saturday delivery and if it can't increase its share at least it can be preserved or maintained."[7]

The result of all this good client advice has been not only good client growth, but good growth as well for Kobs and Brady—in fact, it is now one of the fastest growing advertising companies in the country. This growth took them in just about five years from a new company just starting up to the largest independent direct marketing agency in the country. This was about five years ago. At present they're coming up to their tenth birthday and are now part of London-based Saatchi and Saatchi, the largest communications company in the world. The jury remains out on whether their loss of operating independence will serve their clients well, or not. Recent management and creative shifts suggest that change will be rapid at Kobs and Brady.

# Creating Distribution Channels ▬▬▬▬▬▬▬▬▬▬

Occasionally, a marketing strategy will come along that's so powerful as to revolutionize an industry. Companies have been routinely advertising on television since the medium first came into active use in the 1940s. But it wasn't until 1986, with the creation of the Home Shopping Network (HSN), that television changed from being only an advertising medium into an actual store as well—one that came right into your home.

The Florida-based HSN, a specialty retail marketer, distributes a wide variety of consumer items by means of live interactive television programs. According to HSN, "Viewers purchase merchandise by calling a toll-free number and placing an order with a company sales representative. HSN's two networks are available via satellite live 24 hours a day and now reach both cable and broadcast viewers."[8] Roy N. Speer, chairman of the board and Lowell W. Paxson, president and chief operating officer of HSN, have described their spectacular results as follows: "We have been able to realize what few entrepreneurs ever dream of accomplishing: We have created a whole new industry. As the leader in the industry we have, in a very short time, enjoyed phenomenal growth in sales, created a strong customer base, and formed a solid corporate infrastructure."[9]

HSN's financial results are nothing short of incredible. Formed in 1982, the company developed net sales of $898,000 and lost $220,000 in the first year of operation. By the end of 1986 sales had reached $160 million and profits $17 million for the year. Their simple marketing approach? "Join the home shopping club—America's original live discount shop-at-home TV service." An inventive and entertaining way of merchandising, HSN has demonstrated the power of persuasive marketing at its best.[10]

Innovation is at the heart of the marketing mentality. Tom Monaghan didn't invent the pizza, but through marketing innovation he's developed a massive billion dollar business. He simply gets a warmer pizza into your home more quickly. Ray Kroc didn't dream up the hamburger, but he did learn to serve it up to Americans in a very different way.[11] Kroc's company, whose corporate charter calls simply for "Courtesy, cleanliness, and service"[12] quickly became a billion dollar corporation. Before his death Kroc said, "One of our secrets is 'nook and cranny expansion'. There are countless nooks and crannies throughout the country that are possible locations for it and we fully intend to expand into them."[13] The marketing mind instinctively understands the importance of paying attention to nooks and crannies.

On another level, Kroc has demonstrated how effective the franchising technique can be. Franchising is a method of increasing growth for a product or service that has already been tested and confirmed in a home-based, controlled, start-up situation. Fast rollouts, (consisting of very heavy marketing investment in building rapid sales) such as those engineered by Kroc and Monaghan, are legion in the United States. The introduction of franchising techniques to foreign markets has also proven effective. Robert Payton, who was born in Troy, New York, and worked for J. Walter Thompson in London, eventually formed the London based "My Kind of Town Ltd.," a pizza and ribs chain that went from $2500 a week to $25,000 a week practically overnight.[14]

Franchising is basically a method of marketing and a method of financing. It has grown at a dramatic rate in the United States, and many of the fast-growth companies with whom we spoke have been able to finance new growth of their own by selling franchises to new operators. Steven Galante in the *Wall Street Journal* recently described franchising as an accepted way of financing expansion, and distributing products, with new service companies springing up as a result of people's interest in franchising. Galante cites Francorp. Inc., a franchising consulting company in the Chicago suburb of Olympia Fields, Illinois, run by Patrick J. Boroian, which has had dramatic growth and now receives approximately 7,000 phone calls a year from people who would like to get going with their own franchise. Boroian's company sales have quintupled since 1982, to $5 million a year, making it the largest U.S. franchise consulting company.[15]

# New Products for New Markets ▬▬▬▬▬

The timing of marketing decisions has proven to be the key to growth for some companies. Len A. Ganote is president of Hawaiian Pacific Elevator Corporation, an elevator installation company based in Honolulu, Hawaii, that grew from $200,000 a year in 1979 to over $4 million in 1986.

Ganote explains, "Hawaiian Pacific Elevator Corp. started in business as a maintenance company in 1977. In 1979 we looked at the competition and decided to enter the new elevator installation market. We picked up the Dover Elevator distributorship, built an aggressive marketing plan, and Pacific Elevator's new installation sales have climbed dramatically. We've hit $4 million a year in just five years. Market timing and the decision to enter the new installation markets when we did was the most critical factor in our growth."

Others have found that growth came with providing incentives to the people who were making their marketing programs function. Rex Maughan, chairman of Forever Living Products Inc. of Phoenix, Arizona, has said, "We developed the finest program for compensating distributors for the effort expended in sharing our products and opportunities with others. We then found a natural product, stabilized Aloe Vera, which improves the health and lifestyle of those who use it." Maughan's company, founded in 1978, achieved $8.4 million in 1979 sales and dramatically expanded sales to $90.4 million by 1983.

**57**

Some companies have discovered new advertising and marketing techniques, including telemarketing, an industry that has grown to several billion dollars within the past decade. Jimmie Dale Weir, vice president of Quality S. Manufacturing, Phoenix, Arizona, has noted that "Our company took off in 1983 when we started manufacturing trailer kitchens and marketing them by phone. We went from three dealer/distributors to over 2000 in one year, and phone marketing sales jumped from $140,000 to $3,000,000 in this time period."

Another company that cashed in on a newfound ability to sell by using telephone marketing techniques was the Shelby Group International of Memphis, Tennessee. The company's president, Hilliard Crews, has said, "We recognized a growing acceptance of imported work loads for industry and we were a leader in telemarketing to our industry. We were able to achieve a 109% compounded growth rate in the first five years and a 47% growth rate in our second five years."

# The Importance of Advertising

Everybody knows you have to advertise. But a lot of advertising money is wasted if companies don't develop a keen sense of just which part of their advertising is effective and which part isn't. Advertising can be used to create inquiries, draw customers, and build an image and cement positive ones in people's minds—it's a cornerstone of a good marketing program. But many fail to ask themselves the fundamental question of what they want their advertising to achieve.

Larry Kaplan, president of Tele America Inc., Northbrook, Illinois, which provides telemarketing services to its clients said, "An advertising program with *Fortune* and *Inc.* magazine, giving Tele America national visibility led to our marketing growth breakthroughs. We picked up two accounts from that advertising, both of which were listed on the New York Stock Exchange, and from this very small base we sold new accounts on the success of their programs. In 1980 telemarketing was an infant industry and the ad campaign gave us a much larger appearance than we really had." The Illinois-based service company has grown from two employees to over 200 during this period.

Intelligent marketers try to get across benefits, not just features in their advertising program. One sage described this as "selling the sizzle, not necessarily the steak." Robert B. Spizzo, president of Whitebirch Inc., a company specializing in time-sharing and campground development in Breezy Point, Minnesota, said, "We used aggressive marketing of a 'quality of life' that emphasized fun and relaxation combined with first class product, conceived, built, marketed, and maintained by a professional staff that was results oriented. We've become the largest employer in northern Minnesota and have made the *Inc.* magazine 500 list for the last two years." Spizzo's marketing techniques brought Whitebirch to over $18 million in 1985 sales, and the growth rate continues.

Even local advertising, done effectively, can build a small company into a fast-growth company. Donald L. Rosenberg, president of The Record Exchange of Roanoke Inc. in Greensboro, North Carolina, said, "We used local advertising to turn a small market (collectibles and records) into [one with] a much broader appeal. We used the profits from the used records to allow us to sell new records at significant discounts, insuring a good supply of used records for the future as well as a continuing supply of new product buyers." The Record Exchange now has seven retail stores that buy and sell new and used albums, tapes, and compact discs. Its greater size makes for greater buying power. The Record Exchange, founded in 1979, had 1980 sales of $108,000 and 1984 sales of $806,000.

Mira Flores, a design company based in Danville, California, used its advertising and marketing to establish an unmistakable image. "We were a design-oriented firm," said John Hewett Chapman, chairman of Mira Flores, "and with good advertising and good customer contact we created the image and mystique of the highest class, highest quality company in our field. We were perceived as being the 'Rolls Royce of our industry.' We targeted the highest quality hotels (Four Seasons, Sheraton, Hyatt), which provided us with great endorsements. It was just a matter of time before other hotels followed." Mira Flores has shown strong growth—it went from $177,000 the year it was founded (1980) to $6.8 million in 1984.

## Creative Copy ████████████████████

Creativity is another factor that can lead to sales breakthroughs and fast growth for many companies. Tom Collins, cofounder of Rapp and Collins, one of America's premier advertising agencies, described creativity to me once as being less an innate quality than one likely to have developed from having to write 100 different headlines for the same product. Tom has been behind the fast marketing growth of many national companies. He personifies the impact a fresh piece of copy or a new offer can have, and the breakthroughs it can create. "Exaggerate, expand, take apart, miniaturize . . . push your brain beyond *normal* ways of thinking," said Tom recently.

Many of the fast-growth companies with whom we spoke cited creativity. Patrick J. Gorman, chief executive of American Leisure Industries Inc. of Lanham, Maryland, a provider of travel services said, "We had a dramatic breakthrough in 1984 primarily because we hired a creative guru and expanded our sales rep force, both of which critically contributed to over a 100% increase in revenues and net profits for the next two years." American Leisure did $35 million in 1986 sales.

Ron Hume, founder of the Hume Group, which markets high-ticket investment courses in Toronto, Canada, said, "Our advertising program was going nowhere. Fortunately, we were able to connect with the Wunderman Agency in New York, which developed an entirely new creative approach and direction for us. That was a turning point for our company." Hume will do close to $80 million in sales this year.

Sparkling advertising copy has brought many people into the fast-growth lane. There's probably no better example of this than Gary Comer, founder of the Land's End catalog of Dodgeville, Wisconsin, who in 1963 as a copywriter at Young and Rubicam decided to push out of the advertising business and devote himself full time to his love of sailing. Two partners put in $3000 each to form a sailboat parts catalog company called Land's End, which grew quickly but was losing money fast. Comer was able, for $15,000 each, to buy out his two partners, who quickly tired of the business and were delighted with the return on their investments.

A turning point for the company came when Comer sensed that, with great copy and graphics, he could sell many more turtlenecks and slickers than sailboat parts. In 1977 he dropped the boat hardware business completely and pushed out with stylish clothing for sailors.[16] His idea was right on target. The business exploded, to $72 million in 1982 and $265 million in 1986. Although Land's End's product selection was good, so was that of thousands of other catalogs, from Carroll Reed to Spiegel. So why the enormous success? The keys here were creativity, copy, and exceptional catalog marketing.

Comer, who has been called the L. L. Bean of the Midwest, wrote all the copy for the early catalogs. "It was kind of fun. I went out with a camera interviewing people."[17] In 1986, Land's End went public, with its shares listed on the NASDAQ. One year later, in October 1987, it applied for a listing on the New York Stock Exchange with expected 1987 year-end sales of $300 million.

## Other Important Factors

Positioning, which Lyman Wood used to describe, alternately, as "grabbing the center of the stage," or "finding a good parade and getting out in front of it" has been central to the marketing campaigns of many fast-growth companies with whom we talked. John Zenger, president of Zenger Miller of Cupertino, California, a developer of management training systems, said, "Our sales grew from nothing in 1979 to over $10 million in four years because of our unique ability to position ourselves in the marketplace. We developed a quality product and positioned ourselves as simply a more flexible and customer-responsive company in a market which was dominated by one supplier who behaved inflexibly toward its clients."

Other companies have focused on market research. Gary Jacobsen, president of Abacus II Computers of Toledo, Ohio, says, "It all comes down to market research. I've always been fascinated by computers. The fascination led me to study it intently, and into the realization that there was a real opportunity here.

## MARKETS

After years of looking at potential competitors, we launched in 1980 and followed the explosive growth of the micro computer industry. We were sharp enough to recognize the growth opportunity in this industry as opposed to a different industry through market research." Jacobsen's Abacus II Computers reached $12.5 million in 1986 sales and continues to move forward, fast.

At the other end of the product spectrum is Island Water Sports, Inc., of Deerfield Beach, Florida, which, instead of high-tech products, sells just plain good surfing shirts and accessories. According to President Kirk G. Cottrell, "We tried to differentiate ourselves from the very beginning in the retail surf apparel area with aggressive off-the-wall marketing. Plus once we hooked our customers we had good people and good products to back up our claims." Island Water Sports, Inc., which also sells water sporting goods, did $10.4 million in 1986 sales.

Others have used cooperative promotional arrangements to grow. Arnold Johnson of PNS Inc., a packaging and shipping firm based in Racine, Wisconsin, said, "The active promotion of our program by cooperative organizations, particularly hardware stores such as Century and American Hardware, coast to coast, gave us the greatest boost during the past three years." PNS did $3.8 million in 1985 sales, after a very fast initial growth.

Some of America's most dramatic marketing successes have occurred when an entrepreneur has taken a fairly standard product and created a powerful new way for a consumer to buy it. Harry Sherman, founder of the Book-of-the Month Club, did nothing other than take books and make them available to customers on a subscription basis, which he called the "Book-of-the-Month."

His concept, launched in the late 1920s, was a strong initial success, whose growth was later fueled by World War II, when reading became the primary source of entertainment in the United States. Growth in the war years served as an impetus to later growth, and finally, in 1977, to a sales level of $60 million, at which time the Sherman family sold it to Time Incorporated for a wonderful return on beginning equity. Incredibly, the company had a loss of $24,000 in its first year, and then proceeded to make money every year, without fail, for over 50 years.

It's also noteworthy that many people in the publishing business thought that the success of Book-of-the-Month Club, in bringing large volumes of books directly to the consumer by mail order, would lead to the death of retail book selling. As it happened, however, just the opposite occurred. The heavy advertising of new books, the premium enticements, and the member-get-a-member offers caused book consumers in general to be much more attuned to new titles, which they could get through either the club or their local bookstore. A new interest in book acquisition by consumers and the generally rising tide of public interest proved healthy for all forms of distribution.

Sales are the principal beneficiary of marketing programs. Ron Farmer, president of fast-growth U.S. Signs, of Houston, Texas, says that it was really just selling that gave his company an advantage. "Even though we were selling in declining markets, we were able to grow (almost doubling every year) by capturing an ever-increasing share of the market through emphasis on *sales*. We were also able to overcome my lack of training and knowledge in production by subcontracting any new product line until we had captured enough volume in this line to bring the production in house, often buying out our subcontractor." Farmer's electronic sign manufacturing concern, founded in 1980, achieved sales of $187,000 that year, and $2.2 million by 1984.

# Pinpoint Marketing

Pinpoint or "target" marketing—what Lyman Wood used to call "brain surgery"—has led to dramatic growth for many companies. Melvin Edward Spelde, president of Clearwater (Florida) Flying Service, Inc., says, "Our rapid growth was the result of selecting a unique aircraft and then pinpoint marketing its capabilities."

Other pinpoint marketers include Paul Hawken's company, Smith and Hawken, which sells the highest quality gardening tools to serious gardeners. Consolidated Dutchwest uses highly sophisticated list segmentation techniques to identify prospective buyers for its high-quality wood stove line. Bankers Life built a mammoth insurance sales company by funneling just the right number of leads weekly to its direct sales agents.

## MARKETS

Pinpoint marketing was helped along by the introduction of the zip code system. And no company took better advantage of this development than L. L. Bean. Certainly the foundation of the legendary Bean company was product—the Maine hunting boot—and customer service that is *still* unmatched in the catalog world. But Bean's real breakthrough, as we noted earlier, came when the government developed the zip code and put it into effect in 1964. The new zip code system allowed Bean, for the first time, to analyze precisely where their catalogs were going and what the results and implications of this were. Bill Henry, former Bean executive who spearheaded that growth, said to me recently, "Bean started using outside mailing lists with uncanny accuracy and we were on the way from a few million to a few hundred million in a year."

For the first time, Bean analysts could track the response from each of the 40,000 zip code areas, and target future catalog mailings accordingly. On the premise that people who lived, for example, in Short Hills, New Jersey, Birmingham, Michigan, and Kentfield, California, were more alike than different, and that they were the kind of customers Bean was seeking, the Bean mailings became increasingly efficient.[18] Because of this, Leon Gorman, Bean's son-in-law, with the help of Bill End and Bill Henry, was able to lead the company to its enormous growth by strategically following the simple dictum: "The more catalogs you mail, the more orders you get."[19] Bean fueled its growth by renting lists from FAO Schwartz, Yield House, Garden Way Incorporated, and hundreds of other companies.[20]

L. L. Bean himself, back in 1917, was able to get his hands on a mailing list from the state of Maine, which listed Maine nonresidents who, at a cost of $2.00 apiece, had just been issued hunting licenses. Bean was able to pick up 7500 names, a perfect mailing list for his boots, before mail order even got very popular.[21]

Although mail marketing has always been one of the keys to Bean's growth, some parallel developments were going on in the 1970s in product marketing that helped as well. For example, with the introduction of corduroy shirt dresses and other items, a new, female audience opened up.[22] After 1981, 25% of Bean's gross sales came from women, and between 1978 and 1984 70% of Bean's new customers were women.[23] This ability to track demographics and customer preference further accelerated Bean.

Of course, L. L. Bean was one of the great early marketers, a man who understood the value of an advertising dollar. When Henry Luce, a Bean customer, decided to publish a four-page article on Bean in the lifestyle section of *Life*, Bean said, "The *Life Magazine* four-page write up was a big help to our mail order business. One full page showed pictures, descriptions, and prices of nineteen different items from our catalog. To have bought this space would have cost us about $48,000." That was in 1941. The cost of the space today would be a few dollars more than that.

Bean has served as model to many of the mail order entrepreneurs of the 1970s and 1980s. Paul Hawken, one of the most thoughtful, launched his business, Smith and Hawken Tool Company, with an initial investment of $25,000 in imported tools from the Bulldog Tool Company of England and a 1-inch ad in *Organic Gardening, The New Yorker, New Farm,* and a few other magazines.[24] As Hawken puts it, "We showed a picture of one of our forks with the header 'English Gardening Tools. Send for a free catalog.' We ran the ad for four months and received 497 requests for the catalog, but we didn't have a catalog. We had to create the business first."[25]

As we noted earlier, Hawken is a pinpoint marketer who has built his business with unusually high-quality product, imaginative copy, and very sound marketing. Its $30 million plus a year in sales makes it the unquestioned leader in the garden tools catalog business.

# Multilevel Marketing ▰▰▰▰▰▰▰▰▰▰

Many producers rely on two-step marketing, where a distributor or dealer network is brought into play. Finding those dealers can be hard work, however. E. T. "Bud" Bennett, chairman of the board of the Bennett Funding Group, a municipal leasing company in Syracuse, New York, has said, "We started to contact the manufacturers directly, thereby picking up 300 to 500 dealers at a time with about the same effort that we had been exerting to sign up one dealer. We also became the leader in municipal leasing, an area most leasing companies shied away from. The company grew dramatically, from $186,000 a year in sales to $26 million. It was marketing!''

Other marketers use a slightly different two-step approach. They go after the consumer directly through advertising and mailings, and then refer that respondent to a dealer in their area. Richard Considine, president of Lincoln Logs, Ltd., has built his business through the use of that dual marketing technique. Considine, who has 200 dealers around the nation, has been innovative in the use of informational marketing products, and in his pursuit of the customer through follow-up mailings.

Considine told me, "Our best offer ever was a rebate idea that I got at the end of 1978 when we were into business about a year and a half, with marginal cash flow, but we had lots of visitors coming up to the Adirondacks in the summers. We kept their names. September came and all of the summer visitors went home and things were getting tight. I picked up my local paper and saw an advertisement from Lee Iacocca providing a $1000 rebate to everyone who bought a new car that month, so I decided to try it myself. I offered a $500 rebate on a new log home and we sold 27 houses in the month of September alone. This was our breakthrough!''

Other marketers have used multidimensional marketing, the most exciting recent example of this being Royal Silk, founded by Prakash "Pak" Melwani. Melwani, born in Bombay, became a street-smart rag merchant on the West Side of Manhattan, sharpening his retailing skills there. We recounted earlier his initial advertisement in the 1978 issue of *Cosmopolitan*, which launched Royal Silk and which subsequently became a supplier (to CBS). "But I really didn't want to be a supplier, I wanted to run my own business," said Melwani. So he went back to being a merchant and direct marketer. Since then he has also become a retailer—today he has 21 stores, which produce 50% of his volume. He has also just issued a video cassette (which he sells for $5.95) as a "living" catalog. Sales went from $0 in 1978 to over $40 million in 1986, a 1076% sales growth in a five-year period. Melwani said, "I use as many different marketing methods as it takes to get the message of Royal Silk out to people.''

# And Then There's Packaging

Another critically important marketing consideration is packaging. One fast-growth company that focused very heavily on an imaginative packaged product was Celestial Seasonings, a tea company started by Morris Siegel in Boulder, Colorado. Celestial Seasonings went from startup to $10 million and then $25 million a year by creating unusual herb tea products and using innovative packaging.

"Siegel started with an herb tea which he called Moe's 24 and then developed Red Zinger, and 50 additional tea products, each individually packaged, including Mandarin Orange Spice which, for instance, was packaged in an orange and black box sporting an illustration of an Oriental girl framed in white orange blossoms, bluebirds, and branches heavy with fruit."[26] Siegel eventually sold his company for a high multiple of earnings to corporate giant Kraft Inc., which could never run it with the entrepreneurial zest of the founder.

Another fast-growth company that recognized the importance of functional packaging is Calibrake Inc., of Independence, Missouri. Steve Frisbie, the president said, "We have always tried to differentiate ourselves from the competition in order to get people to say 'Hey! Look at them, they're different.'" An example of this was the marketing of disc brake calipers for automobiles. "We sold directly to the auto parts jobber rather than the warehouse distributor. To get through to the distributor we decided that we had to package and market in a non-traditional way, so we put a cardboard sleeve around a pair of our calipers packaging both right and left sets together and for a price of a $.15 piece of cardboard we got a big jump on the competition that we still hold today." This seeemingly minor packaging concept dramatically fueled Calibrake's growth, from startup to nearly $2 million in 1985 sales.

Once a year our company holds a creative packaging session with Orrie Stone, of Middlebury, Vermont, who helped design the Marlboro flip-top box. Orrie, who has spent five decades in packaging, never fails to come up with an imaginative new way of packaging or repackaging our books. This has allowed us to achieve much wider distribution in non-traditional markets, including hardware, drug, and feed and grain stores, where countertop displays are relatively more important to a book's success.

Visionary redesign perspectives on traditional products are what have helped some companies make a needed breakthrough and go on to grow successfully. Ron Hume, president of the Hume Group, while working early in his career as a hired hand at McGraw-Hill, which was already involved in lower level correspondence courses, in Washington, D.C., noticed that editorial properties that came in for publication consideration could also just as easily be spread out in a continuity or correspondence course format.

"We could take the same idea and make a 350-page book out of it which could fetch a price of $9.95 or turn it into a 24-volume continuity correspondence course which could sell for $395.00," says Hume. "Clearly the margins, particularly on paper and ink products, were greatly in favor of the correspondence school format."

Hume eventually took his idea, for selling upscale financial courses, tested an investment correspondence program, and launched the Hume Financial Services Correspondence Course, which grew from startup to $80 million in 1988 sales in just 12 years. One of the techniques that Ron used effectively along the way was to create "The Hume Advisory Board," using the faces and credentials of very well-known leaders of industry and finance to give consumers a feeling of confidence. People like Archie R. Boe, director of many U.S. corporations, Morton Shulman, Kingman Douglas, Jay Trevor Eyton, and the honorable John C. Stetson comprised a board that gives people who have never heard of Hume the confidence to do business with him.

More recently, fast-growth companies such as International Masters, of Los Angeles, California, have applied the same concept to the sale of recipe cards. The company turned what could have been a $3.95 paperback book, or a $14.95 hard cover, into a series of cards that could be shipped monthly for years, resulting in $150.00 of eventual sales.

Marketing brings out the color, soul, and true personalities of people. Here we've seen some of the rich diversity that fast-growth companies enjoy: the many different kinds of marketers, ranging from those who like the slow-and-steady approach to those who like to test fast and roll out quickly; from those who prefer single channels of distribution to those who like multi-media; from young phenoms to octogenarians; from Yale-educated corporate captains to street-smart Indians from Bombay. In the next chapter, we'll learn where the money came from to fuel their fast-growth ideas.

# Money

**4**

The key to growth is quite simple; creative men with money. The cause of stagnation is similarly clear: depriving creative individuals of financial power.

—George Gilder[1]

Gilder's landmark book, *The Spirit of Enterprise*, focused closely on about a dozen unusual entrepreneurs. In the course of our research we spoke with literally hundreds of creative people, all with—at one time or another—money problems. None of these people viewed the nonavailability of money as a primary obstacle to fueling their dreams. But virtually all of them ran into this problem early on, as their businesses unfolded. It's described by various terms: cash flow problems, working capital pinch, slow receivables, tax problems, debt versus equity, liquidity, alternative sources of capital, high interest rates, and so on. Whatever it's called, almost every growth company has experienced it at one point or another, and been almost brought to a grinding halt because of it and its underlying basis—the absence of cash.

Traditionally, businesspeople have been more preoccupied with operating margins, profits or losses, than with cash flow. In large corporations only one department even thinks about it! But the availability of cash is vital in sustaining an enterprise's growth. Steven C. Brandt, author of *Entrepreneuring; The Ten Commandments for Building a Growth Company*, put it this way:

"Cash flow is the blood of a growth business. A company's ability to continue is determined daily,—not at year end. Keeping money in hand or readily available for planned and unplanned events is not only prudent, but necessary."[2]

The imbalances that develop in many companies, precipitated by overdue receivables, inventory obsolescence, or inability to quickly produce the product that's needed, can lead to serious disruptions in a business. People who are able to build cash reserves as they go along find that these imbalances and "fits and starts" can be overcome. It's very difficult to pay suppliers and to take care of employees with either overdue receivables or slow-moving inventory. Cash, in the end, is king.

Prescott Kelly, owner of the Institute of Children's Literature in Redding, Connecticut, a $10 million per year correspondence school, advised, "Build a cash reserve as fast as you can. Think of it as you would personal savings. Have at least a 6-month emergency fund on hand."

# Money Problems: Getting Started

Problems with capital availability are inherent in virtually all of the entrepreneurial businesses we spoke with. Perhaps the most difficult thing is just getting going in the first place.

Dennis W. Bakke, executive vice president of Applied Energy Services, of Arlington, Virginia, told us, "Our biggest challenge was financing our first three projects, depleting our cash reserves completely and threatening our financial viability." Applied Energy, which operates independent power facilities, is now generating revenues of over $22 million annually.

Everett G. Jewell, of Jewell Building Systems, said, "We had an incredible balancing act when we had to spend a great deal of money developing the engineering to fully realize the potential of the company. In our business, you have to have the engineering before you can do anything . . . try to get the financial geniuses in this great land of ours to finance a dream . . . no way!"

Others had problems just establishing credit. Daniel J. Robbins, president of Robbins Communications of Pittsburgh, Pennsylvania, said, "We just didn't have cash to support our growth. We failed to develop financing in the earliest years when it wasn't needed, plus we had no track record for the bank to look at. We should have borrowed early and established a credit line from the very beginning." Robbins, which installs telecommunications cable, is now doing in excess of $5.5 million.

# Money Problems: Continued Growth ━━━━━━━━━━━━━

For companies on the fast-growth track, money problems can arise from a variety of sources and can take many forms.

For some companies inadequate accounting and financial systems can create difficulties and lead to money problems during their fast growth. Phillip B. Crosby, Jr., of Phillip Crosby Associates Inc., said, "We had no ability to maintain an accounting and a financial system that could keep up with the growth and still provide timely and accurate data for decision making."

Ken Rehler, president of RVBK Inc. Architects, echoed this, saying, "We couldn't keep a handle on our costs, nor did we save for hard times for the future."

Cass T. Casucci, president and CEO of O/E Automation, Troy, Michigan, said, "We couldn't get a handle on cash flow or on inventory control and as a result we had obsolescence." O/E Automation, which does office automation and consulting, has grown very rapidly to over $50 million in sales.

When the systems caught up, the companies were able to regain control.

Some companies simply become overextended, not knowing how much debt might be too much debt. Len Wallace, president of Condor Power Supplies Inc. said, "We were overextended in our growth when the electronic hiccup of 1984 occurred. The company nearly went bankrupt as a result."

Getting a handle on debt is a very common problem of fast-growth businesses, according to the CPA firm of Arthur Young:

"Highly rich businesses leave no room to maneuver against the unexpected, like fluctuating interest rates and falling markets."[3]

Some companies overlook something as simple as insurance. "We started with only $5000," said Ronald Farmer, president of U.S. Signs Inc., "and all of the equipment and supplies this money had purchased had been stolen the night before we opened up for our first day of production. We had no theft insurance, so we were in the hole from the beginning. We survived this, but rapid growth has forced constantly increasing needs for larger plants and more equipment."

Occasionally, the problem is simply financial credibility. For example, the lack of an early reputation for financial stability limited the initial growth of one company in terms of attracting new business. W. Allan Vandenburgh, chairman of the Crosby Vandenburgh Group Inc., of Boston, Massachusetts, said, "Our biggest challenge was convincing the TV cable operators that we had the capability of implementing a major project and internally managing this enormous growth out of current cash flow since we didn't have reserves available to fund dramatic growth." Crosby Vandenburgh, which publishes magazines, guides, and directories, has now surpassed $13 million in sales.

Charlie Winton, founder and president of The Publisher's Group West, of Emeryville, California, a marketer and distributor to the book trade, started his business with only $500 capitalization in 1977. "Financial credibility is critical to organizations such as ours, which handle other publishers' assets . . . inventory and receivables. In our business, the ability to pay people on time and the appearance of financial stability is absolutely critical to drawing new clients. We just had to be good financially." They have been, and, as a result, will approach $25 million in 1988 sales.

Casucci, of O/E Automation, notes how important an early reputation was to his company: "Obtaining major contracts with highly respected, large companies gave us a reputation that very few startups are lucky enough to have. We started at the top because we had strong financial backing which allowed us that luxury."

Many entrepreneurs have had to learn to think like bankers. Steven A. Bright, president of Electra Form Inc., of Vandalia, Ohio, said, "Our company was undercapitalized and this was a real problem as we struggled with banking relationships. On the eve of our first real opportunity for success, we ran out of cash and were virtually abandoned by our banker. We survived and installed top financial talent who taught me how my banker thinks. We had five banking relationships in seven years. I used to make bankers nervous, but now use my 'track record' as a calling card, and strangely enough, don't find the need to change banks anymore."

Gary A. Hale, chairman of the Alamo Consulting Group, echoed this feeling, saying, "Financing has always been a problem. The constant work that you need to do with banks and stockholders detracts significantly from the time and energy that you could be spending on more creative pursuits."

Others are hesitant to share any equity, and have had to limit their growth to some degree as a result. David W. Berkus, president of Computerized Lodging Systems Inc., of Long Beach, California, said, "We could have grown faster but we hung on to 100% of the equity, borrowed little, and grew from cash generated by the business. It would have been easy to do otherwise, but the latitude for decision making, the extra opportunities were worth the more conservative approach we took." Computerized Lodging, which resells computer systems, achieved $8.6 million in 1985 sales.

Some companies have trouble maintaining a good profit margin while expanding. John Whelchel, president of An Environmental Marketing Group Inc., of Boca Raton, Florida, said, "Our biggest single problem was maintaining the estimated profit margin from the bidding process through project completion and startup." Environmental has built sales rapidly in their wastewater treatment business.

Jimmy Dale Weir, vice president of Quality S Manufacturing, of Phoenix, Arizona, manufacturers of trailer kitchens, said, "Maintaining a good profit margin while expanding procedures, adding machinery and space, is a big challenge." Quality S has surpassed $3 million in sales.

And Bill Bohlman, president of Waterbeds Plus Inc., of Oshkosh, Wisconsin, said, "We've always had the challenge of maintaining a level of profitability we felt comfortable with."

Still others have suffered from timing problems. Charles R. White of the Faster Industrial Corporation said, "Our biggest problem was maintaining an adequate cash flow due to our overseas buying. The rapid growth caused us to buy more overseas product which, in turn, created a money shortage due to in advance drafts."

Stephen Kellog, president of YWC Inc., of Monroe, Connecticut, said, "We had a hard time funding all of our new ventures. The timing was tricky. In the environmental service business, timing is essential. YWC did not want to give up equity or go to venture capitalists until we had been successful in accomplishing our objective."

For most entrepreneurs, fast growth means surviving in uncharted waters. Some looked to help from their board of directors. R. C. Anderson, director of Data 3 Systems, of Santa Rosa, California, said, "We looked to our directors to recognize the exact time as to when continued growth and expansion required funding by the infusion of outside capital."

Harry Patten's corporation took advantage of the expertise of 70-year-old Herman E. Anstatt, Jr., who had been chairman of the board of Midland Bank and Trust Company of Paramus, New Jersey, as well as other senior, seasoned executives.

As many of the entrepreneurs have found, there are always trade-offs involved. Frank Oropeza, CEO of Transpo Electronics Inc., which chose to grow through internally generated funds, said, "We got going on a $20,000 loan and launched Transpo. In the beginning I was the only manager responsible for everything . . . product design, new product ideas, manufacturing, marketing, business and finance management. Transpo still remains a closed corporation without investors."

Roger Turner, president of Western Controls, said, "Managing cash flow was tough. It became a very difficult situation since the company didn't have very much starting capital, lacked experience and assets for a bank loan, refused equity investments, and didn't want slow growth. Hard to have all things for all people at all times." Despite all of these challenges, Western showed up on the *Inc.* 500 Fast Growth list.

Still other companies become overextended on credit. William H. Wilson, president and CEO of Pioneer Eclipse Corporation, of Sparta, North Carolina, said, "As we grew, so did our inventory and our accounts receivable, our bad debts and so on. We've been in one continuous building program for six years. Despite all our problems, somehow we've managed to do it." Indeed. Pioneer, which provides high-speed floor maintenance and industrial cleaning equipment, has surpassed $16 million in sales in a short period of time.

Other companies have shifted from one kind of sales distribution to another, which required sizable investments. Wayne E. Alter, president of Dynamark Securities, of Hagerstown, Maryland, said, "We changed from a dealer-based company into a franchise operation. In addition to convincing each dealer to become a franchisee, we were faced with the task of researching and complying with an immense number of federal and state franchise registrations and compliances. The legal expenses for this ran into the hundreds of thousands of dollars while, at the same time, the demand on our own internal resources was vast and unprecedented." Dynamark, which provides electronic protection devices to homes and offices, quickly surpassed $5 million in sales.

Rising interest rates can cause problems as well. David C. Duxbury, president of Comstock Leasing of San Mateo, California, ran into very fast growth and was heavily leveraged when interest rates skyrocketed in 1980 and 1981. His small-ticket leasing operation was hit hard.

Gregory Paul Hilts, president of CIT Construction Inc. of Stafford, Texas, started his general contracting business in 1980 when interest rates were 23%, and survived. His firm is doing well over $10 million in sales today. He was not alone. Corporate interest expense, as a percentage of pretax profit has tripled since the 1960s.

# The Realities of Cash Flow ▬▬▬▬▬▬▬

Entrepreneurs need to learn about cash flow if they're going to succeed.

One group of entrepreneurs, corporate managers who move to start up their own firms or to buy existing operations, have to first unlearn corporate habits. For example, most corporate managers never have to deal with the realities of day-to-day cash flow. In most large corporations, there's a controller's office, a chief financial officer, and established lines of credit for various working capital and other special needs.

Additionally, corporate managers are taught only the importance of profit and loss statements and do *not* become facile with asset and liability sheets and cash flow projections. Life begins and ends with the profit contribution, an unfortunately belated reflection of true business health. This hit me like a ton of bricks when, as a young, green manager, I was sent from the heady atmosphere of the Time Incorporated headquarters at Rockefeller Center to a newly acquired book club operation on the 8th floor of $5.00 per square foot space at One Park Avenue. I learned pretty quickly the difference between a "pro forma" profit and loss statement and one's ability to pay bills. Time Inc. had paid a cool $1 million to George Braziller for the opportunity to try to renovate his aging Book Find and Seven Arts Society Book Clubs and quickly discovered that there would be considerably more capital required to actually run the business.

I felt very much like the ill-fated Greek messenger when I had to return to the 34th floor of Time-Life to seek additional capital ($250,000) to pay bills and take care of payroll the first week. Time Inc's sharp controller, whom most "profit managers" had never had to meet, was David Dolben. Dave looked at my request and said to me, "How much more do you think this operation's gonna need?" I had to honestly answer him by saying, "How would you know?"

Dave smiled and suggested a fast course in cash flow planning and asset and liability management. Time, of course, had infinite resources to back up these kinds of cash flow problems and acquisition transitions, and eventually the learning experience with Braziller's clubs led to the successful and happy acquisition of Book-of-the-Month-Club several years later for over $60 million. From Time's point of view, the first couple of million was simply an intelligent toe in the water.

Bill Blair, who with Dick Ketchum launched Blair and Ketchum's *Country Journal Magazine* in Vermont back in the early 1970s, put it slightly differently in a conversation, "Most corporate people are keeping their eye on the profit and loss statement. Most entrepreneurs learn to keep their eye on daily receipts." Blair and Ketchum were able to grow their business, *Country Journal*, through the careful conservation of cash and the elegant crafting of a distinct magazine profile, and ultimately sell it, at the peak of the market, for over $5 million to the

Historical Times publishing company in Harrisburg, Pennsylvania.

The short of all this is, as Steven Brandt, the president of three fast-growth companies of his own, put it, "It's less adequate to state how you are doing on your profit and loss statement. Now you must project how you expect to do with the assets and resources at your disposal."

Entrepreneurs learn quickly that assets mean leverage. Bankers, notorious for their unwillingness to fuel new ventures, are nonetheless very happy to provide financing when real assets develop. Typically, bankers will fund accounts receivable to the tune of 80% of face value and inventory to the tune of 60%. When we acquired the assets of the Garden Way Publishing Company from Garden Way, Incorporated, in 1983, there was some question as to whether Garden Way, Incorporated, would try to collect its old accounts receivable. At the last minute they decided not to. This left us in the position where, in order to buy the receivables from the company, and complete the buyout, we needed considerably more financing than we had already negotiated.

Nervously, as the deal was now contingent on financing the receivables, I approached our First Vermont banker, who had already stretched to his own limit in providing money to help us get going, and said, "We're going to need to find a way to come up with another $500,000 in order to buy the receivables." I sat there hopefully as the brief silence seemed to last an eternity. Then banker Knute Westerlund, to his everlasting credit, said, "Well, if the rest of the deal makes sense, this certainly makes sense!" As it turned out, we were able to negotiate a discounted price for the receivables, get them financed, and during the next five months collect enough to make a significant early profit on this real cash flow, which fueled our earliest days of growth.

Harold Geneen, the corporate mastermind behind IT&T's growth, has noted the critical nature of cash: "The only irreparable mistake in business is to run out of cash. Almost any other mistake in business can be remedied in one way or another But when you run out of cash, they take you out of the game."[4]

Virtually all of the fast-growth companies with whom we spoke have felt the cash pinch. Many entrepreneurs have operated on adrenaline alone for periods of time, or have done everything—performed every function in the company—themselves. All have faced the prospect of being taken "out of the game."

Gary L. Pittman, president of Publications and Communications, Inc. (PCI) of Austin, Texas, told us, "No question but that my biggest single problem was trying to find capital funding for all of the opportunities that have come our way as a result of our success." Pittman's success is built on the publication of trade journals for the computer industry, which grossed him over $5 million in 1986 sales. Printing companies, Pittman's key vendors, are notorious for their hopefulness about the success of new publications from companies like PCI—*and* equally notorious for their desire to get paid on time.

Entrepreneurs, more than most, have eyes that are always bigger than their stomachs. Even when their plate is completely full, an opportunity that beckons and provides distraction can be very tempting. In many cases, the lack of cash at a point like this is actually the *best* limit to risky growth. We launched a publication at the outset that we hadn't completely thought through. Thanks to our lack of cash, we made that mistake just once. Three years later we launched a publication that we had thought out more carefully and were profitable with the first issue. Others have been less fortunate. David Tresamer launched Green River Tool Company in Brattleboro, Vermont, and may have had too much cash. Rather than testing cautiously, he expanded his catalog mailing to unqualified lists of consumers, drew a very weak response, and, as Geneen put it, "went out of the game."

Another entrepreneur pointed out to us the flip side of cash availability problems, and that is the problems that can occur when cash begins to roll in more steadily. Wayne L. Staats, president of Advanced Computer Graphics, Inc., told us, "Growth provides significant cash flow that can easily mask inherent problems. When growing rapidly, one is less inclined to pay attention to details, which can add up to big hidden costs." Founded in 1978, the firm does over $2.2 million as a service bureau for computer graphics.

Sometimes cash flow problems don't show up right away—in fact, sometimes at first they don't seem like problems at all. One of our earliest entrepreneurial efforts was a monthly publication called *The Practical Gardeners' Newsletter.* To get this project off the ground, we had financed it from our own savings, to the tune of $25,000. In went the $25,000 and back, in the first week of response, came approximately $15,000. We felt as rich as Croesus.

Unfortunately, the feeling didn't last long. Only three weeks later, when the bills for printing, paper, and advertising came in, we realized that the number of subscribers—and the money we had counted on—had fallen far short of expectations. The pressure was on. In the process, we had also created for ourselves a subscriber liability—that is, we now had to provide future issues of the publication to the respondents. It's the kind of situation that doesn't go away by itself.

Gary Jacobsen, president of a fast-growth computer company, Abacus II, in Toledo, Ohio, told us that "Our growth and profits came so fast that it seemed that we could do no wrong and therefore the money would always be coming in at that fast rate. When this condition exists, you can afford to make a lot of mistakes because the profits cover up the mistakes." If structural problems aren't paid attention to, on the other hand, profit margins and cash will eventually dwindle. Abacus II reached $12.5 million in sales by 1986.

# Growth Financing ■■■■■■■■■■■■■■■■■■■■

So where does financing come from? One source is the growth financing business. Providing cash, in the form of growth financing, has become a very strong growth business in itself, according to the accounting firm of Arthur Young in its *Guide to Financing for Growth*.[5] Venture capital as an industry went from below $500 million in 1975 to $4.5 billion in 1984. There was a reason for that dramatic growth, according to *Venture* magazine: the cut in capital gains rates in 1978 to 29% from 49%, which "produced a startling 15 fold rise in new venture capital followed by a cooling off period the next year."[6]

*Venture* goes on to point out that in addition to the increase in the size of venture capital pools, initial public offerings (IPOs) went from only 30 in 1975 to over 833 in 1983, and to 500 in 1984.[7] IPOs tend to go up and down with the market, and we'll see later how two similar land development companies, the Patten Corporation of Stamford, Vermont, and Properties of America, of Williamstown, Massachusetts, were dissimilarly treated by an up market in 1986 and a down market in 1987.

Venture capital pools and public offerings, however, provide only a fraction of the money for fast-growth ventures. By far, the greatest sources of funding for such ventures are retained savings, personal savings, family, and friends. Personal savings, helped more than a little by the proliferation of two-income households, have increased dramatically during the past ten years, going from $300 billion to over $750 billion in 1984, and help to explain the entrepreneurial boom.[8]

David Birch puts it a little differently: "The sums of money required to support our entrepreneurial habits are not insignificant. Assume that each of the approximately 800,000 annual startups of corporations and partnerships need, on the average, $25,000 to open the doors—that comes to around $20 million in net new capital. Now add another $25,000 per business in expansion capital for approximately 300,000 rapidly growing businesses or $7.5 billion. So we are talking about a total of some $28 billion in net new venture capitals per year."[9]

Birch, who has analyzed fast-growth companies for the past two decades goes on to say, "In its best years, the formal venture capital industry raised $2 billion for new and ongoing firms. Banks and other financial institutions (pension funds, government agencies, insurance companies, etc.) provide, at most, another $4 billion. This leaves the 'informal' capital network with the task of providing $22 billion each year. Some comes from the sale of equity and debt on the capital markets, but we have found that the bulk of the $22 billion comes from personal savings, friends, relatives, or local informal venture capital groups formed by doctors, lawyers, or business people."[10]

Thus, virtually anyone with start-up and fast-growth objectives, which we have seen to be the primary trigger for job growth in this country, more often than not is turning to personal savings, second mortgages, home equity, friends, family, and relatives to provide the capital needed to either start up, get through a crunch, or fuel continued growth. Many of the fast-growth companies with whom we spoke were started or fueled in that fashion.

We'll see later how many of these companies outstripped the initial capital available from traditional sources and have had to learn to borrow, to provide equity in their corporations for investor cash or to enter into unusual, even extraordinary, financing arrangements. In our own case, an initial working capital line of $300,000 was quickly doubled to over $600,000 in order to support the last-minute inclusion of an accounts receivable acquisition from the seller. Within another week, we needed an additional $75,000 to support a paper purchase on which, as a new company, we had been denied standard trade terms and required cash. Had any of these been denied, our game could well have been over practically before it began.

# Venture Capital ▬▬▬▬▬▬▬▬▬▬▬▬

Many fast-growth entrepreneurs turn right from the start to venture capital. And often they'll turn to it at times of cash pinch as well. Venture capital represents the personal or corporate resources of outside investors who are willing to accept high levels of risk for a high potential return. The investors may be passive or they may be active, eager to become involved in management in order to meet their own goals.

The variety of public and private corporations that provide capital is limitless, but the list includes conglomerates, insurance companies, foreign corporations, and, most notably, investment banks and venture capitalists. Venture capitalists and other outside investors purchase their equity in the form of common stock, preferred stock, convertible stock, or stock with stock warrants.

The types of relationships that occur between outside investors and the management buyers may range from a close partnership to a passive funding role, or from a majority of seats on the board of directors to a teaching role.

There are currently approximately 700 U.S. venture capital funds seeking long-term, growth-oriented investors (see *Pratt's Guide to Venture Capital*, Venture Economics, Inc., Wellesley Hills, Massachusetts). The funds may be organized in many different ways, among them as a business development corporation (BDC), a small-business investment company (SBIC), or even a public venture capital partnership, where private and public money are raised and combined.

State venture capital funds have been formed in many of the more aggressive states looking to encourage development. This money is available despite lots of "red tape" to qualifying companies. In fact, "Since 1980, the size and number of state-sponsored capital programs has increased dramatically. Before 1980, only Connecticut, Massachusetts, and Wyoming had them. Since 1986 many more states have adopted the plan."[11]

Vermont and Massachusetts, where we have chosen to work and operate, now both have a large number of government-affiliated state and local development corporations. Vermont's Industrial Development Authority looked particularly attractive to us at the onset, but, in the end, we didn't need to get any financing from them. Besides, as noted, their paperwork requirements are ferocious.

However, a good, fast-growth corporate neighbor, the Delf-tree Corporation, of North Adams, Massachusetts, which specializes in growing and marketing gourmet shiitake mushrooms, was able to get fresh venture capital through a combination of private and local development sources that enabled it to buy out and recapitalize a business that came close to folding with the untimely death of its founder. The business is now shipping over 2000 pounds of mushrooms *weekly* to gourmet outlets all over the United States.

Not everyone is happy with venture capital. Some people knowledgeable in business feel that entrepreneurs should avoid venture capital. They feel that the very *first* step for an entrepreneur is to find a good investment banker—someone with no existing ties to any corporation—who has been recommended by a friend, or a friend of a friend.

Venture capitalists are looking for capital gains. They want to turn over their portfolios at regular (about five-year) intervals, and they look for a gain of seven to ten times their original investment.

Competition for venture capital is fierce. Of the almost 700 venture capital firms nationwide, most of them will typically finance only three to four new ventures a year, although they might read 20 business plans each week. Fast-growth entrepreneurs realize early on that competition is high, and must be prepared for rejection.

What do venture capitalists look for in a company? James Anderson, of Merrill, Piccard, Anderson and Eyre (a venture capital firm), speaking at the Stanford University School of Business, said, "The key ingredients are (1) an experienced management with relevant industry experience and actual job function experience; (2) a distinctive product line that fills a real need, that is unique, defensible so that it can't be copied, cost effective, and provides a dramatically superior solution to the customer's problem; and (3) large and expanding markets."

Don Dion, who helped engineer the dramatic growth of the Patten Corporation of Stamford, Vermont, said that he looked at the alternatives of individual venture capitalists, private bankers, and the public market. And he puts it differently. "Venture capitalists are looking for people who are willing to work seven days a week, 12 to 15 hours a day, that have superior problem-solving ability and can tough it out in difficult situations. They'll also insist that you have a big chunk of your own money in the venture, and at risk." Patten eventually went public, but not before Dion had gotten a very good look at the world of venture capitalists.

Venture capitalists have a tendency to want to help the business grow to a certain point, but then they want to go public or sell the business to a larger firm. "Venture capitalists are a breed apart," said Dion. "They'll want to get a majority of the equity in the business, be represented on the board of directors, and get fast information on the company's ups and downs." Thus, with heavy venture capital participation, founding entrepreneurs and subsequent management risk losing control of the business.

In addition, the intricacies and technicalities of venture capital financing can confound the average businessperson. "It isn't easy," said Dion, "and you'll need help from your accountant and lawyer on the 'term sheet' and purchase and sale agreement, working and legal understandings. These require negotiations on many points, including percentage ownership, price to be paid, and who will be on the board of directors. This is a long and complicated process. Ask your lawyer and accountant for help."[12]

Industry observers predict the venture capital boom, which began in 1978 with reductions in capital gains taxes, will not last, especially if taxes are raised again to help fund federal budget deficits.

Today, following changes in tax laws, initial public offering and venture capital funding is somewhat less attractive for start-up companies than it was just a few years ago. Additionally, most venture capitalists are now looking more seriously at investing in companies that are already well established, for expansion purposes.

## Personal Financing

Certainly, far friendlier than the world of venture capitalists is that of personal financing—that is, getting money from friends and relatives. David Birch points out that money for start-up operations and for continued growth comes, overwhelmingly, from this source. Says Birch, "The raising of venture capital depends crucially upon the ability of private individuals to accumulate discretionary wealth."[13]

A typical illustration of self-financing is Orlino C. Baldonado, president and chief executive officer of the E. C. Corporation, based in Oak Ridge, Tennessee. E. C. provides technical and managerial services as well as specialized products to government and industry. The company grew from a startup in 1977 to approximately $16 million in sales in 1986. It began as a part-time job for Baldonado.

He told us, "I incorporated it in 1977, but it's hard enough to get a business going if you do it full-time; it can't be done if you do it part-time. As a result, nothing happened to E. C. between 1977 and 1979."

Baldonado funded his earliest activity through the accumulated vacation pay awarded to him when he left his engineering job to devote all his time to the new venture.

"I opened the office with myself, a secretary, a manual typewriter, two chairs, and about 20 boxes of miscellaneous documents I had collected through the years." Baldonado eventually drew on most of his personal savings, including all of his government savings bonds.

"We needed operating capital most of all and there was nothing more for me to give or pledge. I borrowed to the hilt; the house, wife, and kids were in hock, I believe."

Today things are different. E. C. has about 200 employees, has exceeded $16 million in sales, and has computerized accounting systems, financial controls, and a fuller range of growth company financing options. Each new project for E. C. can run several hundred thousand dollars, and much of the start-up financing required for new projects is the type that banks are not enthusiastic about or particularly well equipped to provide. "This has forced us to do the planning necessary to meet the immediate cash flow needs in starting up large new projects."

## Financing from Business Acquaintances and Customers ▬▬▬▬▬

Financing can occasionally come from business acquaintances and customers. For example, the previous owner of a venture may be willing to help with funding. John Castalucci, a Californian, was able to buy a bankrupt public company by signing a $100,000 note to be paid over a long term; this allowed him to borrow $5000 from a finance company on his signature, and he was in business.[14]

Castalucci leveraged all of this debt, made possible by the owner's willingness to finance the earliest days, into a company that became one of the fast-growth companies of the 1970s. Called La Mesa Energy Corporation, Castalucci was able to grow, through very heavy leverage sales volume, to $100 million.

Sometimes there will be an "angel." As Joe Musolino, president of Techne Electronics Limited of Palo Alto, California, puts it: "We were quite lucky to have the help of an understanding individual who gave us a great deal of financial support when our internal cash flow was not sufficient to fund the kind of growth that we were experiencing. Had we not had this support, or had we lost it, we would not have been able to grow as fast as we did." Techne, which provides security systems for vehicles, was founded in 1975 and had grown to $2.6 million by 1985.

Other fast-growth companies have looked to their suppliers for support. Pak Melwani, whose Royal Silk went from startup in 1978 to $40 million in 1987, said, "The bankers just did not understand the nature of the business we were in. It was pointless to even think about talking with them. Two of us started the company with $10,000 apiece, but to get the money we needed for inventory, as well as for growing and developing the business and financing equipment, was difficult. No banks were interested. In fact, banks are *only* interested in lending me my own money, so we talked our printer into advancing money to us. He liked me. We had 75,000 pieces of catalog mail to get out, and I looked him in the eye and said, if you aren't able to give me the credit I think it's too bad for you."

In fact, money means very little to Melwani, and he has no interest or intention of going public. His business, which is perking along at the $40 million mark now, has allowed him to do everything he's ever wanted to do and he has no interest in relationships with investors, venture capitalists, or bankers.

Ray Kroc, the franchising genius behind McDonald's, ran into a cash pinch once when the owners of a piece of property he had recently leased and began to build upon pointed out to him that he really didn't have clear title. Kroc and partner Harry Sonnenbron remembered it this way:

> "What the hell are we gonna do now, Harry?" I shouted. "How much money are we talking about?"
>
> "Well, Ray, it's going to be at least $400,000," he said.
>
> "Jesus!"
>
> "Ray, I have an idea that I think can pull us out of this. We can ask for a loan from our McDonald's suppliers. I figure $300,000."[15]

At a time of financial crises, suppliers can be some of your very best allies (which argues in favor of maintaining good communications with them so they know exactly where you are). Grolier's chairman, Robert Clarke, was able to get strong supplier support when his publishing empire was approaching bankruptcy. This support, ultimately, saved the company.

Others have experienced this, too. Michael H. Duweck, president of All Star Printing, Inc., of Lansing, Michigan, said, "In view of the fact that we were small and minimally capitalized to start, financing our growth was the biggest challenge. Because we chose to be a private, closely held firm, we relied on our credit lines with vendors to see us through the cash flow trials we encountered. As a result, we maintained 100% ownership while achieving profitability and are well on our way to a sound balance sheet." All Star has now surpassed $2 million in sales.

Still other companies have turned to their customers to help with their financing. We developed a customer financing system at Garden Way, Incorporated, during the 1970s when we were selling major pieces of gardening equipment by mail. We asked our customers to advance 20% of the total cost of their Troy Bilt Rototiller as an advance, a reservation to hold their "spot in line," and to guarantee that they'd get their tiller in time for spring planting. We had, at any point in time, between $2 and $3 million in customer deposits to finance our growth, which was rapid (from startup in 1966 to $130 million in 1983).

Sound pushy? Virtually every magazine in America is financed in exactly the same way. Think about it. If you take out a three-year subscription and pay for your subscription up front, the magazine has a deferred liability of perhaps $100, which reflects the fact that you have lent them money and they owe it to you over a period of time in the form of monthly issues. Multiply this by 100,000 subscribers and you have some significant amounts of cash.

Just for the fun of it one day, Lyman Wood, the marketing genius behind Garden Way decided to try out a plan whereby the customers would finance the business to an even greater degree. "We'll send them out phantom stock certificates," said Lyman. "They only have to send in $1000 apiece to become a good gardening stockholder." At the time, we had well over a million customers. The lawyers wouldn't buy it, and Lyman's accountants just scratched their already hairless heads. No one could ever accuse Lyman of thinking small.

Dick Considine, of Lincoln Logs, Ltd., borrows from his customers in the same way. "We ask them to give a 'pre-cut' notice of intention to buy, at which point they send in 20% for a log home that might sell for $75,000. That's real helpful cash flow for us."

## Financing Through Partnerships

Other fast-growth companies have looked to partnerships to help in their financing and management. John W. Hies, general manager of DDF Transportation, Inc., of Tonawanda, New York, a freight company that grew from $271,000 in 1982 to $6 million in 1987, told us: "I accepted a partner into the business in 1983, and it's quite apparent that our growth began in 1983. Let me elaborate. My philosophy in accepting a partner was based on a Mark Twain quote I read several years ago. 'If you allow a person to row the boat, they don't have time to rock it.' This is the primary philosophy of running our business today. I went so far as to not telling him about substantial losses that we had in 1982 and 1984."

Some might consider this less than an honest, open partnership, but Hies maintains he didn't tell his partner about these periods because he was concentrating on positive selling. "I thought this bad news might have detracted from his ability to perform honestly in the sales and marketing capacity with our customers. We worked closely together as partners but realized early on that cash flow was going to be a critical problem. We've now determined that 30% growth a year eats all of your profits. If we want to maintain rapid growth, we have to stay within the limits of the 30% growth factor or we fail to pay the bills on time. We also recognized early on that banks are not venture capitalists. They're in the business to make money on loaning money and will not take large risks, or even medium risks with small companies."

Hies has looked at fast-growth alternatives and the trade-offs involved. "So we stay within our calculated comfort zone, or else we'll have to think about going public, making preferred stock offerings, all of which dilute our ability to control and manage in the style we know is successful and right." Heis sees the value of a certain limited kind of partnership.

Paul Hawken sees other benefits. "You will need a partner. You shouldn't even think of going it alone. I say this even though I've been burned by a partner. Partners make the good time more fun, the hard times more bearable. A partner is someone to talk, debate, noodle, and argue with. Someone to grow with."[16]

In my own case, I'm fortunate to have a partner that I've known for over three decades, since I was 13 years old. She's my wife. A relationship based on working as married partners certainly faces new challenges, as well as the potential for additional stress. Nevertheless, many have done it, maintaining their personal relationship despite business partnership and fast business growth. Notable in this group are Patricia and Mel Ziegler of Banana Republic Travel and Safari Clothing; Bill and Genevieve Gore of W. L. Gore (Gore-tex) and Associates; Debra and Randall Fields of Mrs. Fields Cookies; and Reuben and Rose Mattus, who founded Haagen-Dazs Ice Cream. (A very well researched and written book on the subject is *In Love and In Business*, which I can strongly recommend to you.)

Bringing in actively participating owner-managers is another way of financing growth. This is what Hume Associates of Toronto has done.

"The way I look at it," said Ron Hume recently, "is that I would much rather have 20% of a $100 million company than 100% of a $1 million company. And rather than simply getting passive partners to invest, I prefer to bring in managing partners, whose skills complement, and in many cases are sharper than, my own."

Hume's technique is to ask managers to become partners by buying their way into the company on a book-value basis; he demonstrates to them what can happen to the book value over a period of time and with successful profit contributions from their operating units. Hume also allows them points at which they can cash in their stock to the corporate treasury.

"I think it makes a big difference to ask people to buy in rather than simply being awarded equity," says Hume. "They appreciate it more and immediately feel that they have a personal stake in the long-term health of the company. Their stock goes up in value in proportion to their profit results. And so does mine!"

The formula works. Hume has grown from a start-up situation 13 years ago to a company that is doing more than $80 million, with operations in Los Angeles, Atlanta, and Toronto, Canada.

# Financing Through Investors and Banks

More than one partner gives you investors. Ray Kroc tells about the time when he had the opportunity to buy out the founding shares from the California-based McDonald Brothers but didn't have the money to do it.

"Three insurance companies would lend us $1.5 million in exchange for about 22.5% of our stock. I would contribute 22.5% of my stock, leaving me with 54.25%, Harry (Sonnebron) would put in 22.5% and June Martino would give up 22.5% of hers. It turned out to be the best deal those three insurance companies ever made. They sold their stock a few years later for between $7 million and $10 million on the basis of $1.5 million in."[17]

McDonald's as we know it probably never would have happened without that infusion of money. "That loan could be called the lift-off of McDonald's rocketlike growth in the sixties. It took a lot more financial trust to put us into orbit, but we would never have gotten off the ground without it."[18]

Many people operate exclusively with local banks. We did, with the First Vermont Bank of Bennington, Vermont, five years ago and quickly became one of their larger accounts.

Another fast-growth business, founded in the 1970s, is C. B. Sports of Bennington, Vermont, which sells skiwear nationwide. This company used local banks and then regional banks to cross-collateralize in order to fuel the fast growth they were experiencing with their quality skiwear line. During some years, C. B. Vaughn, founder and president, would borrow up to half of the operating revenues of the company on this cross-collateralized basis in order to "make things happen." C. B. hit

$35.5 million in 1987 and expects to exceed $40 million in sales in 1988.

Paul Hawken believes in the local approach, too: "If your town truly has a local bank, you may fare better there because the social bonds that hold a community together allow for greater latitude in dispensing loans and other banking services."[19]

In our own case we prefer debt over equity simply because we want to hold on to as much of the company's control as we possibly can—100%, for example. Arthur Young CPA firm points out additional advantages of debt over equity:

1. A debtor has no direct claim on the future earnings of the company, only repaying the amount and interest.
2. Interest on the debt can be deducted from the company's tax returns. It lowers the real cost to the borrower.
3. The lender has no direct claim to the equity of the business.
4. Interest in principal payments are, for the most part, a known amount so you can plan for them.[20]

We've been able to generate all the working capital that we've needed on the basis of the 80/60 receivable/inventory rule; that is, we've been able to borrow 80% against our accounts receivable and 60% against our inventory. This is fine for "business as usual," but we find ourselves hard-pressed when faced with the need for a major expansion of facilities or new capital equipment. Many other companies with whom we have spoken have experienced short-term pressures ranging from inventory imbalances and obsolescence, to bad debt financing, expansion financing, and new product development.

However, there are some disadvantages to debt over equity, which Arthur Young also points out:

1. Interest is a fixed cost and therefore raises the company's break-even point. This can increase the risk of insolvency during a financial crisis.
2. Cash flow is required for both principal and interest payments and must be planned for.

3. Debt is not permanent capital with an unlimited life: It must be repaid sometime.

4. A business is limited as to the amount of debt it can carry. The more risky the company the less a creditor will lend you.[21]

# Going Public

Other fast-growth companies have found that going public is really the only way for them to raise the capital they want or need. The Patten Corporation of Stamford, Vermont, for example, has a global vision, and has successfully raised over $150 million on public markets in the last three years to help it to achieve that vision.

Timing on a public offering can be critical. Patten's initial public offering (IPO) came out in 1985, along with a flood of other new offerings. Don Dion selected Drexel Burnham, a rising underwriter that had been showing good recent success on Wall Street. The initial public offering was overwhelmingly successful and was followed by Patten's New York Stock Exchange listing in October of 1986.

Phil Grande, president of a smaller competitor, Properties of America in Williamstown, Massachusetts, which made the *Inc.* Fast Growth 500 list for two years in a row (1986 and 1987), had been using the same successful land sales approach as Patten, but ran into very different sledding with his IPO. In the post-October 1987 world very few IPOs were being made. People simply weren't buying new issues. Additionally, Grande went to Sherwood Securities and Wolf and Company, both of which were less powerful than Drexel. This, coupled with the fact that investors had far less in the way of liquid assets and did not want to invest in land, made it a much tougher market to sell. The result? POA went from a high of 6¼ to a current level of 3¾.

Going public involves selling shares of the business to investors in the various stock markets. The cash generated in the public offering is used to expand, to strengthen the balance sheet by removing leveraged debt, and to pay off the owner-managers, sometimes at very significant multiples of their original investments.

Preparing to go public, however, is costly in time and fees, and it can erode many of the entrepreneurial incentives that created the business in the first place. This is *not* the route designed to guarantee owner-managers the retention of maximum control of their businesses. In many cases, the entrepreneurs take on new masters, or exchange one boss for another.

Many fast-growth companies have tried public offerings. Michael J. Collins, president of the CEM Corporation of Matthews, North Carolina, a firm that provides microwave-based instrumentation for lab testing and analyses, determined that his company's growth, which had been rapid and which at that point put them at $9.3 million in sales, was fundable only through a public offering. So in July 1986 CEM went public and raised $4.8 million, primarily for working capital and to strengthen its balance sheet. "The firm held no long-term debt at the end of fiscal 1987, and its working capital measures nearly $8.4 million."[22]

Without this funding it's unlikely that the firm could have grown to its current $10 million in revenues (with net income of $1.3 million), particularly given its strong emphasis on new products (the company spent more than 8% of revenues in fiscal 1987 on new product investment).[23]

# Franchising ▬▬▬▬▬▬▬▬▬▬▬▬▬▬

Franchising is another way to go about raising money for expansion. Ray Kroc didn't invent franchising, but he wrote the book on it. Amazingly, it was with a little more than $1000 that his franchise realty corporation was started. As Kroc himself put it: "We parlayed that cash investment into something like $170 million worth of real estate ... We would induce a property owner to lease us his land on a subordinated basis, he'd take back a second mortgage, then we'd go to a lending institution and arrange a first mortgage on the building."[24] In this way, McDonald's raised large amounts of capital in the earliest days.

And started a fast-food industry. Today 130,000 fast-food outlets cover the country. In 1987 Americans spent $55.7 billion on fast food. McDonald's did $14.3 billion in sales in 1987, feeding more than 17 million people at 10,000 restaurants, which represents 25% of the entire fast-food market. All of this from a 1952 startup![25]

Franchising has proven successful nationwide. It became very popular in the 1960s as an additional way "for entrepreneurs with limited capital to operate a business with the amenities of a large corporation."[26] *Venture* magazine, which tracks fast-growth franchisors every year in its "Franchise Fast-Track" March issue, identified seven franchisors from 1986 who repeated on the 1987 "Franchise Fast-Track": Park Inns International, Cindy's Cinnamon Rolls, Lightning Lube, StellarVision, Timbermill Storage Barns, Service Coffee, and Perkits Yogurt. Seven companies went from the Franchisor 50 (February 1987) to the Franchisor 100 (November 1987): Novus Windshield Repair, Americlean Mobile Power Wash, T. J. Cinnamons Gourmet Bakeries, Allison's Place, Penguin's Place, Frozen Yogurt, and the Box Shoppe.

The article goes on to point out the hazards of fast growth: "Managing growth can be a little like trying to keep a roomful of children away from hot cinnamon rolls. By nature, franchising is litigious, and the slightest misstep can result in unhappy franchisees, broken laws, or both. The temptation is to grow too fast, take the easy money, and put off the hard work." Five companies from last year's list are no longer franchising.[27]

One of *Inc.* magazine's Fast Growth 500 companies, Dynamark Security Centers Inc., of Hagerstown, Maryland, attributes its growth to franchising. "We began to grow rapidly in 1979 when we changed our strategy and started offering dealerships to entrepreneurs. Within two years we had over 200 dealers nationwide. In 1984 we franchised the operation, which increased our rate of growth and afforded us national name brand recognition." As a result of all this, *Venture* magazine named Dynamark, which offers electronic protection and security devices, the fastest growing franchise organization in America in 1986. According to Dynamark president Wayne E. Alter, the firm has surpassed $5 million in sales.

# Other Methods of Financing ▬▬▬▬▬

As in many other areas, entrepreneurs are limited only by their imaginations when it comes to methods of financing. In addition to the major methods we've seen, there are a number of others. In this section we'll examine some of them.

Some firms decide to throw in their fortunes with larger firms, merging in order to gain the funding and financing they require for faster growth. Motion Designs, of Fresno, California, manufacturer of Quickie Wheelchairs, which had become the 72nd fastest growing private business in America, merged with Sunrise Medical Inc. in 1986, the seventh fastest growth public company in California. Grown from a backyard operation, Motion Designs, which produces ultralight wheelchairs, had achieved $15 million in sales by the time of the merger. The principals, founders Don Helman, Jim Okamoto, and Marilyn Hamilton, saw Sunrise as a new source of financing as well as a way that would enable them to "compete with other industry majors."

Other companies look to their own profit margins to generate adequate funds. Dr. James E. Jewett, founder and vice chairman of the Telco Research Corporation, said, "Financing our rapid growth, which was 60% a year for three years running solely on the basis of internal funds required incredible cost control and developing a culture where we could attract top talent, get them to take as much as 30% pay cut to come with us, and then give them a five-by-six-foot cubicle."

Not many corporations can do this. "We did it," said Jewett, "without turning to an outside source of financing until we had achieved dominance in each of our chosen market segments and had achieved margins that demonstrated beyond a doubt that we were a good bet for an outside investor. We proved this by first doing a successful placement, and then within months, being equipped by NYNEX [New York New England Exchange]." Telco, a producer of telecommunications software, in Nashville, Tennessee, was founded in 1977 and had 1984 sales of $5.4 million.

Others eschew growth in favor of control. One of the old masters, L. L. Bean, managed to hold on to his company privately through the 92 years of his life. At the same time, however, the company, which is still privately held, did not grow a lot under him. "L. L. had gotten away with being a one-man show by living until he was 92 and by keeping the company the same size for the last 40 years of his life."[28]

In fact, as former Bean executive Bill Henry pointed out to me recently, "There just aren't too many American companies that have had only two chief executives covering an operating period of 75 years."

When Leon Gorman arrived on the scene, one of his first moves was to hire a controller, the first in the history of the company, to help in "what had been, for 60 years, a series of guesses—how many employees should be hired, how much extra warehouse should we build or lease, how much cash would be needed to pay for goods delivered?"[29]

Bad guesses can be expensive, particularly for fast-growth companies that have no cushions to buffer operating mistakes. To fund your own growth, you must do a superior job of managing the cash that does come in daily. This means providing some professionalism in the area of managing inventory, accounts receivable, accounts payable, and daily cash.

In some cases, financing for growth can be quirky. One of the more unusual companies that we met, the Foreign Candy Company Inc. of Hull, Iowa, enjoyed incredibly favorable foreign exchange margins as a result of importing Black Forest Gummy Bears from West Germany into the United States. According to President Peter W. DeYager, "To our advantage, the dollar's value to the deutsche mark climbed all the way up to deutsche mark 3.45 between 1983 and 1985 and we were importing over two hundred 40-foot containers of Black Forest Gummy Bears per year. Our sales grew from $3 million to $9 million the next year and $16 million the next year."

Some companies have gone to European and international money markets to raise capital. The ICN Corporation, producers of pharmaceuticals and biomedicals, undertook a major debt and equity offering in Europe in 1986. According to Milan Panic, chairman and president, "We raised $60 million in Swiss francs, $33 million in Dutch guilders, $40 million in European currency units, and $75 million in Eurobonds in order to become a world leader in the rapidly growing market for anti-viral pharmaceutical products."

Foreign money is also flowing heavily into the U.S. business market. "During the past five years, close to $800 billion in foreign capital has come in to the United States," according to John Burgess of the *Washington Post*.[30]

"The Japanese alone have put $31 billion of capital into the United States economy in the first nine months of 1987 alone. And, not to be outdone, the Europeans hold $745 billion in assets of all kinds in the United States as of September 1987."[31]

## A Success Story

One of the fastest growth stories we found is that of the Patten Corporation, of Stamford, Vermont. According to Don Dion, chief financial officer of the corporation, the company grew from $1.9 million in sales in 1981, with a profit of $200,000, to a company that will, in 1988, achieve $120 million in sales, with an income-before-taxes figure of more than 20% of revenues.

How did Patten do it?

During the early 1980s, Harry Patten, who had perfected his formula for selling land on a small scale locally, wanted to get bigger.

According to Dion, "Patten was very focused. He understood his niche. He sold Vermont land, 20 acres a shot, for $15,000 ... 'will finance.' There was one office in Stamford, Vermont, which was throwing off enough cash for a nice living for Harry, but he wanted more. Patten had already developed a clear vision of taking his backwoods realty firm global.

"We met in Nantucket in early November of 1984 and he was very direct. He said he was looking for a guy to help take him global, who understood capital markets. In a little less than a month we had a handshake agreement and I had 15% of the company."

Patten needed money, and it was Dion's job to get it, from the bankers whom he had worked with during his CPA days at Arthur Young and his lawyering days at Warren and Stackpole in Boston. As a lawyer and CPA, Dion had "for years provided advice to so many guys who had gone out, used my advice, and become fast-growth companies. I decided to trade in the action on one side of the street for action on the other."

Dion determined which six New England bankers should hear the Patten story, and created a carefully orchestrated package, complete with financials, land acquisition plans, and aggressive sales and marketing strategies. "Our pitch lasted about 20 to 25 minutes, and we went in looking for $5 million in initial financing. We all thought it was great!" To his surprise, he got six rejections.

"The bankers simply didn't want to lend money on raw land," said Dion. "They considered it too risky."

Dion was slightly depressed and more than a little nervous. He had had a strong feeling, on the basis of the attractiveness of the presentation and the strong growth record, that financing for Patten would be forthcoming. "We needed cash, and fast, so I went to seven or eight local bankers in the Berkshires, and all of us went on the line with personal guarantees. We got $1 million out of First Agricultural Bank, $200,000 out of Vermont National, and got everyone with whom we had existing line relationships to double their commitment to us within the next four months. We were able to pick up $10 million in financing that way."

But to do what Patten wanted to do, they needed more, much more. They began to think about going public.

"Harry had been intelligent. He had written an annual report every year despite the fact that he was a private company and didn't have to. We hired Arthur Young, one of the top 'big eight' CPA firms, and an absolutely top flight director, Herman Anstatt, who had significant business experience and great contacts.

"We prepared our case for the investment bankers, a thing about which, frankly, I knew very little," said Dion.

"I began making cold calls to New York City," he went on, to firms such as Dean Witter, Morgan Stanley, Goldman Sachs, First Albany, and Morgan Keegan. "I'd tell them, 'I'll be in New York tomorrow and could stop by to see you if you have some free time.'

"Once someone said O.K., I'd get myself into New York, fast."

A number of firms showed passing interest, but only one showed significant interest. "That was Drexel Burnham," said Dion, where a young man by the name of Mark Goodman, a CPA as well as an MBA, with whom Dion related easily, saw great value and potential in the company.

"It looked like we'd team up with Drexel Burnham and Oppenheimer. But Oppenheimer, at the last minute, after a verbal yes on the telephone and a handshake, said no, because one of their senior guys decided that Oppenheimer ought not to be involved in land. So we wound up doing a deal with Drexel Burnham and First Albany and raised $12 million."

Now going public may not be for the average fast-growth company without a strong stomach and without a very serious consideration of the expenses involved. "Our legal bill was $150,000, the accounting bill $60,000, travel and entertainment ran $30,000, and the bill for financial printing services was $120,000," said Dion.

"We did a final proofreading at 5:00 A.M. in the morning and 60,000 copies of our printed prospectus were delivered to every brokerage house in the country by 9:30 A.M., four hours later," he went on.

The critical first wave of financing was complete. The stock was offered at $4.00 a share in its initial public offering in 1985. It reached a high of $30.00 a share, which made it the New York Stock Exchange's best performing new stock of 1986. (It was NYSE listed on October 28, 1986.)

"In a sense we were surprised," said Dion, "in another sense we weren't. We knew we had a strong company with a strong, well-focused idea that could be replicated in most parts of the country and around the world. We had strong leadership from Harry Patten, who wanted to grow the business and who was willing to share it with younger people, myself included."

As the public offering money came in, out went the personal guarantees to the bankers, and the book value of the company increased from $1 million to $30 million in a very short time.

Later in November of 1985, the company raised an additional $8 million; then in May of 1986 it issued a convertible debenture offering for $35 million. In December of 1986 Drexel sold $25 million of Patten accounts receivable, again providing fast cash to the company (and an improved balance sheet), and in May of 1987 $46 million worth of convertible debentures were sold publicly. "We were simply borrowing money from the public," said Dion.

With virtually all of its debt retired by May 1987, Patten was able to invest heavily in new land acquisition and, based on their successful formula for fast turnover, dramatically increased sales and earnings. Another $50 million worth of stock has been sold since May 1987, in what has been a good public market. This has allowed Patten to raise $150 million in cash in a remarkably short period of time.

In the process, Patten and other senior people have been able to take some chips off the table, and a half dozen people in the corporation have become seriously wealthy in a short period of time.

"It's not all roses," said Dion. "During a public offering, you're working seven days a week, perhaps as many as 20 hours a day. You're on the road constantly. A routine week is now 70 to 80 hours. A lot of people pay a high price in terms of family life and the forsaking of other interests.

"But, we're all excited. It's a fast-growth company, we're dealing with the best agencies and firms in the world, and we're on the cutting edge of the financial world. Right now we're raising money worldwide in London, France, and Switzerland for continued expansion," said Dion.

So much for money. Throughout this chapter we've met entrepreneurs who have funded their fast-growth dreams in a wide variety of ways. Yet in virtually no case have we seen anyone whose primary motivation was money. Or anyone who has been held up or stopped by the lack of it. Most simply want to be innovative builders of new corporations for the future. Their efforts are being funded in dozens of different ways, and are resulting in fast growth, new jobs, and, in the process, a renewed and revitalized corporate America.

# Goods and Services

5

In New England, where we run our communications company, the landscape has changed dramatically over the past 20 years. The old 19th-century textile mills, clinging to the banks of the many rivers throughout Vermont and Massachusetts, are all long gone, having fled South during the 1950s and 1960s to lower heat and lower labor costs. What they left behind was warehouse space, as much as you'd like. Mike Meehan and his wife A. J., good business friends of ours, picked up 250,000 square feet of old mill space five years ago for their Meehan and Company Packaging business, and have just added another 100,000. Significantly, the price of the second building was up markedly over the price of the first, as today's entrepreneurs and small fast-growth companies have discovered this solid, low-cost space.

Thus, textiles and tanneries have yielded to warehouses and entrepreneurs. And the old buildings have become the homes of fast-growth businesses such as *New England Monthly* magazine in Haydenville, Massachusetts, an award-winning and fast-growth circulation monthly; C. B. Sports in Bennington, Vermont; and the Delftree Corporation in North Adams, Massachusetts. But this is only the beginning, as many of the mills will serve as incubators to hatch even more fledgling businesses.

Change, particularly in business, is obvious and expected. In fact, the keynote of the entire American experience has been change—from frontier days and the westward migration to the

## GOODS AND SERVICES

Industrial Revolution and into the new age of communications with telegraph, telephone, radio, and television. And change will highlight the new decade and the coming century as well. In addition, its pace has accelerated and will continue to accelerate. And in the process, people's tastes for goods and services will continue to change dramatically.

David Birch put it this way: "The technologically based university is to the waning years of the 20th century what the Mississippi River was to exporters of grain in America's Midwest in the mid 19th century, the Mesabi Range to the steel industry in the late 19th century, and the oil fields to Texas in the early 20th century, namely a priceless resource."[1]

Birch has tracked small fast-growth companies over the last two decades. His huge MIT data base has revealed some interesting data on which goods and services are most likely to be the bases of new businesses and which businesses are most likely to survive in the coming decades. Currently, the top five most frequently started types of businesses are (1) miscellaneous business services, (2) eating and drinking places, (3) miscellaneous shopping goods, (4) automotive repair shops, and (5) residential construction.

Those most likely to succeed, however, are (1) veterinary services, (2) funeral services, (3) dentist offices, (4) commercial savings banks, and (5) hotels and motels.[2]

Birch goes on to point out that the businesses most likely to grow significantly in the days ahead are (1) commercial savings banks, (2) electronic component manufacturers, (3) paper board container manufacturers, (4) computer and office machine manufacturers, and (5) miscellaneous paper product manufacturers.

The companies that we've met, and spoken with, include many of these. They range from floor shining services to high-tech computer design; and they span the country from Austin, Texas, one of the nation's fastest growing areas, to Chestertown, New York, one of the more static. Rather than a cohesive pattern, what emerges is a gigantic puzzle with no particular rhyme or reason to it.

Fast growth isn't limited to high tech, any more than it is to high population areas. Rather, it has something to do with the nature of an entrepreneur's vision—the ability to spot a problem or a need, and the capacity to deliver high-quality goods and services.

## Finding the Right Business ▰▰▰▰▰▰▰

There is no single or simple procedure one can follow to decide what business to get into, to determine whether that business is going to succeed, or to establish how fast it might grow. Consultant Mack Hanan, who nudges sleepy *Fortune* 500 companies into faster growth areas through his Wellspring Consulting Group, asks the question, "Is there an ideal growth business?" Hanan notes that such a company will be:

1. A near monopoly that, like Xerox and Polaroid, can dominate its market because of patents.
2. A business whose earnings from sales represent a large proportion of total sales revenues; where, for example, a 20% increase in sales can yield a 50% increase in net income.
3. A business that can grow relatively independently in the economic cycle.
4. A business that has a consistently high rate of inquiries and incoming and repeat orders.
5. A business that's in a field about which few brokerage reports are written.
6. A business that is dependent on management talent.[3]

Attempting to develop products and services that fit into these categories is both difficult and expensive. According to the SAS Institute, research and development spending in advance of marketing can run as high as 55% of budget for research and development businesses that concentrate, for instance, on the development of software.[4]

An added difficulty is the dramatically accelerated life cycles of products, which we have seen in recent years. That is, the rate at which products are launched, rise, saturate the market, and then fall has been greatly speeded and compressed from earlier eras. As Hanan puts it: "From now on the base line of virtually every product life cycle will be drastically foreshortened. The former rounded curve is becoming saw tooth, bobtailed, primarily by technological innovations and changing market needs. This reduces significantly the amount of marketable time available to recover a product's up front investment."[5]

Thus, while trying to achieve a lock on the market with a unique or otherwise unavailable product is tempting, it is also extremely expensive. One entrepreneur, Jim Cook of Investment Rarities Inc., of Minneapolis, Minnesota, has said, "Developing a new product offers an incredible challenge to an entrepreneur. Follow the '5 and 10' rule when considering new products or services. 'It takes 5 years to get into the black and 10 times as much money as you initially budget.' "[6]

Ron Hume told us his rule of 2½: "Everything takes twice as much time, twice as much money, and is half as profitable as you think."

The real objective of many of these entrpreneurs is simply to gain a very significant position in a market while building a valuable company. Years ago, Andrew Carnegie said, "I believe the true road to preeminent success in any line is to make yourself master in that line."[7]

Paul Hawken, founder of Smith and Hawken, has put it slightly differently: "Take any business—pet shop, flower shop, window washer, or bicycle shop—and make yours the most thorough, best inventoried, highest profile sort of business in its area. Become the arbiter by which other competing businesses are measured."[8]

McDonald's grabbed its market share—now over 38%. Federal Express grabbed its share. Both started with a simple view—of goods in one case and services in the other. Be the best. Deliver the best.

# The Role of the Entrepreneur

Entrepreneurship today has become more of what one critic calls, "Building something fresh of value ... less 'be your own boss.' "[9] Those who are looking solely for independence are represented by the group David Birch calls, "income substituters."[10] These are people who want to do without the hassles of corporate life, and who seem happy to simply replace their corporate income with the same level of income from their own business. This is not the group that we're studying. Our group is definitely out to build: something new, something fresh, something of value.

Very few of these entrepreneurs think strictly in terms of commodities or pure products. As Theodore Levitt said in his book *The Marketing Imagination*, "There is no such thing as a commodity. All goods and services can be differentiated and usually are."[11] Federal Express has helped people like Land's End, Williams-Sonoma, and even BMW distinguish themselves through a heightened awareness of distribution strategies and overnight delivery.

# Products Chic and Otherwise

The range of entrepreneurial ventures that we've seen runs the gamut from the glamorous to the mundane. Jim Leahy moved to Taos, New Mexico, a decade ago and got the idea of developing a better, higher quality, and better designed line of leather jackets and coats. He opened the Overland Sheepskin Company, aiming at boutique retail operations in Aspen, Colorado, as well as other, similar "jet set" or "in" spots around the country. He began designing a beautiful basic product, and then extended his product line. The Overland Sheepskin Company today is a great success from Manchester, Vermont, to Boulder, Colorado, and is growing rapidly.[12]

Other fast growers are less chic. William H. Wilson, founder of Pioneer Eclipse Corporation, of Sparta, North Carolina, developed a system of high-speed floor maintenance that has revolutionized the way floors are maintained. As Wilson says, "We simply built the system that produces the shiniest of floors in a fraction of the time of conventional methods. Cleaning is 90% labor. Our system usually cuts labor by 30% to 50%. We developed the system in the late 1970s, put it on the market in 1982, and sales have soared." Pioneer's innovations have resulted in the company's surpassing $16 million in annual sales.

Or take Peter T. Worthin, CEO of Schreiber Corporation of Trussville, Alabama, whose company was formed in 1980 to manufacture and sell waste-water treatment equipment in the United States, Canada, and Mexico. His product, while hardly glamorous, is the most energy efficient system available and immediately took off. Schreiber recently surpassed $10 million in annual sales.

## Finding a Niche

We devote an entire chapter later in the book to niches, but the subject is relevant here as well. Some of the fastest product growth has come from people who have carefully defined a narrow niche and then moved quickly to fill it. Pak Melwani, founder of Royal Silk, was amazed when he came to this country from Bombay to find that silk, a natural fiber from his own area, was considered affordable only by the very rich. From his point of view, synthetics were no longer inexpensive, and with his own retail merchandising experience and realization that women were moving back into the work force in large numbers in the late 1970s and early 1980s, he launched his high-quality company with a single product: a woman's classic silk shirt, for $22. "I knew, deep within me, from the moment I got the early and strong response that we were underway. We now have a 40-page catalog focusing completely on silk that includes blouses, skirts, sweaters, dresses, and accessories," said Melwani.

"It all started with the product. It was beautiful, surprisingly affordable, and aimed at women—all women." Melwani has since broadened the line to include men's products as well, and used many fresh marketing techniques that have taken him well beyond the original *Cosmopolitan* ad.

Melwani's breakthrough centered on the fact that silk had always held a unique appeal, unmatched by any other fabric in elegance or luxury, and Americans were simply not used to it.

Melwani, who had a small import shop down in lower Manhattan, immediately saw the potential with mail order catalog selling and lined up excellent access to a wide variety of silks. His sales grew dramatically, from startup in 1978 to over $40 million in 1987.

"One thing I wanted to avoid from the very beginning," said Melwani, "was simply having 'me too' products. I enjoyed searching, designing, and offering uniquely beautiful products."

One of Melwani's early challenges was matching price, color, and style within an emerging product line that was no longer just one item. He was able to overcome this early challenge (six sizes, five colors, 30 stock-keeping units) through sheer "number crunching" analysis and was able to grow the company based on his unique understanding of silk and his awareness of the working woman's similar fascination with it.

"Money means little to me." said Melwani. "I've had a great time building this company. It's given me everything I've ever wanted and I'd like to think that we've added a lot of value to a lot of people's lives as we've gone along."

Other fast-growth entrepreneurs have identified similar small niche opportunities. Gary L. Pittman, president of Publications and Communications Inc. of Austin, Texas, told us, "We were the first to try the concept of vendor-specific publishing within the computer industry. It was a gamble but we found a niche and then worked very hard to concentrate on extracting all the revenue we could from that niche. . . . We stuck with it. I believe you gotta dance with the one who brung ya." PCI has danced through the $5 million sales level with its computer trade journals.

Niches emerge in the service area as well. Judith E. Berger, president of MD Resources Inc., of Miami, Florida, said, "We recognized the need for specialized health care recruiting and saturated the market before other firms became involved. Our head start gave us tremendous advantage." Her company has grown from a 1979 startup to over $1 million in sales.

# Quality ▬▬▬▬▬▬▬▬▬▬▬▬▬▬▬▬▬▬▬▬▬

Some of the largest corporations in the world simply depend on getting the product basics right in the first place. Ray Kroc, who founded McDonald's at the age of 52, went meticulously through every single step of preparing french fried potatoes "to get it right" before he signed anything. Kroc put it this way, "To most people a french fried potato is a pretty uninspiring object. It's fodder, something to kill time chewing between bites of hamburger and swallows of milkshakes. That's your ordinary french fry. The McDonald's french fry was in an entirely different league."[13]

Despite lots of effort, Kroc was unsuccessful in getting the french fries to taste right, but he didn't give up easily. He tracked down potato experts, and finally discovered that the original McDonald brothers had stored their potatoes in shaded chicken wire bins, which, surprisingly, improved the taste of the potatoes as they dried out and as the sugars inside changed to starch. "The McDonald brothers had, without knowing it, a natural curing process in their open bins, which allowed the desert breeze to blow over the potatoes."[14] From such details, fast-growth empires get built.

Most entrepreneurs stress "highest possible quality and good follow-through." Joe Musolino, president of Techne Electronics, describes his fast growth as coming from "Building a quality product and following it up with as much dealer support as is necessary. This enabled us to establish a strong dealer base that was in place when the auto security market took off." Techne, based in Palo Alto, has grown dramatically.

Other companies have grown simply by providing a better tasting product. Ben & Jerry's Homemade (ice cream) Inc., for example, was launched in a dilapidated gas station in Burlington, Vermont, and is now one of the fastest growing premium ice cream producers in the country. Recently, the company announced it was going to open stores in both Russia and Martinique. Several of the ice creams, particularly Dastardly Mash and White Russian, are growing favorites throughout the country. Ben and Jerry's will do $30 million this year.

A revolutionary product improvement, introduced specifically for a delimited market that had been overlooked by everyone, led to the dramatic success of Motion Designs Inc. of Fresno, California. Motion Designs brought out a modular frame, ultra-lightweight folding frame wheelchair into an industry that had been stagnant for 30 years and has had enormous market success by providing users with this high-performance adjustable and portable wheelchair. The company, founded in 1980 by Jim Okamoto, Don Helman, and Marilyn Hamilton, has grown from a backyard operation to over $15 million in sales.

Quality is critical for service companies as well. Larry Miller, president of Corinthian Communications of New York, a media-buying firm, said, "We remain dedicated to a quality product. In a service business, like our communications company, one is likely to confuse the real product with the appearance of service. We demand a quality product of ourselves first, then we service the client." Corinthian Communications has grown to $112 million in annual sales as a result of this view.

Dr. Gerald R. McNichols, chairman of Management Consulting and Research Inc., another service provider, echoes this thought. "Quality of our product, mainly superior analysis and study results have helped us grow at 100% per year from 1979 to 1983. We've deliberately slowed our growth to about 37% per year from 1983 to 1987." McNichols is looking for a mere 30% in growth over the next five years.

# Outperforming
## the Competition ▬▬▬▬▬▬▬▬▬▬▬▬▬▬▬▬▬▬▬

Some fast-growth entrepreneurs attribute their growth to simply outperforming the competition. One of these, Mark E. Hamister, president of National Health Care Affiliates, of Buffalo, New York, provides long-term health care and residential facilities in the East. Hamister says, "By going to great extremes to provide a home-like environment, our health care facilities have become places where people want to live. NHCA has not and will not sacrifice quality in order to further the growth of the company." Following this operating rule has proven profitable for Hamister, whose firm will do $40 million this year.

Another company, Original Copy Centers of Cleveland, Ohio, which provides legal and corporate copy services, was able to grow from a startup in 1975 to $2.5 million in 1986 and $4.4 million in 1987. Nancy Vetrone, president, cites a small but significant breakthrough that allowed her to beat the competition. "We began offering evening pick-up service and guaranteeing overnight printing. We placed distinctive metal 'overnight copy' boxes in the lobbies of 14 major downtown office buildings.

Collections were done each business day at 8:00 P.M. and finished product was delivered the next day by 10:00 A.M."[15]

David Nelson, president of Comlinear Corporation of Fort Collins, Colorado, agrees that outperforming the competition is important: "We entered into a crowded market dominated by several large companies and dozens of smaller ones. To even be considered, we had to offer products that outperformed our competition by a factor of 10 or more. We are able to do so and have been able to maintain the advantage through innovation." Comlinear, which manufactures single data-processing components, surpassed $5 million in sales.

Tom Blagge also bases his spectacular growth with Blagge Enterprises of Rancho Cordova, California, on outperforming the competition: "As a distributor of audio and video tapes we only sell service and price. Through primarily hard work, we have offered better service at a better price than our competition." Biagge did $12 million in 1985.

# Unique and Hard-to-Find Products

Sometimes businesses grow because they're able to provide consumers with goods and services that are unique or hard to find. Product uniqueness can be a major factor in fast growth. R. C. Anderson, founding president of Data 3 Systems Inc., in Santa Rosa, California, told us, "Our company took off when we developed a state-of-the-art application software package for manufacturing industries, to fill a demand that was simply not being filled by any other vendor at the time." This uniqueness allowed Data 3 to skyrocket in sales, from $113,000 in 1980 to $6.2 million in 1984.

Mike Collins, president of the CEM Corporation of Matthews, North Carolina, said that his fast growth resulted from "the development of a unique product that had a broad market, and ... the technology in our initial product allowed us to develop new products with even larger market potential." He's been running consistently at 30% to 35% growth a year, and has surpassed $10 million in sales.

James R. Ebright, CEO of Software Results Corporation said, "We were the first vendor to supply a non-deck data communications product for the VAX. For several years, sales doubled every nine months. We simply hitched our wagon to a new computer that Digital was introducing, the VAX, and rode along with it." Sales rose from $470,000 in 1979 to $3.2 million in 1983.

Some entrepreneurs have gone to foreign places to find products that the American market is not used to. Melwani went to Bombay for his silk. David Smith and Paul Hawken went to England for high-quality English gardening tools. As Hawken puts it, "I was in England touring British estate gardens and arboretums . . . the gardens were splendid and the craft of gardening was more highly developed than any I had ever seen, even in Japan. As I watched the gardeners work, I studied their tools. I hefted a spade, the tool of choice. It seemed unusually heavy and it was sharp as an axe, shiny with the patina of constant use."[16]

So into an America that was experiencing a renewed interest in gardening came Smith and Hawken's first shipment—everything from "a 13 pound Sri Lankan solid metal Tea Plantation Fork with thirteen-inch tines, as thick as a baby's ankle (later dubbed and sold as the Monster Fork) . . . to long-handled Irish Dunse Slashers, Scottish Manure Forks, British Mail Rabbiting Spade, and more."[17]

From the very outset, Hawken determined that he would introduce only the highest quality, even if unusual, products to the American gardening marketplace. His company is now approaching $30 million in annual sales.

Another entrepreneur who found success with an unusual product is Peter W. DeYager. DeYager, a school teacher, went to Germany in 1978 trying to find a money-making project for home and discovered the Black Forest Gummy Bears. DeYager brought in a stock of Gummy Bears to sell as fund raisers and found that other colleagues, professors of German, around the country were very successful in doing the same thing. Later, in 1983, he asked himself, "Why not sell Gummy Bears to retail stores if they're doing so well as fund raisers?" By developing the absolutely best available German candy, the Foreign Candy Company of Hull, Iowa, grew from $3 million one year to $9 million the next and $16 million the year after that. His growth continues today.

Other entrepreneurs have built companies simply by finding products for their customers that were otherwise hard to find. Pierre de Beaumont founded the Brookstone Company, which specializes in hard-to-find tools. "With $500 in capital, he and his wife built the company to $2.5 million by 1969 and $27 million at its peak, eventually selling to Quaker Oats."[18]

## Timing

Often the key to growth is timing. Getting to market first with the right product, for example, can be a huge advantage. Robert S. Maltempo, chairman of the Vantage Computer Systems Company of Wethersfield, Connecticut, said that after years of unchanging, traditional life insurance products, a new product, universal life, was introduced by an aggressive West Coast company. "In early 1981, based on what we had heard from the marketplace, we developed the first commercial software system for this new product in anticipation of many other companies offering it. We had the first system on the market and sales jumped from $2 million to $7 million in one year."

Kathleen Allenbach, founder of Allenbach Industries, of Carlsbad, California, said that she simply rode the wave of very rapid growth in the microcomputer software industry. "We were the first and only company in the industry offering duplication services to software publishers for about three years." The result of that was dramatically increased volume, from $199,000 in 1979 to $3.8 million in 1983.

Gerald D. Cohen, president of Information Builders Inc., of New York, told us, "We designed a computer software program to be used by computer service bureaus at the time when there was a booming growth industry and a need for software products to re-sell." Information Builders, which manufactures computer software, had reached $72 million in sales by 1985.

Often the key is introducing products and services when market conditions are ripe. Take, for example, Network Rental, Inc. of Atlanta, Georgia. President Perry J. McNeal told us, "In 1980, with the prime interest rate increasing to 20%, we knew that consumer credit would be hard to find and therefore the 'rent to own' industry would grow larger by increasing the percentage of the population that would have trouble securing credit for home furnishings." His company has grown dramatically to $12 million per year based on this strategy.

Another entrepreneur, W. Allen Vandenburgh, of Crosby Vandenburgh in Boston, said, "In 1983 with the growth of cable television we identified the need for cable TV guides that could be used by cable operators, not only to deliver program listing information but also to be used as strategic marketing tools." Vandenburg quickly got to $13 million in sales.

Ernst Volgenau, president of SRA Corporation, told us his systems research and applications company, which provides technical services to the federal government, "achieved much of our growth because of dramatic increases in the defense budget during the early 1980s."

Stephen Kellog, founder of YWC Inc., of Monroe, Connecticut, an environmental services firm, believes that much of its growth came from "our foresight into environmental regulations, primarily on the federal level that got us into several businesses and markets ahead of others. We had the first municipal wastewater treatment plant, private sector contract operations project on the East Coast. This knowledge of legislation and regulations put us way ahead of the game." YWC grew from $333,000 to $5.3 million within five years.

Another regulation reviewer, Thomas Spann Duck, started his Ugly Duckling Rent-A-Car system in Tucson, Arizona, watching carefully as the state mandatory liability insurance requirements, which had been built over a 25-year period and which forced people to rent nothing but new vehicles, began to change. "We put together the first 50-state, million dollar rental car insurance program and moved quickly." Ugly Duckling has franchised rapidly and increased its sales even more rapidly. Founded in 1978, Ugly Duckling reached $64 million in 1985 sales.

# How *Did* They Do It?

Entrepreneurs and their companies achieve success with products and services in a variety of ways. In addition to the more general avenues to success that we've examined, there are an unlimited number of individual paths. In this section, we'll look at some of these.

Sometimes growth is the result of getting exclusive rights to a product. Charles R. White, owner of the Fastec Industrial Corporation, told us that he became a manufacturer and then distributor of a fastener product called a Quadrex in 1984 and 1985, respectively. "The uniqueness of this product, capable of being used anywhere in the U.S. and overseas and the fact that we had gained an exclusive on it, was a big part of our early sales growth." Fastec, based in Elkhart, Indiana, went from $273,000 in 1979 to $11.5 million in 1983.

Some entrepreneurs learn early on to give their customers more than the customers expected. Richard M. Henley, chairman of Northland Pure Water, told us that his company "has centered on the unique packaging of distillation equipment and always providing the customer with more than he or she expected." Northland's efforts in extra service and enhanced products has paid off.

Jerry Hardy built in this concept of giving more than expected from the beginning at Time-Life Books: "Tell 'em it's 128 pages and give them 144," he'd say. Here at Storey, we add a booklet or bulletin to orders, at just a few pennies of additional expense, that the customer didn't order, and we build enormously loyal customers in our publishing business.

Some companies have grown rapidly by paying attention to forgotten markets. Cathy and Bill Simmons have built their Group Benefit Services of Charlotte, North Carolina, by providing third-party administrative health insurance and related fringe benefit programs for trade and professional associations.[19] Their volume is now at $20 million a year, from startup in 1981.

A superior guarantee or warranty feature is part of product value, and sometimes that's the key to fast growth. Troy Bilt Rototiller introduced a superior rear tine design that takes the drudgery out of turning over one's garden, and discovered that customers found it just too good to be true—they didn't believe it! So the company announced an unconditional warranty on any part or system in the machine. Chrysler's Lee Iacocca, at last check, is up to "seven years and 70,000 miles" with his warranty.

This technique for reaffirming product strength has not escaped the notice of smaller operators. Bill Bohlman, president of Waterbeds Plus Inc. of Oshkosh, Wisconsin, one of the nation's fastest growing companies, said, "We recognize the need for good product at a fair price coupled with service in an industry that was plagued with unkept promises and poor customer service after the sale. Our policy of 'if you don't want it, send it back' has not only won us customers, it has kept them." Bohlman's business went from $1.3 million to $7.9 million in five years.

Once stabilized, many companies begin to look for additional products to fit their existing manufacturing capacity and help speed their growth. Ronald E. Wysong, president of R. L. Drake and Company, identified satellite reception equipment that had "terrific market potential, and at the same time was perfectly suited for our existing design and manufacturing abilities." Drake, of Miamisburg, Ohio, raced from sales of $9.5 million in 1980 to $69 million by 1984.

One company was able to identify a problem that existed for a number of companies, and by applying "win, win" problem solving, was able to build a fast-growth company. Virginia M. Lord, senior vice president of Wright Associates, told us that her company took off in 1981 when "we identified the need for career management services (outplacement) for employers who, for financial and other reasons, had to terminate employees without the risk or fear of litigation, negative community and customer impact, financial jeopardy, and negative press." The company's volume is up a whopping $26 million today.

One of the classic ways to achieve fast growth is to develop something you feel strongly about and then let some of your friends try it. Carole Ziter's Sweet Energy company in Essex Center, Vermont, picked up steam when her friends wanted to know where *they* could get dried apricots. L. L. Bean tried his Maine hunting shoe himself, had a few friends try it, and then rented the Maine hunting license list and began selling shoes by mail way back in 1912.[20] Bean's personal experience allowed him to become the spokesman for this product.

Occasionally fast growth is a direct result of the simplicity of a product or service. Harry Patten boiled his land sales business down to "20 acres, $15,000, we finance." Pretty straight-forward—and worth $125 million a year.

Speed in servicing has become a characteristic of one company's success. The Perry Morris Corporation of Newport Beach, California, began in 1981 with $2000 in capital. Monthly invoice sales are between $5 million and $6 million today. They've become the largest independent equipment leasing company in California. According to a company spokesman, "The biggest single factor in our success is service. No other lender will do what we do because they are unwilling to make the instant decision. Other lenders generally take from one to four weeks to approve a transaction because they review by committee or by a series of credit analysts. Perry Morris will approve within 24 hours because there *is* no committee structure, and because we package a transaction creatively."

C. B. Sports, of Bennington, Vermont, started by C. B. Vaughn, Jr., in the late 1970s, came out with a line of ski and sportswear that has resulted in annual sales of nearly $36 million. His line was simply more stylish than anyone else's.

In Chapter 7 we'll discuss customers, and give examples of truly superior customer service. But Rubbermaid, one of the nation's largest corporations, had doubled its sales and tripled its earnings in the past six years based on what the company calls, "constant attention to customer needs."[21] Rubbermaid pays an enormous amount of attention to its customers, through consumer complaints and customer ideas. According to one reporter, Rubbermaid "has a fetish of keeping in touch with customers," which helps them live up to a claim of a 90% success rate with new products.[22]

Stanley Galter, CEO of Rubbermaid, says, "Our formula for success is very open: We absolutely watch the market and we work at it 24 hours a day."[23]

Some products offer greater efficiency. We came across a company, Pro-File Systems Inc. of Conshohocken, Pennsylvania, a fast-growth company that provides records management and color-coded filing systems to businesses that have problems with the management or storage of their records. Pro-File is generally able to reduce floor space by 50% and increase the efficiency of finding and returning files by 40% to 60%. Founder Phil

Pressler has based his growth on this overnight or over-the-weekend complete file conversion. They've surpassed $2 million in sales in a short period of time.

Some companies have made their products user friendly. Dynamark Security Centers headed by Wayne E. Alter, Jr., has grown dramatically in the past several years by developing a nontechnical "user friendly line of advanced programmable electronic protection devices that can easily be armed or disarmed by authorized business or family members." The company started in Hagerstown, Maryland, in 1977 and had surpassed $5 million by 1984. The company is still growing dramatically through its successful franchising operations.

One company has grown quickly by handling difficult problems. Akal Security, of Albuquerque, New Mexico, offers a highly effective security program for companies and organizations. Akal puts a tremendous effort into the training of its security force, which is geared to "the diffusion of anger and frustration, and avoidance of the resulting conflict." Because of the success of this unusual service, Hari Harkaur, Akal's president, has built the company into a multimillion dollar business. Akal Security, founded with a $1500 loan in 1980, had surpassed $2.5 million by 1986 and is still moving forward.

Selling a service requires constant attention to promotion, marketing, and sales. One public relations company, Watt Roop of Cleveland, has grown from $100,000 in 1981 to $2.7 million in 1987, and according to its founder, Ronald W. Watt, "We built a 30-year-old business in six years!"[24] Watt and his partner Jim Roop believe in just plain hard work. "I'm of the opinion that workaholism is good," Watt said. "Workaholics almost always enjoy what they're doing."[25]

In many of the cases we've just looked at, the product or service that ignited the fast growth derived from the personal interest of the founder. You often do better at things you like. In the next chapter we'll take a look at customers, and learn why the old homily that "the customer is always right" has proven to be a primary commandment for fast-growth entrepreneurs.

# People

**6**

**P**eter Chan is one of the best gardeners and best human beings that I know. He left Communist China in the mid-1960s and immigrated to Portland, Oregon, where he eventually got himself a modest ranch-style home. There, with his wife Sylvia, he's brought up three handsome and intelligent young men.

When I first entered Peter Chan's garden, I couldn't believe my eyes. "This was a rubble-strewn lot when we began," said Peter. "Now it's a thing of beauty!"

He was too modest. I walked slowly around the yard and took it all in. Was this Eden? Hundreds of different plant species—flowers, perennials, shrubs, vegetables, lawns, pools, paths, fruit trees—all beautifully orchestrated by Peter, the master gardener. I said to Peter, "How do you find time to manage all of these plants and all of this growth?" He frowned and scolded me saying, "You do not manage plants—you coach them, and let them reach their potential."

While Peter is not the head of a fast-growth company, I have a feeling that with that attitude he could be. Every time we chat he reminds that unlocking the potential of plants leads to the same harmonious conclusion that working well with people produces.

This chapter is about people, not management. The companies that we will focus on here are among those who have understood Chan's simple growth principle: unlocking talent rather than creating structures and managing people into them.

# Today's "People"

David Birch, on the first page of his treatise on job creation, says, "Twenty million Americans leave their jobs every year, half of them voluntarily. Ten million change their careers."[1] At one point the *Wall Street Journal* estimated that 80% of American workers were unfulfilled in their work. Senior executives at sleepy corporations are told after years of service that "the chemistry isn't right." Occasionally, if they press for more of an answer, they are told, as was Lee Iacocca by Henry Ford, "I don't like you."

Birch indicates that virtually all job creation in America has come from enlightened entrepreneurial companies. Most of the job losses, conversely, have come from corporations who have "had to adjust." Birch cites Polaroid which went from a peak of 22,000 employees in 1978 to approximately 12,000 in 1985. "Due in part to competition from Eastman Kodak and in part to a stale product line."[2]

Paul Hawken corroborates this point saying, "Thirty-seven percent of all employed men and nearly half of the working women want or intend to start a business. The future of American business is standing at the threshold, not sitting in the boardrooms."[3]

It's been almost 18 years since Robert Townsend wrote *Up the Organization*. It's significant that the book has just been reissued, at a time when large corporations need to understand more than ever how to deal with their own people, and how to recapture their earlier growth trajectories. Townsend's section on people provides insight into the basic wants and needs of people. Townsend's view, that corporations "stifle people and strangle profits," reminds us of Douglas McGregor's classic post-World War II work, *The Human Side of Enterprise*, and his original identification of "Theory X" and "Theory Y" companies. (Simply stated, Theory X, according to McGregor, holds that workers need to constantly be pushed and controlled; Theory Y holds that they are motivated, and simply need a decent working environment in order to perform.) In the corporate America of the 1940s, this difference among companies was just being discovered. In the corporate America of Townsend's 1960s, companies were just beginning to view their people differently—as productive people who actually *wanted* to work and to be productive on their jobs. By believing in them a bit more, companies were releasing the talents of their people.

But it took Bill Ouchi's "Theory Z," ten years later, to point up an even greater difference in how companies deal with the people who work for them. He compared traditional American approaches with the Japanese approach to working with people. In doing so, Ouchi, a friend and former classmate at Williams College, introduced American corporations to the concept of Japanese teamwork, Japanese consensus, Japanese pride in work, and Japanese desire for "everlasting customers." Ouchi, now a professor of the School of Management at UCLA in Westwood, California, consults with the top corporations of America, quietly advocating his Japanese business ethic, which begins with people. Much of his work has been adopted into today's corporate America.

As we approach the 1990s, it is clear that American workers are looking for more out of their companies than just money. Certainly the days of a Christmas party and a gold watch are long gone. Smart, fast-growth companies understand this.

What do people in fast-growth companies want? In short, they want more flexibility, more recognition, more participation, and the ability to take complete pride in their company and in their products. We saw this again and again, from Bean in Maine to Eckerd in Florida, Nordstrom in Washington, to Celestial Seasonings in Colorado.

## More Than an Employee

People want to be treated as more than just faceless employees. The entrepreneurs we met have looked into the needs of their people and their rapidly growing companies (just as Peter Chan has looked into the inner workings of his plants), to a far greater degree than have the bland policy-formulating "Human Resource Directors" of larger corporations. When asked, many entrepreneurs responded promptly, "Our people needs are too important to assign . . . I do it myself." Most fast-growth entrepreneurs insist on meeting all new hires. One responded, "What the hell do you mean by 'Human Resources Manager'? If you mean working with people, we all do that!"

## PEOPLE

Very few of these companies refer to their people as "staff,"
"personnel," "employees." Most refer to them as "people." Some
even think up imaginative new names for them.

Ray Stata, who has engineered Analog Devices, Inc.'s growth
from sales of $60 million in 1972 to $400 million today, refers
to his key players, his top engineers, as "corporate fellows." In
the entire history of his fast-growth company there has never
been a general layoff. Stata believes deeply in unlocking the
potential of Analog's people.

Harry V. Quadracci, president and founder of Quad Graphics, Pewaukee, Wisconsin, refers to his people as "students,"
"sponsors," and "mentors." You won't hear the term *personnel*
nor see a "human resources department" in his organization.
What you will see is a state-of-the-art printing corporation that
has grown from $11 million in 1977 sales to $261 million in 1986
sales; from $6 million in plant and equipment to $193 million
in the same period. From 140 happy people to nearly 2200. How
did Quadracci do it? "Anyone can buy the same binders, presses,
and buildings but no one can duplicate the blend of people and
other resources that makes Quad Graphics a unique work of art,"
said Quadracci. His plans call for hitting a billion in sales. At
his current rate of growth he'll be there in four years!

# Recognition ▬▬▬▬▬▬▬▬▬▬▬▬▬▬▬▬▬▬

People want attention and recognition. The classic psychological
research study that took place at the Western Electric Hawthorne
works in Chicago during the 1930s certainly demonstrated this.
The study, performed by Harvard researchers, was geared to an
assessment of productivity in the workplace. I remember my dad,
Matthew J. Storey, who worked at Western, telling me about this
when I was a young, and green, businessman. "Make sure you
pay some attention to your people on a regular basis," said my
dad, who rose to the controller level within the Western Electric Company. "When they ran the experiment out at Hawthorne,
it wasn't a matter of whether the researchers turned the lights
up or down, people's productivity went up anyway. . . . It was
simply a matter of somebody coming through the offices and paying some attention to them," he said.

Certainly, Federal Express understands this principle and has become a prime example of what Tom Peters and Robert Waterman first described as "management by walking around." In talking with Pete Willmott about his experience as chief executive of Federal Express during its remarkable fast growth during the 1970s, he said, "You learn far more by going down and talking to the mechanics in the hangar maintenance area than you do by sitting at your desk and reading your in-box. We insist on getting out and meeting our own people, who know far more about what's going on in the business than the accountants."

In the beginning, it surprised the mechanics and grease-gun specialists when Willmott would show up. After awhile, however, virtually everyone in the company knew him on a first name basis. "Helluva guy," said David Parrish, a transportation and security specialist at Willmott's new company, Carson Pirie Scott, of Chicago. "He's only been here a short time and he knows everybody already."

The average Federal Express employee deeply appreciates that kind of personal attention from a Pete Willmott or a Fred Smith, who began the company. I know also from having spoken with Pete that Federal Express' unique "guaranteed fair treatment program" and record of no layoffs over the life of the company, helps to explain its dramatic growth. The company today employs over 30,000 people in the United States, and has never had a general layoff.

People like it when a company gets the right person in the right job at the right time. Don Dion revealed that when he was a lawyer in Boston, and Analog Devices was beginning its dramatic growth, President Ray Stata went out to find the very best chief financial officer in the country. This happened to be a man by the name of Joe Hinchie, who simply had no interest in moving from his beloved Texas, where he was happily ensconced at the larger Texas Instruments. Stata felt that $1 million in stock might show his seriousness. It did—it caught Hinchie's attention and Stata got him. The $1 million in stock proved, eventually, to be a small price to pay for someone capable of guiding the company through its dramatic growth period.

But actually Stata does well with all his employees. One form of recognition, for example, is sharing in the company's success. People like it when there has been a good harvest and when the managing or founding entrepreneurs share that harvest. So they certainly like working under Stata, who, in 1984, launched "the investment partnership." This is "a tax deferred long-term savings program under which the company makes a monthly contribution equal to 5% of each employee's earnings, and also matches employee contributions up to an additional 2% of earnings."[4]

At Garden Way Incorporated, during our fast growth from $30 million in the early 1970s to $130 million in the early 1980s, key performers were awarded significant bonuses. It was not unusual for a high-producing sales performer to get as much as 25% of his annual income from a bonus. At the same time, *everyone* in the company was recognized with a year-end bonus averaging 3 to 5 weeks salary, as well as a "two-for-one" vacation policy, which awarded two weeks pay for every one week of vacation earned, paid on the day an employee left for vacation. The philosophy was that "if you don't earn these bonuses, you really shouldn't be here."

Sam Walton, who has built Walmart into one of the nation's premier retail operations with sales in the $5 billion range believes deeply in the profit-sharing and stock purchase technique. "The employee profit sharing trust, one of the largest owners of Walmart stock, has increased from $4.4 million in 1977 to $158.3 million in 1984," he said. "The company's contribution to each associate's account represented 8.4% of his or her earnings for the year."[5]

Jack F. Gold, chief executive officer of Contract Furnishing and Systems Ltd. of New York, another fast-growth company, understands the effectiveness and corporate self-interest of sharing: "Recognition on our part of how important people and their development were to our success, led to the creation of an environment that not only allowed but encouraged our people to personally profit and benefit from the successes they brought to our company." Gold's company, founded in 1978 is now approaching $20 million.

Many companies have struggled with appropriate incentives for their top producing salespeople, and general rewards for others. Jeffrey DePerro, owner of Aim Executive Inc. of Toledo, Ohio, told us, "Because our staff is composed of very high achievement sales personnel, our biggest challenge has been to effectively manage the unique types of personalities that are inherent among top salespeople. Equally as challenging has been our efforts to maintain the 'spark of enthusiasm' among top salespeople who frequently meet or exceed their personal financial objective." DePerro's "sparking" has triggered this executive recruiting and temporary help service firm to $6 million in annual sales.

Lyman Wood placed a very high premium on his sales and marketing people and would regularly remind us all that, "Nothing happens until something is sold." This was reflected by incentives provided to key salespeople to get the "offense" moving. But this can't be done to the detriment of the "defense," or logistical back-up team. There must be a feeling of equity in and among all of the players.

One of the greatest things that ever happened to me was being called into the office of one of the owners at Garden Way and, after a short talk during which I received recognition and appreciation for a job I had recently completed, being handed five tickets to Orlando, Florida, and hotel reservations at Disney World's Polynesian Village for my wife and young family. "Have a great time," said Dick Denholtz. "You've been working hard and you ought to relax a little bit and get a little time with your family." We were on the plane within 24 hours, and as we flew over New York, I genuinely felt "on top of the world."

The Kollmorgen Corporation, a diversified electronics company based in Stamford, Connecticut, rewards its employees for their contributions to the specific *product* on which they're working. "If the product makes a profit (defined in terms of pre-tax return on net assets, or RONA), everybody who worked on the product gets a bonus. Kollmorgen's policy is to pay up to 33% of its pre-tax profits in bonuses."[6] Kollmorgen has exploded in size, now employing more than 5000 people, and with sales well over $250 million.

Remington Products Inc., of Bridgeport, Connecticut, has achieved unusual growth that started when Victor Kiam, now head of Remington, acquired, for under $1 million several years ago, the corporate assets of a company with $25 million in sales. Until then the company had been consistently losing money, but since the acquisition at the end of 1979, the company has "tripled its sales, more than doubled its market share, and is solidly in the black with a payroll that has gone from 499 people to more than 1,100 at the start of 1985."[7] How did Kiam do it?

When we talked to him, he credited the success of this growth to profit sharing and to other participative techniques. As busy as Victor Kiam is, he was incredibly cooperative, talking to us at length from his home on a Saturday just before leaving for a month's sales trip to the Orient. "I think everyone in the organization takes more pride," he said, describing the period following his buyout of Remington, "They are in a stand-alone outfit now. They are making their own way, they know they've got problems, but, by God, they're doing it on their own. They don't have big daddy down the street calling the shots."[8]

Kiam, following significant overhead reduction, began productivity, incentive, and profit-sharing programs that have clearly worked, with base wages running very competitively and with incentive additions taking the hourly rate up nearly 40%. There is no union at Remington.[9]

In addition, Kiam "maintains a $25,000 discretionary fund to give instant cash recognition to workers who have been spotted by their supervisors doing an exceptional job. He calls these people to his office and hands out checks ranging from $200 to $500."[10]

Kiam takes his leadership role seriously. "You have a whole group of people who are dependent on you and your decisions. You've got to bull it through. You've got to keep going. You can't ever show your doubts."[11]

Kiam's leadership has led to very sound growth for Remington after years of malaise. He's gotten rid of the corporate trappings. He tries to let his people have as much fun as he's obviously having.

# Trust

People like to feel trusted. As Paul Hawken puts it: "You ... [must] ... trust your employees. If you don't it stands to reason that you'll try to protect yourself with trick procedures. But these don't protect the business, they isolate it."[12]

People know when they're trusted. At the Donnelly Corporation in Holland, Michigan, which makes accessory products for automobiles, the time clock has been removed, and all the people who work there are on salary. "A Donnelly employee works in a team of 10 people. You are trusted to keep your own records but you are responsible to other members of the team. If you're late because of an illness in the family, for example, your work will be covered by another team member."[13]

All of this trust has beneficial results. In Hawken's case, his company went from nothing to $30 million in a decade. In Donnelly's case, sales between 1965 and the mid-1980s went from $3 million to $75 million.[14]

## Low Overhead/ High Productivity

People like low overheads and high productivity. People on the line are the first to know when overstaffing has developed and when production is about to go down based on slackening of demand. We've made a practice of having no secretaries in our organization; rather, we provide those who want it with a word processor terminal so they can manage their own work.

At Tandy everyone answers his or her own telephone. There is no such thing as calls being screened for executives.[15] And at the Apple Corporation there are almost no typewriters to be seen. Even executives prepare their own letters and memos on their personal Apples.[16] Practices like this help to explain why Apple skipped quickly from the *Inc.* Fast Growth 500 list to the *Fortune* 500 list in less than five years.[17]

## Fun

People like to have fun. Dreyer's Grand Ice Cream Inc., an Oakland, California–based company, which was purchased by T. Gary Rogers and William F. Cronk in 1977, when it was on a sleepy $6 million per year sales plateau, began to launch real awareness campaigns among their employees and customers. "Neighborhood children gorge themselves on banana splits in Dreyer's only ice cream parlor, on the first floor of the Oakland headquarters.

## PEOPLE

Employees get an 'all-they-can-eat' ice cream break every Wednesday afternoon."[18] Dreyer's took off and sailed through the $100 million mark without even looking back.

The Leo Burnett Company Inc. of Chicago, the largest advertising agency in that city, with over 1600 employees, has a happy tradition, now in its sixth decade (!), of an "apple a day." It all started in 1935 when a telephone receptionist began to put out apples for people coming into the Burnett offices. Today, Burnett gives away 1000 apples a day at every one of its offices.[19]

Do all of these niceties really mean anything to the average employee? Well, at Burnett, it sure doesn't hurt. The turnover rate is practically nonexistent. Thirty percent of the work force has 10 years of service, and 133 of the people have been there for more than 20 years.[20]

## Workplace ▬▬▬▬▬▬▬▬▬▬▬▬▬▬▬▬

People, increasingly, like to work in nice locations. The days of headquarters having to be in downtown New York, Chicago, or Los Angeles are over. With telecommunicating and teleconferencing, telex and FAX, and Federal Express and dozens of other suppliers happy to come to places such as Pownal, Vermont, the need for companies to actually be located in a heavily congested urban metropolis is a thing of the distant past. Increasingly, fast-growth corporations are springing up in the places where people want to be.

Morris Siegel, who started Celestial Seasonings, selected Boulder, Colorado, as the kind of community and area where the people working for his company would be happy. This "health capital of the country" seemed a perfect reflection of the products and style of the company.[21] And the area has attracted many other fast-growth companies, including Neo-Data, Spectrum Color, and others.

Siegel did some other things right as well. "On your birthday you receive a $25 check. At Thanksgiving you get a $50 check. And at Christmas there's $100 for everyone. There are no time clocks at the plant. There are no unions. And the place seems to have a sense of humor."[22]

136

We certainly never had any trouble attracting talent to the out-of-the-way locations that Garden Way Incorporated selected: Burlington, Vermont, for its editorial and research groups; Westport, Connecticut, for its advertising, sales, and marketing people; and Troy, New York, for its manufacturing facility. During the fast-growth period of the 1970s, the company attracted to these locations 150 of the best young marketers in the country, and built what, at the time, was the most powerful direct marketing arm of any company that existed in America. Most of them looked forward to removing themselves from New York, Boston, and Chicago and getting into the country.

Bean had the same experience during its fast-growth period of the 1970s. It had little difficulty attracting top talent to its Freeport, Maine, headquarters.

And Glendinning, a marketing consultation firm formed by Ralph Glendinning after he spun off from Procter & Gamble in the 1960s, attracted some of the top marketing talent in America to its spectacular corporate headquarters in Weston, Connecticut.

One of the most shocking events of my life was leaving the extraordinary comfort of the Time Incorporated headquarters at 50th and Avenue of the Americas in New York to go down to "the frontier" at 1 Park Avenue, the "low rent" district, after we had acquired George Braziller's book club operation. Stepping into the order processing and fulfillment room was like stepping into a different era. How could we possibly motivate people with no ventilation, no light, and nothing to uplift their spirits? We picked the processing operation up and moved it to Connecticut, where space, views of the Long Island Sound, light, and air added vitality to a dead business.

Herman Miller Incorporated, of Holland, Michigan, which pioneered the concept of office landscaping, lays its own office space out, not surprisingly, in the same way. Everything is wide open. There are no doors—only light and air and openness. Something must be working right for Herman Miller. Sales went from $40 million in 1974 to $400 million ten years later.[23]

People also like to have an exciting atmosphere in their workplace. A crackling feeling of day to day action and motion. Don Dion says of the Patten Company, "It's energizing to be part of a young aggressive company that's growing at dramatic rates of speed. We'll do $120 million this year, and all that means is enormous opportunity for everyone."

Federal Express is the same way. "They talk of a sense of adventure associated with a company that is changing so rapidly. People work hard at Federal Express and they're proud of it."[24]

## Part of the Family ▬▬▬▬▬▬▬▬▬▬▬▬

People like to have a "family feeling." The larger a company gets, the more difficult it is to achieve this family feel unless individual operating units are allowed to operate as independently as possible.

At Gore and Associates, "The Gores found that the maximum effective group is around 150, and as their company grows, new plants are built to accommodate new associates rather than putting an expanding staff into a larger and larger facility. Plants worldwide number about 40, and in 1985, the company had about 4,500 associates and was increasing at a rate of 25 percent a year."[25]

Time Incorporated tried this approach in the early 1970s with its satellite business operation scheme. The scheme was based on the idea that many small businesses (in the $1 million to $10 million range) could be spread around the country in some of the nicer executive watering spots (such as Greenwich and Darien, Connecticut; San Francisco, California), yet be linked electronically to the mega computers that Time kept whirring 24 hours a day in New York and Chicago.

The *concept* was decent enough, but the expense and impracticability of teleprocessing in the early 1970s proved insurmountable. As a result, many of the lines were pulled back in by the mid-1970s, and most of the subsidiaries found themselves back in New York.

The family feel was maintained at Garden Way for many years. Everyone felt that helping each other was like helping one's brother or sister, and the mood was one of optimism. The feeling was that even large disappointments and marketing setbacks could lead to future successes.

Many companies mention this feeling, even as they become large. The Hallmark Company, founded by Donald Hall and based in Kansas City, Missouri, has managed to maintain that "family" feeling, even though it is now well over $1.5 billion in sales. "Employees . . . say Hallmark is like a family and they speak of how people care for each other . . . they talk with pride about what it means to become a 'Hallmarker.' "[26]

Ron Elgin, president of fast-growing Elgin Syferd, of Seattle, Washington, confided that one of his biggest problems "was to keep the small family feel that helped us to be successful in the first place . . . in blending our two disciplines of advertising and public relations." His firm does over $3 million in sales.

Another fast-growth company, Odetics Inc., employs between 400 and 500 people and works hard to keep them. "In an industry where job hopping is a way of life, Odetics has the lowest employee turnover of any electronics firm in California's Orange County, according to The Executive of Orange County. Associates [the firm junked the term *employee* in 1984] talked of the company as 'the family' and even recruitment brochures talk of becoming part of 'The Odetics Family.' "[27]

# Time Off

People like extra days off. The Reader's Digest pioneered this idea decades ago, with Fridays off in the summer at their Pleasantville, New York, operations. Garden Way Incorporated worked halfdays on Fridays throughout the year. Grolier works four 10-hour days at its Danbury, Connecticut, headquarters and takes Fridays off.

The Marion Laboratories Incorporated of Kansas City, Missouri, also works shortened hours on Fridays during the summer. "It's a program called 'uncommon days'. Instead of the usual 7:00 A.M. to 3:30 P.M. workday, plant employees work from 6:00 A.M. to 12:15 P.M.[28] "Uncommon days" must be working. Marion Labs doubled its sales between 1980 and 1984, and continues to grow fast.

## Extra Benefits ████████████████████

People like benefits that they wouldn't otherwise provide themselves. We recently surprised one of our key employees, who had gone the extra distance on a major project, with a $100 dinner certificate at the best restaurant in our small New England town. She took her husband and told us the next day, "I never would have done that for myself. Thanks."

CIBAR, an artificial intelligence software firm based in Williamstown, Massachusetts, took its entire staff to a country inn for a holiday celebration and invited them to not only enjoy the meal, but spend the night if they liked as well.

Harry Quadracci of Quad Graphics insists that his key managers take advantage of a completely paid-for annual trip for two to New York City. "The company picks up the tab for air fare for two and provides use of the company's apartment on 57th Street. Such trips help acquaint the work force of mostly local Wisconsin youth with the home base of most of the company's magazine customers."[29]

Merle Norman Cosmetics, a California-based cosmetics firm whose sales increased from $30 million in 1978 to over $90 million in 1983, provides its employees with gourmet meals for $.25 *every day!* Few of the company's employees would normally buy entrees such as prime rib, trout almandine, and barbecued spare ribs, but at Merle Norman it's practically free.[30]

Sometimes the benefits are more practical. For example, some companies offer transportation assistance to their employees. For many years, the Reader's Digest Co. of Pleasantville, New York, because of its sizeable processing requirements, has had to reach out to hire people from the surrounding countryside. There was no direct transportation service from many of the towns, and as the Digest pushed from 100 to 1000, 2000, 3000, and 4000 employees, they had to come up with innovative ways to get those employees to work. In talking with Jed Hall, director of personnel there for many years, he said, "We came up with the idea of the subsidized bus system. Digest buses drive all over Westchester County picking up groups of people. They enjoy the service, we go to dozens of different towns, and we charge the employee a very modest amount of money to use the service."

More recently, the Digest has come up with another idea. "It's possible for groups of employees to acquire their own vans to get to work. Parked in the Digest lots these days are 104 passenger vans. The Digesters who use a van to commute, pay for it via payroll deduction. After three years, they collectively own the van."[31]

McDonald's, desperate for employees in Florida, bus people as far as 75 miles to some of their hot spots. And the time clock starts running the moment the employee gets picked up.

## On the Other Hand: Getting and Keeping the Right People

To be sure, fast-growth companies have experienced people problems as well as successes. Finding and attracting the right kind of talent is one that all are challenged by. William H. Younger, venture capitalist, speaking at Stanford University's Conference on Entrepreneurship, put it this way: "As you begin to build your small group, and then a management team, you should do the following: (1) Hire experience, (2) go for quality people especially when they will be hiring additional people, (3) try to match their skill with the company's culture, (4) try to find people you have worked with in the past, (5) keep the team as small as possible, (6) focus on money. Profit is the goal."[32]

This advice comes from someone who has watched an extraordinary number of new projects try to get off the ground and documented dozens of early lessons learned by them.

Jack Rinehart, president of American Computer Professionals Inc. of Columbia, South Carolina, told us, "The biggest single challenge for us was putting together a management and sales team, most particularly the latter. And starting without an organization of people you know, trust, and understand, makes implementation of any plan extremely difficult. As a result, you must be prepared to have high and rapid turnover until you get the proper mix of the very best talent you can find." Rinehart's firm, which provides computer consulting services, has achieved $6 million in sales.

## PEOPLE

High turnover is not at all unusual in the early days of many fast-growth companies. We were told of losses amounting to one-half to one-third of total staff as new companies found their way, defined their purpose and direction, and searched for the right mix of people to achieve it. One of the early problems is the lack of a shared vision among all employees as to what the potential for the organization might be. Later, when objectives have become well defined, and people have bought into the definition, this becomes less of a problem. Just for historical perspective, I checked our records and found that we lost half of our staff in startup year one, 25% in year three, and 10% in year 5. Thus far this year we've had only one person of 35 leave.

Gulab Bhavnani, vice president and owner of Granada Systems Design Inc., said, "Our biggest single challenge was how to attract and keep highly qualified technical talent without sacrificing the quality of our customer service." Granada, which provides software to the communications industry, quickly surpassed $1.5 million in sales.

John R. Oren, CEO of Eastway Delivery Service, Houston, Texas, shared those thoughts: "Our biggest problem was keeping those quality people that bought into my dream. They have stayed to make it happen. Now they should see the benefit of their commitment." Founded in 1970, Eastway is approaching $5 million in sales.

Jiffy Lube, one of the fastest growing franchise operations in the country, found the right people and kept them. The company was unusual in being unable to turn to its franchises and employees during a time of financial crisis. "The collapse of the old Quartz Savings and Loan Company cut off access to all of our funds, crippling our company," said W. J. Hindman, chairman and CEO of Jiffy Lube International Inc. "The franchisees and employees lent the company over $1 million, allowing us to survive the crisis."

The unusual situation led Hindman to a philosophy he's happy to share with anyone who asks "What makes your company successful?" "People," he says. "Surround yourself with quality individuals, that is: people who believe in a common philosophy and mission; people who believe in and strive for the American dream; people who possess the entrepreneurial spirit, the desire to learn and grow; people who are loyal and honest;

and people who want to do good for their country and its inhabitants." Jiffy Lube, based in Baltimore, has reached $30.4 million in sales.

Many other fast-growth entrepreneurs found their challenge to be one of recruiting. Virginia M. Lord, senior vice president of Right Associates, an outplacement firm, said, "Our biggest difficulty was the recruitment and selection of staff entrepreneurial enough in nature and competent in human resources consulting to service our many client needs." To achieve this, Lord developed an affiliate network and a unique compensation structure that has attracted the people needed to fuel the company's growth.

Other fast-growth entrepreneurs have not had an easy time dealing with people once growth began. Melvin Edward Spelde, president of Clearwater Flying Service Inc. said, "Our biggest problem is dealing with people—the constant fight to balance the interest of all company contributors—owners, employees, customers, vendors, government agencies, and lenders. The task is never over and there is always someone who believes they're not being dealt with fairly."

# Developing Managers ▬▬▬▬▬▬▬▬▬▬▬

Developing management personnel is sometimes crucial to a company's success. But for some, the planning and timing of staff additions has proven tricky. Crystal S. Ettridge, vice president of Temps and Company, said, "Our biggest problem was a shortage of trained managers. In our third year of business, we built sales to $2.5 million with a permanent staff of only five or six people. The following year, when we were doing $5 million we still had only 10 to 12 permanent staffers—a small enough group for me and my brother Steven to manage hands-on. We thought we had planned for everything, but we forgot to develop enough managers. We realized the depth of our mistake after we were irreversibly committed to several new offices. We muddled through, but it was a real trauma. We still haven't fully recovered from the effects of our poor planning." Temps did $19.4 million last year.

William F. Simmons, president and CEO of Group Benefit Services Inc., of Hunt Valley, Maryland, agreed. "The development of a middle management team was certainly my most difficult task. As the sales volume grew we added clerical and salespeople easily, but finding and training people to manage them seemed almost impossible. Cathy and I were burning ourselves out. We did find them. They are in place and we are growing." All of this seems to have contributed to the right kind of direction. Simmons has had a 6000% growth rate since 1982 and made the *Inc.* Fast Growth 500 list for the second year in a row.

Perry J. MacNeal, president and CEO of Network Rental Incorporated, Atlanta, Georgia, said, "I underestimated the need, both in quantity and quality, of the people that it would take to achieve our anticipated growth. If I had been able to see this in our third year and taken the necessary steps to recruit heavy-duty experienced management people, the company would have sacrificed a little in profits but would be considerably larger in our sixth year." Network did $12 million in sales in 1986.

Some companies have tried to avert "span of control" problems by earlier and better planning. James A. Poure, CEO of General Alum and Chemical Corporation, said, "We accomplished the development of an extremely young management team through our 'mentor system.' Mentors were recruited from a cadre of retired former chemical associates and family friends who possessed skills that would complement our young, inexperienced management team's needs. Each manager was assigned a mentor who worked as a consultant and project coordinator. Thus, we were able to expedite the development of our managers to match our corporation's growth." The Holland, Ohio, firm reached $7.5 million in sales.

Others have recognized the need for training. Betsy Morris, vice president and general manager of CPA Services Inc., of Brookfield, Wisconsin, says, "We spend much time, effort, and money on training to ensure consistently high editorial quality and relevance to our accounting profession." This *CPA Newsletter* publisher surpassed $1 million in sales in 1986.

Marshal Lasky, president of Vocational Training Center of St. Louis, Missouri, says, "We have trained 99% of our own employees rather than taking them from other businesses. They learned our way of thinking and doing things. Most promotions come from within the organization, thus many people feel they have the opportunity to grow and be promoted." Lasky operates vocational schools and achieved 1986 sales of $10 million.

Fueling the people growth from within is a characteristic common to many fast-growth companies. Identifying that talent is no easy task, however. V. Beecher Wallace, CEO of Northwest Gears Inc. of Everett, Washington, says, "Finding the necessary personnel to staff our facility has been hard work, but in large part this has been done by selecting employees that possess the potential to learn and grow within the company." Founded in 1979, the firm has done $1.5 million in sales.

Invariably, promoting from within gets more difficult as the technical requirements go up. Susan W. Bowen, president and CEO of Champion Awards Incorporated, Memphis, Tennessee, says, 'We have had the most trouble finding qualified people to work in an extremely technical business. We must train every employee very fast." Champion, which sells printed apparel and awards, did over $4 million in 1986 sales.

Norman G. Wolcott, Jr., president of Nor-Cote Chemical Company Inc. of Crawfordsville, Indiana, agrees. "Assembling a small team of young technically competent individuals who care about the product and are willing to make personal sacrifices for company success has made the difference in our organization. We deal in innovative products and we must gain customer acceptance and it took great people to do that." Nor-Cote manufactures special inks and coatings and had 1986 sales of $2.8 million.

Sometimes management problems derive from the fact that many fast-growth entrepreneurs have difficulty in yielding responsibility to key people, and thus ensuring good supervision down the line. Most of them had to resolve this problem before they could unlock the true growth potential of their company. Ronald W. Watt, chairman and CEO of the Watt Roop Company of Cleveland, Ohio, said, "If you want your firm to grow, the simple answer is: Get good people and let them go to work for you; don't hamper them, don't nitpick; be supportive and attentive, be a mentor and advisor; make them feel free to talk to you whenever your input can be helpful, but damn it, let them do their jobs!"

Bill Gore, who founded W. L. Gore and Associates, Inc., which produces Gore-tex, takes this message of freedom of action to what some might consider an extreme. According to Jack Doherty, now advertising and marketing director of Gore-tex Fabrics, "When I showed up for the first day of work at Gore, Bill Gore shook my hand and said, 'Why don't you look around and find something you'd like to do.' "[33]

People must be finding things they like to do at Gore. Founded in 1958 in the Gores' Delaware basement, the company's sales reached $150 million by the early 1980s and is still growing.[34] The company's now famous "lattice" approach to organizing is built on four people-related principles:

1. Sincerely strive to be fair with each other, suppliers, customers, and all persons with whom you carry out transactions.

2. Allow, help, and encourage associates to grow in knowledge, skill, and scope of responsibility, and range of activities.

3. Make your *own* commitments—and keep them.

4. Consult with associates before taking actions that might be "below the waterline" and cause serious damage to the enterprise.[35]

## The Problem of Family

Sometimes people challenges arise when family members are involved. "My best advice," said Don Dion of Patten, when we were talking recently about family businesses, "is to avoid them. I've not yet seen a situation where the second generation had the same strength that the first generation did. One business, south of Boston, had a unique technology that could have been expanded dramatically, in that they invented a machine to print on cable and wire. Their sales of $3 million were based on this one product and one idea and has not changed for many years. They just can't grow the business because they're unwilling to add managers outside of the family," said Dion.

Conversely, Alan Stone, chairman of the Taft Hamilton Merchandising Group of New York, said that the single thing that caused the rapid growth of his company, a licensor of corporate names and trademarks was "the injection of youth and their competitive, ambitious, industrious attitude and performance into their father's business. Two of my sons, Michael and Robert, joined my company five years ago and my sales volume jumped from $2 million to $10 million in a couple of years." Stone, who launched Taft Hamilton a few years ago, has developed this licensing agency into one of the leaders in the field, and $10 million in annual sales.

In this chapter we've seen how entrepreneurs help release the talents of their people, and how they face the challenges and hard work of relating to them on a day-to-day basis. Virtually every entrepreneur we spoke with, either personally or through key assistants, spends a good portion of his or her time on the people in the company. The coaching analogy came up regularly: Provide the younger people with advice, tips, counsel, suggestions, mentoring, but don't interfere. "We've got to help them with their back swings," Lyman Wood used to say.

Conversely, in virtually all of the high turnover corporate situations that we saw, we heard words like *power, control, agendas, blocking, accountability, reconciliation,* and so on. This is the "management" that has become so stifling and that has replaced a great deal of the fun work in corporate America. It has also led to the loss of many jobs for many people.

Perhaps the model of the fast-growth entrepreneur, forging ahead with vision and energy, and with people as partners, will provide the model for 21st-century American companies. I hope so.

# Customers

7

I was ready to depart for New York City on a business trip recently and had already made hotel reservations when, in my mail, there arrived a special announcement from the Hyatt Hotel chain. I opened it and found a cheery letter and certificate, "Good for upgrading from a standard to a superior 'Regency Club' room during your next stay with us at Hyatt."

Coincidentally, my meeting the next day was to take place at the Grand Hyatt in New York, so I picked up the telephone, called the special 800 number indicated on the direct mail piece, and spoke with a very accommodating customer service representative, buried somewhere in the heart of the Hyatt organization, who said, "Yes, Mr. Storey. I have a room available for tomorrow night and you will be able to use your upgrade certificate on it."

Terrific, I thought. Upgrading from a modest room downtown to a first-class room right in the heart of midtown Manhattan. I enthused over my good timing.

As I approached the clerk at the front desk of the Hyatt the next day, I turned over my "Upgrade Certificate" and he said, "I'm sorry, Mr. Storey. These certificates are good at most other Hyatt hotels, but not here. Please read the fine print on the other side."

I turned the certificate over, and sure enough, in the *very* fine print, it said, "All Hyatt Hotels except the U.N. Plaza and Grand Hyatt."

"But I checked with your 800 number before leaving Vermont, *and* before changing my reservations from another hotel," I said.

"I'm very sorry. I don't know what I can do," replied the desk clerk.

"Well, one thing you might do would be to tell me the name of the general manager of the hotel so I might discuss this with him." My polite but firm reaction let him know I was serious.

"Let me see what I can find, Mr. Storey." Moments later I walked into my huge room on the 27th floor of the Grand Hyatt, a room large enough for my entire company. We could have held our Christmas party in it!

Now, the point of this story is simply that most American companies have awakened to the need to make instantaneous, on-the-spot customer service decisions that will allow them to retain me and you as customers. Greater discretion for making such decisions has been given to desk clerks, phone clerks, shipping clerks.

Those companies that haven't done so just don't understand the cost involved in acquiring—and then losing—a customer, and for this reason they are doing severe damage to their own growth potential.

Lyman Wood used to say, as we handled the daily incoming inquiries, "Just think of all of those coupons as $10 bills. That's what it cost us to get them." People hearing that suddenly began thinking about inquiries and customer orders in quite a different way.

# High Expectations

Gone are the days of the "Please allow four to six weeks for delivery." Here today are the days of "Check here if you'd like overnight express mail service."

Virtually all companies are now going well beyond the minimum delivery and customer servicing standards required by the various governmental agencies. There is a considerably rising tide of customer expectations as to the service that corporations can provide to them. Customer service expert Milind M. Lele, author of *The Customer Is Key*, believes deeply that companies are seeing it to be in their own self-interest to provide superior customer service. He tells the story of a Kodak customer who purchased a Kodak camera in West Germany, and who, while using it as he traveled throughout Europe, had it fail suddenly when he arrived in London. He was amazed when he brought it into a Kodak office in London and the clerk replaced it on the spot without any questions asked.[1] This incident shows how far companies have come in the last decade. In the process, the customer is the big winner. And through renewed and repeat business, so is the company.

Richard Thalheimer, president of The Sharper Image, one of the fastest growing catalog companies in the United States, put it this way. "People expect a certain reaction from a business and when you pleasantly exceed those expectations, you've somehow passed an important psychological threshold."[2] Thalheimer has certainly pleasantly exceeded many customers' expectations if his business growth, from nothing in 1979 to over $125 million in 1987, is any indication.[3]

## Building a Relationship

The customer relationship begins with the advertising a company uses to bring attention to its products and services. Much of American advertising is overstated, and smart customers sniff that out very quickly. James R. Cook, author of the American Management Association's book *The Start-Up Entrepreneur*, says, "Get into the habit of understating your claims and promotions. Decrease your numbers of assertions—check ads and everything for total honesty. You cannot excel in business without unswerving integrity."[4]

This was written in 1979. By 1989, America had come around to understatement as the norm. Paul Sampson, head of the Direct Marketing Association Education Committee, always used to point this out to us as we tried to write copy for our various product lines. "Give away the little ones," said Paul. When he gave his advertising seminar within Garden Way, he would take a piece of copy in which someone had described an attachment or a snow dozer blade for the rototiller and say, "Here's what's wrong with this. It says it can do everything. Well, in fact, it can't. Let's write it this way. 'Try the dozer blade attachment on the front of your rototiller if you have only a little bit of snow. If the snow gets too deep, say much beyond six inches, this attachment probably won't give you very much satisfaction. On the other hand, it only costs $110, which is considerably less expensive than a snow blower, and if you have time, and don't mind sticking with a job, it does a fairly decent piece of work." Understatement. Honesty. Giving away the small ones. All of this works.

We all found that building our integrity and credibility with the customer on the smaller items—those for around $100—even if the customers didn't buy them, made it easier for us to sell the $1000 products, which is exactly what we were doing. We were consciously allowing the customer to take advantage of the company in a way that worked to the benefit of the company in the longer term.

The beginning of the conversation or dialogue with the customer is one of the most important times for customer psychology and understanding. I remember vividly when we were relaunching the Popular Mechanics *Do-It-Yourself Encyclopedia*. I hired one of the most expensive copywriters in New York to describe the product. When I received his copy, it had a kind of "high falutin' " air to it. So we brought in a group of people, a so-called focus group interview session, at which ten of our typical *Popular Mechanics* magazine subscribers came to discuss the idea. The idea didn't get very far with them.

"The problem with the brochure that you've got here," said one of the "dirt underneath the fingernails" guys, "is that it's written for people who take taxi cabs. Most of us use the subway!"

The copywriter was sitting behind a two-way mirror watching the session, and I'll never forget the look on his face when he heard that comment—suddenly he was sitting a little less comfortably.

Paul Hawken puts it differently: "Watch the customer's hands, eyes, feet, and body. See what people do and don't do—the attractions and repulsions—and observe the minutiae of daily life so that you can say, before the buyer even knows it, 'This is what you want.' This is what we try to do with our Smith and Hawken gardening catalog."[5]

One fast-growth president, Steven A. Bright of Electra Form Inc., Vandalia, Ohio, went to an extreme on this point. Said Bright, "After three years, I came to realize that the initial growth was fed by underdog enthusiasm and decided that I must have a better understanding of my market. I went way out on a limb and hired one of my customers, a man who became our connection to the market and its needs at once. He also helped us deal with *Fortune* 500 companies." We've all heard "If you can't beat 'em, join 'em." In this case, we see "If you can't understand 'em, hire 'em." The firm, which is a manufacturer of injection tooling, went from $1.4 million in 1980 to $10.2 million in 1984.

# Keeping a Customer: Customer Service ■■■■■■■■■■■■■■■■

*Keeping* a customer depends on the satisfaction level with which the original product is received and on the quality and perception of value that the customer feels. Consultant Philip Crosby, in his book *Quality Is Free*, puts it simply and bluntly: "Do it right the first time."[6] Crosby points out the incredible cost associated with product defects, delays, poor customer service, and being buried under third- and fourth-time complaints. He tells the story of one company that got so backed up on its complaints that it decided to begin to deal only with complaints that had been received a third time. They threw out the first- and second-time complaints! The company was soon out of business.

Many of the great mail order successes today have their people begin their training in the world of customer service with the L. L. Bean description of "What is a customer?" which is carried throughout the company's literature and in its store in Freeport, Maine. It reads as follows:

## CUSTOMERS

### What Is a Customer?

**A Customer is the most important person ever in this office . . . in person or by mail.**

**A Customer is not dependent on us . . . we are dependent on him.**

**A Customer is not an interruption of our work . . . he is the purpose of it. We are not doing a favor by serving him . . . he is doing us a favor by giving us the opportunity to do so.**

**A Customer is not someone to argue or match wits with. Nobody ever won an argument with a customer.**

**A Customer is a person who brings us his wants. It is our job to handle them profitably to him and ourselves.**


Many companies have read the Bean "manifesto," plugged it into their own code of doing business, and are listening to the customer as they've never listened before. Peters and Waterman focused on this in their classic *In Search of Excellence:* "These companies learn from the people they serve. They provide unparalleled quality, service, and reliability—things that work and last. They succeed in differentiating—à la Frito Lay (potato chips), Maytag (washers), or Tupperware—the most commoditylike products."[7] Peters came to one of our recent Direct Marketing Association conventions and gave an electrifying presentation on customer service and customer attitudes. "The days of assigning customer service to some department way down the line is gone. Any company whose top leaders fail to focus on the customer as its most important asset is ignorant," said Peters.

American corporate attitude and understanding of their customers has gone way up. Top management is spending time talking to customers. It's not unusual to find a Frank Perdue checking chickens and talking directly to the customers that he serves or, before he passed away, Ray Kroc and other senior managers personally showing up at McDonald's outlets around the country to check on quality and service. As a recent annual report says, "Quality is the first word in the McDonald's motto . . . that's because quality is what consumers enjoy each time they visit a McDonald's restaurant."[8]

Customer contact is essential for any entrepreneurial chief executive. The contact can be made by telephone, by reading the mail selectively, by talking with the customer at the retail level. In my own case, I try to pick up the company mail every Saturday and spot-check through it to see what kinds of inquiries, complaints, and orders are coming from various parts of the country. It's amazing what you can pick up in a half-hour of reading your own mail.

Companies have learned that they must find ways to add value to the customer relationship. David Ogilvy, founder of Ogilvy and Mather, which he built into the preeminent advertising agency in the world, forces everyone in his organization to keep priorities straight when he says, "The agency must live up to the dictum that the number one object is unparalleled client service, not profitability."[9]

Some companies dramatically demonstrate this commitment to clients and customers. The Southland Corporation, which operates the 7-11 Stores, invites employees who have performed superior feats of customer service to join in on a company sweepstakes, with the winner receiving a cool $1 million. "On Friday, February 13, 1987, Deborah Wilson, a Plano, Texas, 7-11 store manager and divorced mother of two, won $50,000 a year for the next 20 years."[10] I suspect everyone in the organization got the point.

Clearly, this kind of attention to customer service requires consistent reminding within the organization. Larry Renbarger, CEO of Shelter Components Incorporated, a fast-growth *Inc.* 500 company said, "We continuously remind ourselves of 'what brung us to the party.' The fear of losing day-to-day touch with our customers was the single most important concern that we had." Renbarger's firm, which supplies component parts to the housing and recreation vehicle markets, launched in 1979, is doing $29.3 million in sales.

Companies today are able to measure the benefits of superior customer service. For one thing, they find that they can charge for outstanding service. "In industry after industry, happy customers are willing to pay extra for the additional satisfaction they derive. . . . Federal Express consistently gets a somewhat higher price for its overnight delivery service than does the competition."[11]

After a company has obtained a customer the game is just beginning. Peters and Waterman cite the case of Joe Girard, one of the best car salesmen in the country: "In a typical year, Joe sold more than twice as many units as whoever was in second place."[12]

Say Peters and Waterman, "His magic is the magic of IBM and many of the rest of the excellent companies. It is simply service, overpowering service, especially after-sales service."[13] According to Joe Girard, "There's one thing that I do that a lot of salesmen don't, and that's believe the sale really begins after the sale—not before . . . The customer ain't out the door, and my son has made up a thank-you note."[14]

It's also becoming increasingly common to receive a thank-you for your order. Bob Sharp's Nissan/Datsun, in Wilton, Connecticut, one of the fastest growing car dealerships in New England, has built his marketing program around thank-you gifts, in the form of cash or accessory offers, to previous customers who refer new customers to him.

Book-of-the-Month Club's entire member-get-a-member strategy is based on the feeling that a contented member will, if the incentive is right, bring in others. And on and on it goes.

Most fast-growth companies view good customer service as an investment, not an expense. Once the accountants and book-keepers understand that the company can get more new customers more easily when there is a high degree of ongoing customer satisfaction, the sooner companies can get on about their business of building value and profits in their organization.

Customers want service with a capital S. Gulab Bhavnani, owner of Granada Systems Design Inc. of New York, says, "Commitment to customer service and product quality in a high-tech computer technology area has led to a steady but rapid growth in our company." Granada, which offers custom software, will do $1.5 million in sales.

Some companies find that sales level out once they tighten their customer service policies. Renovator's Supply of Turners Falls, Massachusetts, once one of *Inc.* magazine's Fast Growth

500, fell from the list in 1984 when sales began to flatten and customer satisfaction with the Taiwan-sourced product line fell. It hasn't returned since.

Robert Hernandez, vice president of customer service at Federal Express, on the other hand, says, "If you look at the quality of service, for example, customer inquiries, information. . . . What we do is we tell customers that we're going to respond to their inquiries within 30 minutes or they won't have to pay. Because we know, and it's repeatedly reinforced through letters and customer contacts and surveys, that the information side of this shipment is as important as getting it to that place; I [the customer] have to know what's going on. So the customer base is asking for that, and we say—we have to do it."[15]

How shocking the old copywriters would find the fact that their standard line of "four to six weeks" for delivery has now been turned on its head by Federal Express and others who promise to today's customer—their own as well as everyone else's—that "All packages sent by overnight service to most destinations will be delivered by 10:30 A.M. or your money back."

Customers today are looking to be treated fairly. Jim Poissant of The Walt Disney Company spoke recently with some of our salespeople in Boston. "Disney has four categories of importance," he said. "Our value system, training, communications, and caring. Each one of these plays a significant role in our philosophy. The value system is the largest category and here are the four most important parts of that: (1) Keep it clean, (2) keep it friendly, (3) make sure you do your best, and (4) give the customer everything you can give them from yourself and from your company."

Pretty simple, clear, and fair. Poissant suggested that other companies ask themselves the question, "What does our company mean to our customers? If it means the same to us as it means to the customer, we're accomplishing our goals."

# Customer Wants

What else do customers want? In this section we'll examine some other things that customers are looking for.

## CUSTOMERS

Customers want peace of mind. One of the fastest growing *Inc.* 500 companies, Dynamark Security Centers Inc., Hagerstown, Maryland, distinguished itself from the rest of the pack by being one of the very first to offer a service to its existing security system customers called "Dynawatch." Dynawatch provides a constant monitoring of the residences of customers who have installed a Dynawatch System. In addition to that, Dynamark has a procedure for allowing its clients to simply push a button for help in case of a medical emergency. This provides the customer additional peace of mind and has allowed Dynamark to become one of the fastest growing franchise operations in the country.[16] Dynamark now does over $5 million in sales.

Customers are anxious for someone to take care of problems that are bigger than they can manage. Asbestos removal, only recently recognized as important in reducing health hazards in older buildings, has become the centerpiece of Frank Duross's business, Oneida Asbestos Removal Inc. of Marcy, New York. The level of customer satisfaction is clear in this letter they shared with us from one of their clients, Robert L. Goolody, resident engineer of the Veterans Administration: "Your company's management and work force cooperated to their fullest to perform a very difficult asbestos abatement project in a safe and professional manner." Oneida is approaching $5 million in sales.

Companies can gain lifetime customers by solving their problems for them. Tom H. Hill, chairman of T. H . Hill Associates of Houston, Texas, said that the biggest single factor that explains their growth was "A continuous focus on working the technical problems of our customers." Hill's management and engineering consulting company has made the *Inc.* Fast Growth 500 list with its $4.3 million in sales.

Michael J. Collins, president of CEM Corporation of Matthews, North Carolina, which has pioneered microwave technology for analytical instrumentation, explains its growth by saying, "Staying close to our customers' needs and maintaining the quality of our service . . . we provide benefits to a growing number of industries by helping them solve problems." CEM is approaching $10 million in sales, and Collins has guided his company onto the *Inc.* Fast Growth 500 list.

Tom Peters puts it this way: "IBM trains its salesmen not to be salesmen but customer problem solvers. 3M has always done the same. A general instruments sales executive captures the spirit of getting to know the customer well enough to really solve his problems."[17]

Roger Holmes, a long-time friend who sold Sprague Electric Company components to IBM, practically lived with his primary client. When the Poughkeepsie-based factory that he served needed close-in consultation, his company had the vision to move Roger's office from North Adams, Massachusetts, to Danbury, Connecticut, within easy striking distance of Poughkeepsie.

Other companies grow by simply providing more convenience to their customers. Nancy Vetrone, president of Original Copy Centers of Cleveland, Ohio, was looking for a breakthrough to get her static company moving and came up with the notion of putting drop boxes in the lobbies of the buildings of all the major corporations in downtown Cleveland. This was accompanied by an advertising campaign that said "If you drop your printing jobs in our overnight box in the lobby of your corporation by 8:00 P.M., we'll have it on your desk by 10:00 the next morning." This application of the Federal Express overnight delivery techniques has caused her business to skyrocket, and has allowed her to jump onto the *Inc.* Fast Growth 500 list.

Customers clearly want communication—in as many and varied ways as possible. Pak Melwani, founder of Royal Silk, was not content with print media, or even direct mail catalog efforts, as a way to reach his customers, so he's now sending out videos, as well as moving into new technologies using computers, phone lines, and video for two-way television ordering.[18]

Some customers feel completely overlooked. Marilyn Hamilton discovered a highly responsive audience, paraplegics, after she herself was paralyzed when she fell during a hang gliding accident. She and her partners Don Helman and Jim Okamoto have focused their California company, Motion Designs, completely on mobility and the needs of paraplegics. "Caring for the person is what did it," said Hamilton. "Often it was the little things that made the difference. For instance, I knew it took six months for me to get my first chair, and that's too long. You want it in the hospital so you can learn to use it." Motion Designs delivers custom wheelchairs in weeks instead of months,[19] and grossed $15 million in sales last year.

## CUSTOMERS

And, of course, customers want quality. Gerald L. Kasten, president of Night Caps Incorporated, a fast-growth company in Milwaukee, Wisconsin, that sells waterbeds, said, "The market was there and identified. We vowed to produce a quality product at a reasonable price (not the cheapest) with on-time delivery. We never lost sight of this basic goal." The company went from $106,000 to $1.7 million in five years.

People are buying quality control software to ensure customer satisfaction. Perry Johnson of Perry Johnson Inc. of Southfield, Michigan, a $6 million a year company that provides quality control software programs, said, "The company's on-line analyst generates C, U, P, NP, Moving Average, Moving Range, and individual charts: performs Pareto Analysis, CU Sum and linear regression."[20]

Sometimes customers want to be partners with you. Charlie Winton, president of Publishers Group West, looked at a part of the publishing business that he felt was underrepresented—smaller publishers with sales of $300,000 to $3 million a year—and told them he would not just gain them distribution, he would become their "marketing partners." Winton was able, with just $500 of capitalization in 1977, to build a company that's looking at $25 million in sales in 1988, by actually becoming the marketing department of many small presses that otherwise would not receive decent representation.

Clearly, customers also want satisfaction. Michael H. Duweck, president of All Star Printing Inc. of Lansing, Michigan, told us, "Our success is based on our single-minded dedication to giving our clients what they want, when and how they want it. We have charged past our competition because, although many of them know and even understand our philosophy, few apply it with equal consistency." All Star, a commercial printer, quickly surpassed $2 million in sales.

Customers want to be able to return things if they're not absolutely pleased with them. Returns, which are a way of life in the book business, and may *even* affect this volume that you're reading, have also become a standard part of the mail order business. Bean puts a cost on this of between 5% and 6% of its sales.[21] Some catalogers and retail establishments budget 10–15% for returns. The book trade routinely experiences 20%.

Customers want and expect direct access to the companies with which they're doing business. Virtually every major American company and even most of the small ones have 800 telephone numbers—some for customer service, some for sales.

It's not unusual today for even small companies to have an around-the-clock 800 service, and most of these are manned by knowledgeable sales representatives. According to Gerald D. Cohen, president of Information Builders, Inc., "Our customers, through our service bureaus, wanted direct contact with us, and we had to decide to build a national direct sales force. Luckily we did this because the computer service bureaus business has disappeared." Cohen's sales have skyrocketed, to over $72 million a year.

When customers do call, they want to find someone knowledgeable on the other end of the line. And they certainly do when they talk with Smith and Hawken on a gardening question. They do with Bean on outdoor gear. But they don't with all companies. Try calling your own company on the phone, using both your 800 number and your office number to see what kind of response you get to a fairly straightforward question.

Garden Way Incorporated formed a "CCC"—customer contact committee—which met informally once a week to share pluses and minuses from every department on the contacts they had made with customers during the week.

Here at our company, we bind a "We'd love your thoughts card" into every single book that we publish and every year we get thousands of them back. They contain everything from praise to disappointment, suggestions for new books to criticisms of old, and, most important, they keep us more closely in touch with what our customers are thinking.

Robert H. Waterman, Jr., in *The Renewal Factor*, tells the story of the time that a major corporation asked its customers what they thought, and were amazed at the answer. "The company commissioned a study to find out why customers were turned off on Ford.... The good news was that no one had anything bad to say about Ford ... the bad news was that no one had *anything* to say about Ford automobiles."[22] The lesson Ford learned is that if customers aren't talking to them, they had better make extra efforts to talk with the customer.

## CUSTOMERS

Customers also want to have fun. I remember vividly the morning that Lyman Wood came in to the corporate log cabin, where we all sat around two Ping-Pong tables, and suggested that he had a new product he wanted to present. He pulled out a child's tricycle horn, honked it three times for us, and said, "What would you think about offering this as a new option on the Troy-Bilt Rototiller?"

We all sat there in amazement while Lyman awaited our answer. Finally, one of us got up enough courage to ask, "Why would you need a horn on a rototiller?"

"Well for heaven's sakes, don't you know? How else are you going to let the earthworms know that you're coming!" Believe it or not, we actually offered the horn, and customers got a tremendous kick out of it.

Customers want to have an easy time dealing with you. Stanley Fenvessy, who has become the master of customer service within the direct marketing industry and has watched its growth rise from the earliest days to the $100 billion a year level, said to me recently, "There are some really excellent companies in this field, and all of them try to make it as easy as possible for the customer to order." He cited, among others, Bean, The Sharper Image, and Lillian Vernon.

Fenvessy also cited the J. C. Penney Company as one that led the way with expediting customer complaints. "The procedure for returning unwanted merchandise or complaining and the address to which the merchandise and the complaint should be sent, are spelled out on every packing slip accompanying the mail order merchandise."[23] Believe it or not, according to Fenvessy, "This was considered a radical and foolhardy step at the time (the 1960s). Many people felt that it would markedly increase merchandise returns, thereby costing additional expense. However, the test made then, and those repeated since, are showing skeptics that this innovation does not increase returns or complaints. And because the customer is instructed what to do, the transaction can be handled faster and more economically."[24]

Customers, as we've already noted, want things to be convenient. Fenvessy goes on, "Where clothing and shoes are involved, provide careful instructions on how to measure body dimensions for proper sizing. Don't depend on a customer's recollection of his or her size. . . . Penney's, Sears', and Ward's general catalogs do an excellent job. The clever approach taken by the Haband Company . . . includes a paper tape measure 50 inches long, folded in with many of their direct mail offerings."[25] Fenvessy introduced Bean to a two-part service action form that allowed them, during the peak of their growth years, to stay up with customer volume. Fenvessy says, "Where internal action, such as adjusting the customer's account, preparing a refund, or reshipping merchandise is called for, complete a service action form that, in one writing, will both: (A) Inform the customer and (B) Direct other departments to take the required internal action."[26]

Customers want a predictable atmosphere. This in large part explains why stopping at a McDonald's, whether in Portland, Maine, or San Diego, California, is the same experience and why so many other people strive to recreate the McDonald's image and atmosphere.

# The Loyal Customer

Companies that satisfy all these customer wants develop customers who are extremely dedicated and loyal. Bill Ouchi, an expert on Japanese management techniques, talks in terms of "the everlasting customer." The Japanese have known for a long time what Americans are only recently discovering, and that is that customers don't want to jump around from company to company but prefer a longer term relationship.

I became a convert, and then a true believer, after eight years at Garden Way Incorporated, where customer satisfaction was a passion. We would get personal correspondence every day from people who were responding to the direct mail letters we had sent out to millions of people. Most of these people really believed that we were writing to them personally. There could be no greater compliment to our copywriters than that. One of my favorites came from an elderly gentleman in Kansas. He said, "Enclosed is a picture of me and *both* of my big reds" (the Troy-Bilt Rototiller was painted bright red and was referred to by many as "big red"). In the picture, the man had his one hand on his rototiller and his other hand on the head of an Irish Setter

## CUSTOMERS

dog. The letter went on, "Last week big red, my dog, passed away after 16 happy years. You'll be happy to know that I used my big red, the rototiller, to dig a hole big enough to bury my old friend Red. Yours Faithfully, . . ."

When companies that are mailing tens of millions of pieces of mail a year can get that kind of response, you know they're on the right track with their customer attitudes.

# Niches

8

**W**hen I was sent down from the opulence of the Time-Life Building in Rockefeller Center to the dingy quarters of the Book Find and Seven Arts Society Books Clubs at 1 Park Avenue, Margot Sandick, the long-time bookkeeper that George Braziller had doing petty cash and billings in his club operations, looked at me squarely and said, "Mr. Storey, may I ask you a question?"

Now understand, I was as green a trainee as they come, but in Time Inc.'s view, God bless 'em, ready to go out and "run an operation."

"Sure, Margot," I said, with all of my 26 years of life experience.

"Where did you get your business degree?" she asked.

"Well, Margot, I don't really have a business degree," I responded.

She looked perplexed for a moment and then said, "Well, where did you learn accounting?"

"I'm not really an accountant either," I confessed.

"Bookkeeping?" she said hopefully, and I had to tell her, "No, Margot. I don't know a thing about bookkeeping either."

"Mr. Storey, would you mind my asking what you majored in in college?" said Margot.

"No. I don't mind. It was American history and literature," I said, with all of my pure liberal arts background coming through.

She thought for a moment and then said, "Well, at least you got the literature part!"

So there I was. With my Time-Life training, experience, education, master's degree, and no dirt underneath the fingernails. Thrown together with Margot: no education, years of hands-on bookkeeping experience, street-smarts, and people savvy. Certainly not the first time in business history that this confrontation has occurred, but increasingly common with people who truly want to make their businesses grow. In short, without the development of that savvy, that experience, that skill, fast growth just doesn't occur.

Now I count myself fortunate in escaping from the Time-Life Building. My Time Inc. buddies sent me their regrets. "One Park Avenue—Jesus, you are out of it!" I heard. My concern was that many people went through their entire careers at Time Inc. never having learned to use a calculator, never having met a single outside supplier, never having spoken with a customer. It could easily have happened to me. When that important contact with the outside is missing, you find the homogenized, ho-hum, predictable corporate approach that is resulting in a good deal of the job loss of America. Few of my friends actually got away. Richard Stollenwerck went to France to run Time-Life Books' Paris office. Peter Barnes went out to Haverhills (a mail order catalog) in San Francisco. Kevin Dolan was sent up to run Little Brown in Boston, and Larry Crutcher sent over to run Book-of-the-Month—both have done admirably. But most would tell you that 50th and Avenue of the Americas, the Time Life headquarters, is where the action is. Why leave?

# The Importance of Trade Skill

Paul Hawken describes what most Time Inc. people never learn: "trade skill." Says Hawken, "Trade skill is really the set of skills that spell the difference between success and failure in a business. It's that knack of understanding what people want, how much they'll pay, and how they make their decisions. It is knowing how to read the signals of the marketplace, how to learn from those signals, how to change your mind. Trade skill gives you a canniness about how to approach your given product, market, or niche."[1]

Trade skill certainly does not come from sitting behind a large corporate desk and methodically filing through your in-basket. Yet this is what most corporate managers actually do every day! Think of it—doing what their in-box tells them to do rather than talking with employees, customers, or product developers. Business savvy comes from that combination of knowing your product, meeting your customers, developing a sense of how the money in your business comes in and goes out, and working with your partners and people in your business, sharing the experience that you have as you go along. It leads to very sharp focus.

In our own business, we don't sit around having many philosophical discussions or strategic planning sessions. We have work to do. The work results from people seeking our books, our editorial product line, which are well defined as "Books for Country Living." If a manuscript comes in that's fiction, biography, or esoteric material, however strong, we don't spend any time talking about it because it simply doesn't fit. Our niche is that of providing information to people who are interested in the country. Simple as that.

## Developing a Niche ▮▮▮▮▮▮▮▮▮▮▮▮▮▮▮▮▮▮▮▮

Now it's true, many niches, by their very definition, are tiny. *Niche* comes from the Latin "nidus," or nest that is modest in size. It's interesting to note that, according to the *American Heritage Dictionary,* the third meaning of niche is "A situation or activity specially suited to a person's abilities or character."

So if you take the idea of the size, the limits of a nest, and the notion of an activity growing out of a peculiar ability that you may have, you can understand why niching works for people. As Steven Brandt puts it in his *Entrepreneuring,* "Smaller companies become competitive when playing for a limited gain in a marketplace of its own choosing . . ."[2] The point is to pick one's playing field, even if it seems small. Virtually all of our fast-growth entrepreneurs have done that.

## NICHES

A sharp focus is important, not only in the earliest phases of fast-growth companies, but in order to avoid the fatal misstep that could result in trying to be all things to all customers and, in many cases, extinction.

Rippling out gradually is a far preferable means of growing than diversifying rapidly into an area that you know little about. And even rippling out too quickly can have dangerous consequences. The Green River Tool Company, once located in Brattleboro, Vermont, believed that only by increasing its gardening customer list dramatically, by leaps and bounds, could it achieve economies of scale and become competitive with the industry leader, Smith and Hawken. But by rolling out much too quickly, sending an untested catalog to untested lists, Green River took very heavy losses and had to "get out of the game." David Tresamer's wonderful Green River concept had simply gone out of control. Peter Rice of Plow and Hearth in Madison, Virginia, acquired the assets of the company and neatly folded them into his own fast-growth company, which was growing prudently at a well-defined rate. Rice joined the *Inc.* Fast Growth 500 list. Tresamer went to Colorado.

Garden Way Inc. had identical problems with its "Country Kitchen Catalog." We were losing about $1.50 an order, or $150,000 annually. By succumbing to the tempting economies of scale argument, we were able to double the volume—and the loss. In short, there are many who have discovered that increasing the volume to find the break-even point simply doesn't work.

Some of you may remember the traveling salesmen at the beginning of the musical *The Music Man*, reminding each other that "you gotta know the territory." Certainly most fast-growth companies have carved out their own territories. Within the last ten years the world of specialty catalog retailing, for instance, has exploded, to nearly 6000 catalogs—a wonderful example of niche marketing.

There was a time when the big fat Sears catalog made a lot of sense. Sears, Montgomery Ward, Penney, and many other major merchandisers realized in the early 1970s that unless they began to define more tightly those niches in which they could profitably operate, they were simply wasting money by mailing fat catalogs to people who didn't find appropriate most of what they had to offer. The move to target catalog recipients more specifically began with geographics (in other words, why try to sell beach gear to Eskimos?). It was then affected by the development of the zip code, and also by demographic and psychographic analysis. ("Demographic" generally takes age, sex, income, education, and other factors into consideration; "psychographic" tries to add values and attitudes—"psyche"—to the analysis.) Claritas, a Washington, D.C.–based fast-growth research firm introduced the concept of "cluster groups," defining 40 different lifestyles that could be found throughout the United States. With this concept, marketers could target "suburban affluents," for example, for their upscale product offerings, while passing up Newark, New Jersey, and Hayward, California. On the basis of these tightly defined demographic marketing samples, specialty cataloging was created. Brookstone, with its "hard-to-find tools," which we learned about earlier, was one of the first. Lillian Vernon, Norm Thompson, and thousands of others followed.

Renovator's Supply popped up in Millers Falls, Massachusetts, in 1978, when Claude and Donna Jeanloz wagered their last $10,000 on a catalog mailing offering brass decorative hardware that rang people's Victorian chimes. They grew dramatically from $262,000 in 1979 to $10 million in 1983 sales. Williams-Sonoma in California decided to apply the same technique to the world of gourmet cookware, with even more dramatic results. Banana Republic, more recently, seized on the world of travel and travelers and has built a very big, if perhaps faddish, business very rapidly. "It was like turning over a grain of sand and finding an elephant," said one insider.

All of these companies had in common a keen awareness of their niche, and a personal interest in that niche.

## Corporate "Niches"? ▬▬▬▬▬▬▬▬▬

On the other hand, the big corporations that have tried to experiment with "intrapreneuring" have had generally weak results. CBS could not figure out Royal Silk. Time Inc. buried Haverhills. RCA almost killed Random House. Today, General Foods, the mega food marketing corporation of White Plains, New York, lets a kind of "skunk works group" operate in the direct marketing world. Two of these operations, Gevalia (which offers Swedish coffee) and Thomas Garraway Limited (a "purveyor of fine foods"), are trying to operate as entrepreneurs within a $9 billion corporation (owned, in turn, by Philip Morris, a $25 billion corporation!) that truly does not know how to deal with small entrepreneurial businesses. Despite sincere, even valiant, efforts on the part of the entrepreneurs running these modest size businesses, customers who call their 800 lines soon realize that they are not speaking with an expert in the field—that is, fine foods—but rather with a corporate department resigned to "checking their two computers." Shipments are incorrect. Replacement items are delayed. Customer satisfaction low.

Many corporations try niches, and then decide that those niches just aren't big enough to support the overheads that the corporation must charge to the operating unit. Time Inc. acquired Haverhills, a specialty merchandising operation in the late 1960s. The business was doing a nice $1 million a year, hardly big enough for billion-dollar Time Inc. to take seriously. They sent one of their brightest young business managers, Jim Levy, to San Francisco with instructions to grow the business from $1 million to $10 million, and a funny thing happened along the way. They lost several million dollars. The business, founded by entrepreneur Gerardo Joffe, who threw a dart at the map of England to determine a name for the company, had produced a very nice living for Joffe, who signed a fat contract with Time Inc. not to compete for five years. So Joffe sat on the sidelines and watched his baby struggling with its new parents. On the fifth year and first day, Joffe reannounced operations, only the dart hit "Heniker" this time and quickly became a lovely little niche company selling exactly what Haverhills offered years earlier.

Celestial Seasonings, the imaginative tea company, founded by Morris Siegel in Boulder, Colorado, seemed to lose all of its heat when Kraft Incorporated acquired it. Following Kraft's takeover of the business, which had made $35 million for Mo Siegel, and four years of trying its best, Kraft announced in "corporatese" that "While Celestial is an excellent, growing business, Kraft is selling the company because our current objectives call for moving away from the beverage industry," according to Eric Strobel, president of the Grocery Products Group of Kraft, a multinational food company.[3]

Beneath these fine words is a built-in reason for failure that could have been foreseen even before the acquisition took place, and that is that Kraft, an $8 billion Glenview, Illinois–based corporation, is simply not going to be content with a business of $10, $20, or $30 million. The seed of its own dissolution was there from the start: Its growth expectations could never materialize.

So what does Kraft do? It turns around and sells the business to Thomas J. Lipton Inc., a mere $7.3 billion tea maker. This allowed Lipton to plug in Celestial Seasonings as another product line. My guess is that Celestial will be unrecognizable in a short period of time.

# Narrowing the Focus ■■■■■■■■■■■■■■■■■■■■

Fast-growth niche companies behave very differently from corporations acquiring and divesting product lines and businesses. Smaller companies try to thin their seedlings faster. I remember watching master gardener Dick Raymond for the first time, sowing his seeds in the garden in the spring, then coming out two weeks later with a tool he had engineered himself called the "in row weeder," which ruthlessly thinned out weeds and seedlings. I said, "Dick, you're pulling 'em all out." And he said simply, "The strong ones will survive, and I'll have a stronger garden than I ever would have if I let them all crowd each other out."

Small companies experiencing fast growth don't have the resources to allow the weeds to grow, so the weeds, as well as plenty of seedlings, come out in the process. Steven Brandt, describing companies trying to allow entrepreneuring within their established framework, recommends, "Expand from a profitable base toward a balanced business."[4] And this is exactly what the smaller companies do. They plant their seed, nuture the early growth, get rid of the weeds along the way, and broaden their base as they move toward a more balanced business.

The National Title Company, an insurance agency launched in Houston, Texas, in 1978, grew because of its ability to focus on a narrow but profitable market. According to Stephen C. Vallone, president, "Our analysis of the real estate market in Houston indicated that growth would likely take place in the commercial and luxury residential sectors. Therefore we chose to specialize in those limited areas, as opposed to a general practice. We developed a reputation for excellence in servicing to Houston elite, and our profitability zoomed. By concentrating our resources and energies in a narrow but profitable area we were able to outperform those companies who felt compelled to participate on a broad but marginal scale." National Title grew from $341,000 in 1979 sales to $2.0 million by 1983.

One firm went into the field of very narrowly focused software. David W. Berkus, president of Computerized Lodging Systems Incorporated of Long Beach, California, a reseller of computer systems, said, "We created a very feature-rich software package for a narrow industry segment (hotels) and focused on that market alone. It took three years before we were 'suddenly discovered' by the hotel chains. It seems that they were merely waiting for the weak new players to wash themselves out. We were at the right place at the right time, preserved the cash on the way, and took advantage of the window when it opened." Founded in 1975, Berkus pushed the company to 1980 sales of $328,000 and 1984 sales of $4.9 million.

## Doing What You Know

Lyman Wood, who once told me to "find a good parade and get out in front of it," found his niche in applying his mail order copywriting skills and his mathematical mind to an area he had personally enjoyed and studied over many years: gardening. Applying his skill, he got into America's "gardening vein" and mined it deeply for over 20 years. Lyman was also called a visionary, because his original charter for Garden Way read more like a Utopian dream than a business plan. But Lyman never lost the ability to apply hard skills, copywriting and mathematical analysis, to business, which helped explain its dramatic growth under his leadership. Now, after several years of stalled growth, the company is growing again under new management headed by Jairo Estrada, who is using acquisition to fuel the growth.

Other people apply their knowledge of an industry to develop new products. Instead of trying to create products within their industry, they go at it in a different way. Frank Zeeny of Zymark in Hopkinton, Massachusetts, which produces and sells lab automation equipment, brought his unusual knowledge of the waterchromatography business into focus, and said, "We simply know the chemical and laboratory business inside and out. We understand the industry, now let's create a product." He and his partner visited over 100 labs, asking people, "What do you need?"

It soon became apparent to them that the repetitive task of checking test tubes for chemical properties was very time-consuming and costly for lab workers. So the two men came up with a laboratory robot that cost $250,000, a price that, in fact, represented incredible savings to those in the laboratory testing business. In addition, the robot could be used all day long—on a second and third work shift—without supervision. Each robot was custom programmed and, in short, Zeeny started an industry within an industry.

Founded in 1981, Zymark had $163,000 in 1982 sales and $12.3 million in 1986 sales. The company would like to reach $50 million, and may well make it. It's made the *Inc.* Fast Growth 500 list for the last two years in a row, and is currently ranked twelfth. The customer list is one of the finest in the United States, with clients such as Du Pont and Kodak. Venture capitalists have loved funding this business, and one of the pressing issues currently for Zeeny and his partner is when to go public. Growth has been positively affected by stock incentives to key employees and by an inviting factory that looks more like a doctor's office than a warehouse.

Another company that developed an absolutely new technology is General Alum and Chemical Corporation, a chemical producer of aluminum sulfate, founded in 1978 in Holland, Ohio. According to James A. Poure, chief executive officer, "We produced a chemical commodity in a new environmentally sound process with the end result being a high-quality finished product that outperformed competitive products. The acceptance of our product by the pulp and paper industry, water and waste treatment, and food processing industries has allowed us to make great strides in obtaining a substantial share of the market." Sales volume for General Alum has grown from $657,000 in 1979 to $7.5 million currently.

Ted Cross took his particular "trade skill"—lawyering—and asked, "What can I use professionally, as a lawyer, that I can't easily get my hands on now?" Cross built his company—Warren, Gorham, and LaMont (the first names of him and his brothers)—into one of the fastest growing publishing companies in America. Cross had looked at the dearth of law books and at the rapid amount of legal change going on; then he'd looked at the huge number of corporate "dues and subscription" dollars that were available for purchasing helpful legal manuals and guides. He then applied direct marketing skills, which he learned on the job, toward making these technical books available. The offerings were an instant success, and Ted quit his job at Sheraton, ultimately forming as many as 100 minicorporations to represent different product lines. The International Thompson Organization eventually bought his company for $25 to $30 million.

One commentator described Cross's meeting with the Thompson Organization to achieve an "agreement in principle" as a classic. Red Cross, Ted's brother, said to Michael Brown, the Thompson negotiator, "Look, you've made several passes at us. We're agreed that we want to sell and you want to buy, but we're apart by $6 million or so. Let's play two out of three sets of tennis, and the winner will get the $6 million." According to the report, Brown was stunned, and coughed up the $6 million rather than playing!

All of the Cross brothers—Warren, Gorham, and LaMont—signed management contracts but hated the new atmosphere. Nevertheless, Ted has stayed much in the fray. In 1987 he created quite a stir with his run on Harper & Row, which led in turn to Rupert Murdoch's Australian News Company taking over the company through its William Collins subsidiary—all for an incredible amount of money that was measured in terms of a multiple of sales rather than earnings! But it had all started when Ted Cross, a smart lawyer, could see that the legal niche was not being properly served and went after it.

# Filling a Void

Literally thousands of niches get filled every year. Ron Elgin's company, Elgin Syferd of Seattle, Washington, identified a void in its marketplace in 1981 when it recognized that there were good advertising agencies and good public relations firms but no single company doing both. "When a client came to us we would assume they had a 'communications problem' rather than one or the other. We became a one-stop shopping agency for corporate communications needs. The success to our clients was immediate and our success resulted in growing from $223,000 in 1981 to $3.1 million in 1985. After six years we ranked third out of 250 agencies, with $36 million in billings and $5,000,000 in income. We also now own a $10 million design firm and another $8 million ad agency for a total of 125 employees."

David C. Duxbury, founder of Comstock Leasing Incorporated, of San Mateo, California, brought his professionalism and expertise to the small ticket equipment leasing market in 1980—a market that had previously been served only by brokers. "Our kind of professionalism had previously been reserved to lease financings in excess of $100,000. There are now numerous competitors that are subsidiaries of large banks or insurance companies." Duxbury, whose California company has grown dramatically in his defined market niche, grew from $121,000 in 1980 to $1.5 million in 1984.

The T. W. MacDermott Corporation, which manages dining services or contract food services, grew from scratch in 1978 to a company that did $6.4 million by 1983, and $10 million in 1987. According to T. W. MacDermott, founder and president of this Kingston, New Hampshire, firm, "In an industry dominated by much larger companies, in other words ARA and Mariott, we define a specific market: small and medium size colleges and independent schools in a geographic territory—New England, Southeastern New York, and Northern New Jersey. We develop distinctive services, either superior or not available from the majors. We then cold called our way through a sales growth that took us to $10 million in ten years."

Constance Karsh, vice chairman of San Diego Design Incorporated of Santee, California, which manufactures home furnishings told us, "We recognized a void in the furniture manufacturing marketplace. San Diego Design literally created the new category of furniture for all to enjoy—entertainment furniture. We quickly designed new products as the video cassette recorders became so popular. We hired independent furniture sales reps and obtained showroom space in the furniture markets nation wide. Our volume jumped from $6,000,000 in 1984 to $12,000,000 in 1986. The forecast for 1988 is for sales to reach above $25 million."

Philip B. Pressler, president and CEO of Pro-File Systems Inc. of Conshohocken, Pennsylvania, which produces color-coded filing systems said, "Most companies needed help on their filing systems. Our company recognized a need existing in virtually every business across the country for a comprehensive filing system consisting not only of equipment and color-coded supplies, but also the actual physical implementation in a turnkey fashion over a weekend. The need to effectively manage the increasing volume of paperwork in the business environment and our unique total system marketing strategy led to an increase in sales of over 910% in the first five years." Pro-File, founded in 1979, reached sales of $1.9 million by 1985.

Service businesses offer numerous niche opportunities as well. Petrocomp Systems Incorporated of Houston, Texas, formed in 1979 recognized and filled a need providing consulting personnel for oil and gas companies. According to Lawrence A. Youngblood, president, "The oil and gas industry virtually had a hiring freeze for four years, yet they allowed consultants for specific needs. This business was then very complementary to our oil and gas software development division. The software development group also grew very rapidly with our expertise in microcomputers and IBM's entry into this marketplace with the PC product breakthrough. Though there were better PCs at the time, IBM's PC showed their approval and standardized this technology, a big help to us." Petrocomp went from $213 in 1980 to $3.1 million in 1984.

One company took its knowledge of a particular technology to an area of the country that had had no access to that technology before. Twenty years ago, Irv Grosbeck and Buddy Hostetter launched Continental Cablevision of Boston, a business that provides cablevision through satellite dishes to communities without decent reception. They raised $300,000 with the help of the Bank of New England, and found two small towns, Tifton and Fostoria, Ohio, that lacked decent reception. They talked to the town fathers, who agreed to let them build a tower that would enable them to pick up signals from Cleveland. They then rented a storefront and put in eight different television sets showing eight or nine different stations—to the amazement of every single member of the local community. They rented telephone pole space for their cables and invited subscribers to sign up for an installation charge and a monthly fee, up front. They've now become the twelfth largest private company in New England and within the last year they've sold off 25% of their company to Dow Jones. Continental Cablevision, which knew its niche and "knew the territory," is bound for outstanding continued growth.

One region that has seen dramatic population growth and, in turn, growth in consumer marketing opportunities is Florida. John Whelchel, president of Environmental Marketing Group Incorporated of Boca Raton, Florida, took advantage of this growth, forming his company which provides environmental products and services, in 1977. Whelchel said, "The tremendous growth in Florida's private developments has exceeded the capability of existing utility systems. This opened the door for our turnkey water and wastewater treatment plants." In the process, Environmental Marketing has increased its sales dramatically from $580,000 in 1980 to $4.5 million in 1984, a 669% sales growth, with an increase in employees from 4 to only 23.

# Getting in at the Start ▬▬▬▬▬▬▬▬▬

Sometimes timing is the key. A commercial broadcast group, TVX, of Virginia Beach, Virginia, founded in 1977, recognized early in the formative years of VHF television stations "that the most difficult element to find was independent experienced management which could operate without trying to solve problems with money." According to President Tim McDonald, "We replaced capital with hard work, developed systems that allowed us to operate television stations with fewer people and less cash and partnered our stations with people who saw the business opportunity but had no experience. We built more VHF television stations from scratch than any single company in television history." This niche proved profitable for TVX, which grew from $1.9 million in 1980 to $15.5 million in 1984.

TVX developed assets quickly. "We took advantage of a window of opportunity early (VHF construction), contributed to an overbuild during the boom years, and then sold assets to be prepared to buy major assets in a shakeout," according to McDonald. "The end result was a company begun with a capital contribution of $5300 in 1977 that today has assets valued at more than $440 million."

Many niches are somewhat mundane. Dennis E. Bale, founder of Super 8 Motels Incorporated of Aberdeen, South Dakota, which builds and furnishes economy motels said, "We started in business in 1974 when the concept of economy lodging was in its adolescent stage. The extremely successful concept grew from 1% of total rooms (lodging) to more than 16% today. [Between] the growth of our chain of developed total support services (construction, furnishing, telephones, management) [and] our franchises, our growth [has been] dramatic." Super 8 Motels, founded in 1973, has been a consistent *Inc.* Fast Growth 500 list company, growing from $1.9 million in 1982 to $58.5 million in 1986, a growth rate of 2861%.

Other companies have selected more specialized areas. Irvin E. Richter, chairman and CEO of Hill International Incorporated of Willingboro, New Jersey, told us, "Our company grew from a one-man firm to a $50 million consulting firm because we perceived a need in construction and construction litigation for broad professional expertise within one firm. We filled that need and the market exploded. Call it timing, call it good luck, it's the same thing." The company, founded in 1976, has been a consistent *Inc.* 500 company.

# The Government/Industry Connection

Some companies have discovered that the government—defense in particular—occasionally drops some rather large crumbs. Northwest Gears Incorporated of Everett, Washington, started out in the gear business as strictly a job shop for other customers. According to V. Beecher Wallace, president and CEO, "Within the first year of operation (1979) we were given an opportunity to manufacture some complete gearbox assemblies used on naval

radar systems. The confidence our customer had in us to produce these assemblies on a timely basis was respected and had
the greatest impact on our growth in the early years of the
business." Northwest had $189,000 in 1980 sales and raced to $1.5
million in 1984.

Mandex Incorporated was in the same category. This
Springfield, Virginia–based company was founded by Carl A.
Brown, who said, "We received a major boost in 1984 when we
received a $21,000,000 eight-year contract for the U.S. Marine
Corps to install and maintain a world-wide telecommunications
network. We selected AT&T to be our subcontractor and our sales
jumped approximately 100% from $8,000,000 in one year to
$16,000,000 the next." The company, founded in 1974, provides
telecommunications engineering.

Other companies have become subcontractors for industry
giants such as IBM, and have made out handsomely. John C.
Overby, president and CEO of Advanced Input Devices of Coeur
d'Alene, Idaho, said, "Our company took off like a rocket when
we received a contract from IBM to build the PC Junior keyboard
in 1983. They also gave our three-year-old company the credibility
needed to sell to other large companies on a sight/source basis."
Advanced, which was formed in 1979, exploded to a 1984 sales
volume of $26.4 million.

Most companies we spoke with knew how to leverage their
early breakthroughs with major corporations into additional
business. In the case of Storey Communications, a small piece
of consulting work on a new series concept, "Country Pleasures,"
with Time-Life Books, enabled us to talk more easily with Grolier,
McGraw-Hill, Times Mirror, and Doubleday—in fact, with all of
the major publishers of the world. Without that initial piece of
consulting work, which we did at breakeven, many of the even-
tual olives would not have come out of the bottle.

# Other Niches ▰▰▰▰▰▰▰▰▰▰▰

As we've seen, fast-growth companies find their niche in a variety of ways. Basically, however, the entrepreneur looks out at the
world, the country, society, the competition, sees a need, and goes
about filling it.

## NICHES

Some firms take a hard look at the competition, find relatively low barriers to entry, and move right in. Larry Renbarger, CEO of Shelter Components Incorporated of Elkhart, Indiana, which supplies component parts to the housing and R.V. industry said, "The competition was vulnerable. There was a significant shortage of service-minded suppliers to the industry that we were most familiar with. My partner and I felt that this void, coupled with an excellent product line, was all we needed to establish Shelter in the marketplace." They were right. Shelter, formed in 1979, achieved first-year sales of $637,000 and 1983 sales of $29.3 million.

MMS International, formerly Money Market Services, of Redwood City, California, has benefited from the computerization of the international financial community. The firm, which provides on-line market analysis, identified the internationalization of financial markets (bonds, foreign exchange, and stocks) coupled with the increase in demand for analysis behind market movements, and, according to Richard C. Green, president, "With market volatility increasing, MMS International capitalized on an increase in global trading and the associated demand for rapid information on the moving markets by using state-of-the-art technology to instantly transmit information from our global analyst to traders around the world." MMS, founded in 1974, had reached $11 million in annual sales by 1986.

Knowledge of international business has helped a number of companies. For example, Compact Performance Incorporated founded in San Ramon, California, in 1977, attributes its dramatic increase in sales to its selection as the exclusive Bay Area distributor for imported, remanufactured engines coming from Japan and Europe. According to company president Keith Bigelow, "Sales grew from approximately $100,000 a year in 1982 to over $3 million in 1987. We managed to streamline the business so that our work force increased only slightly from two employees in 1982 to five employees in 1987."

Niche publishing has exploded with the total decentralization of the publishing industry and the launch of desktop publishing. One company that has taken advantage of this is CPA Services Incorporated of Brookfield, Wisconsin. According to Betsy Morris, vice president and general manager, "Company president Jerry S. Huss has 16 years of experience as a CPA,

11 of those managing his own CPA firm. He spotted an unfilled niche, a digest newsletter designed to save managing partners time. He developed CPA Digest without the necessity for extensive market research based on his prior experience and knowledge." CPA Services Inc. now publishes five newsletters for CPA firms along with manuals and special reports based on what the customers and prospects tell them they need. Formed in 1979, the company reached 1985 sales of $1.1 million.

Another company, Hanley-Wood Incorporated of Washington, D.C., a magazine publisher formed in 1976, took a look at an opportunity in a somewhat contrarian way. In 1981 and 1982, in the midst of the worst business recession since World War II, Hanley-Wood bought two of the three magazines serving the home building industry (*Builder* and *Housing*). According to Michael Hanley, chairman, "Our volume increased from $1.6 million to $6 million, as a result, from 1981 to 1983." By 1985 they had approached $11 million, a 552% increase.

One company found a niche supplying materials. Straub Metal Service Incorporated of Bear Creek, Pennsylvania, identified a market for a special grade of stainless steel (409), which had limited warehouse distribution in the United States. According to Frederick W. Straub, president of the company, "SMS now stocks, processes, and performs other value-added features for the stainless steel product. Sales have jumped from $300,000 to $2 million in four years.

A technical company in Cleveland, Ohio, Technicomp Incorporated, which provides technical training services, has focused on "the quality movement." "We identified the quality movement early and we created highly effective, reasonably priced training materials on the new technologies of quality (statistical process control, problem solving, measurement analysis), then promoted them effectively. In short, we anticipated a need based on our own experience in the field," according to Eric Berg. Formed in 1979, Technicomp achieved 1985 sales of $1.4 million.

In the end, the difference between these fast-growth corporations and their larger corporate counterparts is that the former have identified a niche that needs filling and have then focused on it aggressively and single-mindedly. The larger corporations, on the other hand, look at growth industries and then try to buy companies that will put them into those industries—in the process they frequently manage to ruin those very companies.

So it's a matter of knowing your "trade skill," digging in deeply in an area that you know and feel something about, and planting seeds that can yield dramatic growth results.

This is not to say that fast-growth entrepreneurship is not without problems. We'll focus on some of these in the next chapter.

# Problems

9

**E**ntrepreneurs are born with a sense of optimism. Without it they are doomed.

On the other hand, there's nothing more amazing than a Pollyanna, someone who goes through life wearing rose-colored glasses. I have regularly been accused of being a Pollyanna, always trying to seek a breakthrough from our worst mailing results, always looking for the silver lining in the darkest of financial clouds, humming "Everything Is Beautiful" when a dirge would be more appropriate.

I remember that during the early days of Time Inc.'s book club foray, when Bob Luce was editor-in-chief, my phone rang one morning, and I was invited in to talk with Bob. There he sat, at ten minutes of eleven, with a Bloody Mary in his hand. He looked at me saying, "Young man, I've just read your financial report for the month. Things look grim."

"Well," said I, knowing full well the depth of our difficulties, "we do have a lot of challenges."

"Challenges my ass!" said Bob. "We've got problems!"

The problems that all entrepreneurs face are real. Here at Storey Communications, just a matter of days after startup, we discovered that our supplier, Westvaco's $75,000 paper bill, on which we had thought we could get at least 30 days trade credit, was due and payable in advance because of the transfer of ownership of the paper contract from our former corporate parent.

## PROBLEMS

At a time when we were already borrowed absolutely to the hilt, I had to go back to the banker and explain why $75,000 was due now, cash up, rather than in 30 days which we might have gained had we been an established customer. Fortunately, our banker was with us; we got the money and the paper, but not without more than a few sleepless nights.

Later, after we had gotten up and going and had proudly loaded lots of data onto our first IBM PC-XT computer and word processor, we had a computer theft. Not only was all of the hardware stolen, all of the software was taken as well! I couldn't imagine a greater problem or setback.

Later still, after we thought we were going to make it through the first year of operation relatively unscathed, we discovered the real nature of returns in the trade book business. Waldenbooks, wanting to clear up its accounts with inventory, sent back $50,000 worth of books—we went from breakeven into an unhappy loss situation.

Every growth company runs into money problems, people problems, product problems, customer problems, leadership problems. Major decisions face every growing company. How will we finance our growth? Can we do it through debt with the bankers or must we dilute our equity as well? How long can we stay private? What's the advantage of going public? Should we slow up our growth? Let's begin by looking at this last question.


# The Problem of Fast Growth

Paul Hawken, whose company has been happily growing for the last dozen years, asks, "Do we have a concept that a slower growing company may be more successful than a fast growing company? Can we even conceive that speed does not equate with quality, steadfastness, maturity, or even ultimate growth in size? Nothing in nature tells us that rapid growth is good, and certainly nothing in human biology. In our own bodies, the most rapid growth of all is cancer."[1]

And yet the temptation of fast growth is irresistible. Believe it or not, for most entrepreneurs, the realization that someone might actually want to buy something from them is incomprehensible. Tom Peters thought perhaps 300 people would buy his book, *In Search of Excellence*. (His publisher, Harper & Row, wasn't much more confident, doing an initial print run of only 12,000 books.) It's difficult to visualize the 10, 100, or 1000 people who are actually going to buy your product. So when sales demand develops, it's very hard to resist the temptation to take it, to take it all, and to take it all *quickly*.

That's when the problems begin. Allowing the logistics of the business—production, order processing, fulfillment, shipping, invoicing, and customer satisfaction—to keep up with the demands on the sales side is one of the biggest problems that most growth companies run into.

John C. Overby, president and CEO of Advanced Input Devices, put it this way. "The biggest challenge was to not only hire hundreds of new people over a period of a few months and to get the product out, but to keep the quality high and make money at the same time. Explosive growth can turn into cancer."

While emphasizing the sales side, profits can flip-flop and cash flows deteriorate. According to William A. Delaney, "Rapid growth does not automatically mean more profit." He suggests not trying to grow too fast. "Though it's hard to turn away unexpected new business, it's better to be disciplined and grow in a steady planned fashion." Delaney goes on. "Slower growth is preferable to bursting on the scene like a skyrocket, soaring high in the heavens and then falling to Earth as a burned out shell. It's better to be a small satellite, climb into the sky slowly and stay in orbit indefinitely."[2]

So we ask ourselves, How fast is too fast? Charles Kyd, in an article of that title suggests that, "You need to be aware of your AGR (affordable growth rate). Sales can grow only as fast as your assets and you must maintain a constant debt to equity ratio. The growth rate of your sales depends on the growth rate of the equity." Kyd goes on to explain what he means by the AGR. "Say it's 24%. That means that if you keep a growth rate of about 24% your financial growth will stay in balance. Faster growth than 24% means you must sell more stock or increase your debt ratio. Slower than 24%, you can reduce your debt ratio and buy your stock."[3]

Before we acquired the assets of the Garden Way Publishing Company, the division had been pushed toward fast growth in order to "reach economies of scale" and "help absorb corporate overheads." This overly simplistic analysis suggested that the more units we pushed out, the lower our cost of production would become, and therefore the more margin we would develop. However, what the parent company failed to realize is that economies of scale may not develop at all in the $1 million to $5 million sales range, and that the overheads that the company was putting on top of the business, including large computer systems, mega telephone systems, and a bloated corporate staff, were far greater than the company could afford. Therefore, for a period, every additional book that was pushed out contributed an additional nickel of *loss* to the company. In the final year, before Storey Communications acquired the assets, the company made its final fast-growth push, taking it to $5 million in sales. It lost over $1 million in the process!

For many, sales growth is just plain heady. John Grant, consultant to the American Standard Company, says, "It has to do with the mindset of this whole culture, this idea that high growth is exciting and low growth is for dullards. But what's the growth based on? Is it real growth based on expanding markets or improved productivity? Or is it house of cards growth that's spun out of the air? Growth for the sake of growth is a loser."[4]

The "volume for volume's sake" trap is enticing and should be avoided. Some of the very best advice we had from our board of directors in the initial meeting was to first downsize the company in volume—to try to determine where the break-even point was. There were some scary moments along the way, and it appeared at times that we would never find the break-even point. But once we did, we had the kernel of a good, solid, profitable business that we could build on. And we have—taking it from just over $1 million in 1983 to $5 million this year.

Eventually, most of these issues of growing too fast lead down the same path. It's called the money path. Whether companies have been launched on venture capital, a handful of private investors, family money, or debt through a local bank, sooner or later the reality of cash flow problems develops.

# The Problem of Money ████████████████

Tom J. Fatjo, Jr., launched a fitness chain in Texas called Living Well Incorporated, which, after just three years of very rapid growth, lost $24.5 million on sales of $148 million in the first nine months ending September 30, 1987.[5] Fatjo had taken the company from a small acquisition in 1982 to revenues of close to $200 million by 1986. During 1987, the company found it impossible to pay even the interest on $72 million worth of senior debentures and notes.[6] One of Fatjo's problems was his excessive efforts to build membership. He decided that new members didn't have to pay cash up front, a critical change from the 30% deposit that had previously been collected from new members. This and his strong marketing push for new members resulted in a severe cash crunch.

A happier story comes from John Hewett Chapman, former chairman of Mira Flores Designs Incorporated, who told us, "We struggled in finding a bank that would provide increases in bank financing to keep pace with our rapid growth. Eventually we did successfully find a bank who understood fast growth, and they supported our needs very well."

Many of the *Inc.* Fast Growth 500 have decided to merge. Motion Designs and T. J. MacDermott fall into that category.

Others have decided on joint ventures. Xscribe Corporation of San Diego, California, did this in order to expand its market but also to share its financial risk. According to Robert F. Mawhinney, "A joint venture with an East Coast company opened up the market for us. It also set the stage to expand throughout the country. Before 1981 we were localized in San Diego." Xscribe, which manufactures computer-aided transcription equipment, has blossomed to $30 million in sales.

Capital needs can overtake growing companies. While in the beginning many companies decide to rent or lease, the temptation to improve margins by investing in capital equipment critical to day-to-day production is strong. Patrick Gorman, chairman of American Leisure Industries Inc., said, "Installing newer equipment was critical to service the needs of our greatly enlarged membership base. The only way to get it was to turn to debt or equity markets." With financial fueling, American Leisure grew rapidly to $36 million in sales.

**PROBLEMS**

A myriad of companies have decided to make strong investments in new capital equipment—at just the wrong time. After seven years of dramatic growth, for example, with volume doubling annually, Garden Way Incorporated hit sales of $60 million. Based on the fast growth, the board of directors decided to increase the size of the plant by 50%, thus increasing productive capacity and the ability to produce not 60,000, but 100,000 units a year. But a funny thing happened on the way to the 100,000 units. Demand slipped. Unhappily, the company stayed, with the newly expanded overheads and debt levels, at the 60,000 level for almost three years. Finally, following a rebirth in the marketing program, Garden Way was able to lift production to the 100,000 per year mark that the corporation had believed possible. The path getting there was pretty rocky, though.

# Going Public ■■■■■■■■■■■■■■■■■■

Many companies are tempted along the way to go public. The Patten Corporation, which had grown modestly for a short period of time decided that it wanted—and could—"go global," according to Don Dion, chief financial officer. "We had proven the formula of land acquisition and land sales. We knew that the formula would work. It was just a matter of convincing other people that this was the case and getting the money to do it."

In Patten's case, his first choice was to go to debt markets. But no one wanted to lend money on "raw land." "I was surprised," said Dion. "These were people that I had dealt with extensively in the past and we believed the prospectus that we put before them was irresistible. I was forced to go into the equity market for the first time in my life." Fortunately for Patten, a bright underwriter at Drexel, Burnham, Lambert saw the value of their proposition and helped them to package a public offering that raised the first of what came to be $150 million in cash over a three-year period.

Many resist going public, however. In fact, of the fastest growing 500 companies reported by *Inc.* last year, only 17 actually decided to go public. A recent survey showed that "more than

50% of the responding CEOs said they had little or no interest in going public."[7]

Some see going public as a fast way to not only retain control of their company but to get rich in the process. Others are concerned that the time, effort, energy, and expense associated with going public will completely take their minds off the business itself. In Patten's case, the offering cost well over $300,000 in legal, accounting, and printing expenses—clearly not something to be taken lightly.

One entrepreneur, Carlton Cadwell of Cadwell Laboratories Inc., put it this way: "The disadvantage to us, if we go public, is that we could no longer be primarily accountable to our customers and our products. You become a prisoner to a quick hit mentality. I'm a long-term planning kind of person."[8]

Another fast-growth entrepreneur, Kenneth George of Burr Wilson, said that he "prefers having a regional firm that affords me the luxury of providing quality service to local clients." He goes on that when you go public you "start peddling whatever the company needs, just to keep the stock moving rather than doing what the client needs."[9]

There is also a fear by many that the financial people, not the creators, engineers, or marketers, will suddenly take over. Jerry Rochte, of Cavro Scientific Instruments Inc., says, "You end up focusing on today's numbers as the be-all and end-all. Companies lose their identities; they're simply chips on a board and you forget that profits aren't everything, survival is everything."[10]

Others suggest that there's not that much to worry about. Harold S. Schwenk, Jr., of BGS Systems Inc., who took his company public, said, "It's all been boringly simple. Maybe the biggest surprise is that there have been no surprises."[11] This decision, like many others, clearly is one of trade-offs. By going public there is instant liquidity, plenty of cash to do all the things that the company wants to do. On the other hand, there's much greater scrutiny of activities. Everything that was ever private becomes public in the FCC Registration Statement, and an owner begins to run the risk of losing control of the company.

The majority of entrepreneurs with whom we spoke had considered going public and had stayed private. One who decided to go public, Judith Kaplan, chairman of Action Packets Incorporated of Ocala, Florida, needed the money to expand the market niche she had found. Kaplan said, "Our company began to grow when we realized this simple formula: Find a market niche and supply it better than anyone else does. Going public and raising capital meant we didn't have to worry about funding our immediate growth plans anymore."

Some companies face stormy market seas after deciding to go public. Properties of America Incorporated, of Williamstown, Massachusetts, which had been on the *Inc.* Fast Growth 500 for two successive years was all ready to go when the market crashed on October 19, 1987. To the company's credit, it faced the wind and sailed into a less than completely favorable market. The initial public offering was November 19, and the company joined the NASDAQ over-the-counter market in late 1987. Properties of America, which operates much like Patten, hit a much less favorable stock market than Patten did, and was not able to raise the amount of money outlined in its original prospectus. Many would have not even tried, but POA sold into adversity with determination, and survived. Today it's the third fastest growing company traded on NASDAQ.

One company that didn't try going public after the crash was Ben and Jerry's Homemade Inc. of Waterbury, Vermont, which had planned to make a $6 million equity offer when the market hit its "black Monday."[12] According to Fred Lager, "We were two weeks from making the offering when the market crashed. We were unable to do that, but we were able to convert it into a $6 million convertible debenture that did well." Ben and Jerry's will use the money to move ahead on expansion of its facilities in Waterbury and Springfield, Vermont.[13]

Most Fast Growth 500 companies eventually decide to stay private. John Oren, president of Eastway Delivery Service Inc., put it this way: "Having total control is where I'm at. The company is a reflection of that." Oren believes that investing in his own company is a better financial alternative than investing in someone else's.[14]

Amar Bose, of Stereo Equipment, was concerned about the short-term emphasis that going public seems to inject. He said, "We win only by staying on the cutting edge of technology, and that can't be done by just following short run goals. Sometimes you have to move backwards to get a step forward."[15]

# Deal Making ▬▬▬▬▬▬▬▬▬▬

Some companies get the financing they need from other sources. Some, for example, consider private placements, which require no registration with the SEC or other federal commissions. Some even create a new holding company, with the partial liquidation of other assets to improve their financial condition. The authors of *The Arthur Young Guide to Financing for Growth* recommend considering a private placement when (1) your company doesn't have the financial strength or reputation to get enough investors for a private offering, (2) you can't afford the expense of a private offering, or (3) you need the money now and can't wait for the lengthy process. They go on to suggest that it's "the fastest and cheapest way to get capital, it's money you don't have to pay back, and there's little danger that you'll lose control of your company to outside investors."[16]

Some companies have given their organizations new life by going through a leveraged buyout. During our research we contacted nearly 200 people who had done LBOs, whereby they had borrowed money on the assets of the company that was to be paid back out of earnings over a long period of time. One of these was John R. Oren, CEO of the Eastway Delivery Group Company in Houston, Texas. "After working for the previous owner of the Eastway for a year, I realized that I had the desire to be my own boss and business owner. After convincing the previous owner to sell this seedling of a business (he had several other thriving businesses) to me, I suddenly came to understand the relationship of top line revenue to my sense of security."

Oren has achieved success and puts it this way: "At age 25, naïveté was the best I had to offer. Since that quiet revelation I've not stopped to look back. My future is growth. My security is higher sales revenue. My solace is achieving my sales goal . . . thus the single most critical factor to my growth was understanding what the consequences were for not selling my service."

There are dozens and dozens of deal makers waiting to untangle financing problems. One of these—Weiss, Peck, and Greer, a private merchant banking firm—focuses on the smaller, faster growth companies in the $10 million to $100 million range. "It's beautiful to watch," says the group's founder. "There's a vast ocean of frustrated middle managers out there and we're helping them become entrepreneurs. It may sound arrogant, but I really think we're dream makers."[17]

# The Problems of Acquisition

A few companies grow rapidly by simply acquiring attractive companies. But they absorb and then must deal with the problems of the other companies. Charles M. Leighton, founder of the CML Group of Action, Massachusetts, in 1969, has taken his business from nothing to over $280 million by 1987 by acquiring a number of specialty retail companies, including Nordic Track, Sybervision, Carroll Reed, Gokey's, Britches of Georgetown, The Nature Company, and others. Leighton's acquisition ability was fine-tuned at Bangor Punta Corporation, which he helped take from $3 million to $70 million through acquisitions in the mid-1960s. "I decided that if I could do it for them, I could do it myself, so we decided to grow by acquisition."

CML has been uniquely successful, with earnings growth of 30% a year for the last five years and a current 2700 employees.

The key to Leighton's plan has been the retention of the owner/entrepreneurs of the acquired companies. He's been uniquely successful in running a company of $280 million with a totally decentralized approach, and a central management team of only 11 people. Each of the companies is run very separately.

Occasionally this management style causes some egg on the face. In the case of Gokey, for example, the absence of adequate financial controls led to a surprise inventory adjustment of over $2 million after the CML stock had gone public. This caused uncertainty as to how much control Leighton actually had. Although Leighton admits to making mistakes, he steadfastly supports the decentralized style and its overall effectiveness. "We've got good entrepreneur/owners who know more about their business than anyone else. We try to coach, and leave them alone."

Interestingly, most of his deals with his founder entre-preneurs are based on earn-outs (cash from future earnings), where the entrepreneur makes more money than he would have at a current valuation, but has to wait approximately five years to do so, based on the positive cash flow of the company.

Leighton is also quite successful in convincing his entre-preneurs to get help when they need it. "In the case of Nordic Track, we had a brilliant mechanical engineer who knew every-thing there was to know about new product development but needed marketing and operating people. He agreed to put them in and has done wonderfully."

Another company that is on the fast-growth track again is Grolier, the $425 million publishing company that, after stum-bling in the mid-1970s and approaching bankruptcy, came back strong under Chairman Robert B. Clarke. According to Clarke, the growth came from acquisitions. In order to strengthen its direct mail marketing operation, Grolier acquired Mystic Color Lab Inc. in 1985 and Child Craft Education Corp. in 1986.

When Clarke acquires a company, he usually leaves the old management in place. "I don't want to cut down on their creativ-ity. The last thing we need around here is a bunch of MBAs and CPAs coming in with formulas, trying to tell people how to run their businesses."[18] Grolier's future growth plans are ambitious, and, significantly, the company is recruiting some of the best peo-ple in the publishing and direct marketing business.

# Coordinating and Controlling Growth

As fast growth develops, managing or trying to coordinate the growth becomes a major problem. Lyman Wood used to tell us, "We can't run this company, we can only run with it." Getting the right people in the right places at the right time. Adding supervisors who can lead other people and who will make deci-sions. In a recent survey of 100 chief executives, a question was, "What single factor do you consider most significant in prevent-ing your subordinates from rising higher in the organization?" Sixty-five percent of them said "indecisiveness."[19]

**PROBLEMS**

Many fast-growth executives complained of this in a number of different ways. Constance Karsh of San Diego Design told us, "Our biggest problem was the inability of our management to develop and mature as quickly as our company was developing in the eyes of the marketplace. As a result, our company went through a period of putting out fires and never really solving them."

San Diego Designs Inc. survived those challenges and at the $18 million mark in annual sales, the company totally reorganized. "We brought in a president whose philosophy is working smarter. The layers of management and supervisors are gone. Direct reporting and accountability have made our workers feel more valuable." Today they've surpassed $25 million in sales.

Many fast-growth executives also complained about a loss of control. Mike Stansburg, president of National Decision Systems, said, "Internally, in a high growth company, the communication, organization, planning, and control is our biggest enemy. Maintaining a proper balance of those factors is our Achilles heel."

Richard DeWolfe of DeWolfe New England said very simply, "Control was our biggest problem. No matter how prepared we felt, no matter how we planned, there were so many variables that we were at the mercy of events. In our case, what we thought were excellent financial systems totally broke down under the complexity of more business and new ventures. Control is really the challenge." DeWolfe is doing $12 million in real estate and financial services.

# The Problem of Quality ▬▬▬▬▬▬▬▬

Many entrepreneurs fear that the worst thing that may happen during their fast growth is the loss of quality standards. W. Timothy Finn II, executive vice president of Professional Bank Services said, "Maintaining the quality standards that created our growth in the first place was a big problem."

Donn Rappaport, chairman of the American List Council, a Princeton, New Jersey–based direct mail list brokerage firm, agreed: "Maintaining the same quality of service and responsiveness to our client needs that provided the foundation for our growth in the first place was really hard." American List has surpassed $16 million in sales.

Dr. Gerald R. McNichols, chairman of The Management Consulting and Research Incorporated Group, noted another aspect of this problem. "Rapid growth typically implies loss of quality . . . a small business often has the reputation of the founder/entrepreneur tied up in the company's products. Thus maintaining integrity and a quality reputation is the single biggest challenge."

When quality suffers, so does business. Robert S. Maltempo, chairman of the Vantage Computer Systems Group of Weatherfield, Connecticut, said, "We had to grow from 50 people to 150 in one year. The reputation for quality, which we had built over 10 years, suffered tremendously, and it took us almost three years to reestablish it again." Vantage has passed the $7 million sales mark.

Some people run into significant competition. Roger F. Naill, vice president of Applied Energy Services Incorporated, said, "Five years after our start, we now face stiff competition in the electric generation market from cogenerators, independent power producers, and utilities. We have to develop a strategy of operating excellence to keep ahead of our competitors." Applied Energy, of Arlington, Virginia, is at the $22 million sales mark.

Sometimes the competition wins. John DeLorean's strategy for his DeLorean Auto Company of starting at the top and competing against the "big guys" failed. As reported by James R. Cook, "DeLorean had nowhere to go but down. He began on a grand scale and had no market gap."[20]

Other fast-growth companies have run into the problem of deteriorating customer service as volume grows. We certainly ran into this at Garden Way when, during the heart of our very effective sales campaigns, we developed a 22-week backlog. We began to experience severe difficulties in delivering not only new products, but replacement parts as well.

Martha Sanders Smith, vice president of Phoenix Advertising Design and Promotion, faced the same problem: "Maintaining the level of customer service for clients was a problem as we grew. We were left with the feeling that many of our clients were not fully developed to their maximum potential."

Kirk G. Cottrell, president of Island Water Sports, told us, "Lack of follow-up by our management hurt us with our customers. It was nuts."

W. J. Hindman, chairman of Jiffy Lube International of Baltimore, Maryland, said, "Maintaining Jiffy Lube's standards of excellence is probably, with our products, service, values, and people, an ongoing effort. The critical issue here is the transfer of excellence through training." Jiffy Lube has surpassed $30 million in sales.

# The Problem of . . . ▄▄▄▄▄▄▄▄▄▄▄▄▄▄▄▄

All sorts of other problems can—and do—arise. One entrepreneur ran into problems of space: where to do and put things. Robert L. Page, president of Replacements Limited, said, "Probably the most pressing need we had was for storage space. I had to add on to my existing warehouse three times in as many years. As soon as I built space or filled it up, we'd be bursting at the seams. I finally purchased a brand new 40,000 sq. ft. building that I hope will hold me for a while."

Often the problem is governmental and bureaucratic red tape. Stephen C. Vallone, president of National Titles Company, said, "The biggest challenge for us to overcome was to defeat the legislative efforts by the large established companies to close the market to new companies such as ours. They came close to passing a bill that would limit whom we could do business with, but the Texas senate saw their effort as anticompetitive and voted it down."

Richard M. Henley, chairman of Northland Pure Waters, told us, "Keeping the federal or state government and agencies from changing the rules repeatedly and getting in our hair, instead of them attacking the nonproductive or criminal segment, which needed attention, was our biggest challenge."

Marshall Lasky, president of Vocation Training Centers of St. Louis said, "The regulatory agencies that slowed us down every step of the way in every phase of our operation made it difficult. The bureaucratic hurdles were constantly in our way and slowed our growth."

Logistical support for the fast-growth company is yet another challenge. Jack F. Gold, chairman of Contract Furnishings and Systems Limited, said, "As a result of early growth, support became our major problem, first in administration, second in management. Without developing a support organization that was as committed to the organization's success it would have been impossible to continue the development."

Others mentioned the problem of communications. Rex Maughan, chairman of Forever Living Products, said, "Proper communications with 1.3 million distributors around the world, along with complying with all the various government regulations and red tape were the biggest challenges we faced."

Linda G. Watkins, president of J. L. Associates Inc. of Hampton, Virginia, told us, "Establishing a communications system to serve our expanding needs was a top priority. Success or failure to meet our rapid growth needs depended on how well we were able to flex or introduce new players and have them work as a team quickly and efficiently." J. L. Associates, which provides management services contracting, has passed $12 million in sales.

Communication problems are increased when a company is decentralized. Richard C. Green, president of MMS International, said, "Our management structure was decentralized and maintaining communications was a difficult and important hurdle for everyone."

One common problem of many fast-growth companies is having sales information pile up so quickly that there is little time to analyze it. Without complete computerization or analytic systems, it becomes difficult to know which channels of distribution are providing the best return on money invested. We certainly faced this problem at Storey Communications, where we were using five different channels of distribution, from mail order through distributors and dealers, and had only the crudest of cost accounting to help us determine where the return was greatest. With the implementation of a Fortune microcomputer system and good new software, we've been able to make headway, redirecting our efforts to the right channels.

In the end, most smaller fast-growth companies realize they just don't have the cushions that the larger companies have and therefore have to make decisions a lot more carefully. "You need micromanagement to survive and grow. You can't make the same mistakes a larger corporation can and get away with them as a small company . . . $50,000 mistakes will kill an infant business."[21]

Other people simply run out of raw materials. This was the case with Crystal S. Ettridge, vice president of Temps and Company of Washington, D.C.: "The demand for temporary office help is so tremendous here that the principal factor behind growth is recruiting enough temporaries. In fact, for the last five years that has been our only obstacle to growth. Last year we grew from $12 million to $21 million in billings while, due to insufficient supply of temporaries, we were canceling an average of $60,000 worth of business each week, which would have added an additional $2 to $3 million on our annual sales figures."

Some companies, buoyed by sales success, begin to relax too much. Larry Miller, president of Corinthian Communications Incorporated of New York, told us candidly, "When we could live off our reputation things got tough. The temptation was to grow and get sloppy. We resisted this but it cost us. We've revamped, which cost us time, but it will be well worth it." Corinthian, a media buying company, has passed the $100 million mark.

# Planning for the Future

Some suggest that the biggest problem of small business growth, however, is that you're so busy working on hourly crises and day-to-day matters that you fail to provide for the longer term. Gerald Letendre, president of Diamond Casting and Machine Company Inc. of Hollis, New Hampshire, said, "We've made near-term compromises on profitability with investments that will pay their way over the long haul. The biggest failing of small business is the failure to take the long-term view. And the smaller the business, the shorter the time horizon."

Ronald E. Wysong, president of R. L. Drake Company, said his biggest problem was "being farsighted enough to plan for the future beyond the near term." Steven P. Johnston, president of S. J. Electro Systems Inc. echoed that, saying, "Our biggest challenge was accurately projecting the planning for the future.

We were required to keep in touch with current market happenings while at the same time utilizing our current information to foresee the future." Johnston, based in Detroit Lakes, Minnesota, manufactures alarm systems and has surpassed $2.3 million in sales.

## Where to Go from Here ▬▬▬▬▬▬

Once companies begin to hit their stride, they generally come to a fork in the road. Do we do more of the same, or try to diversify? Peter Drucker, in talking about diversification says the best question is, "What is the least diversification this business needs in order to accomplish its mission, obtain its objectives, and continue to be viable and prosperous?"[22]

Fast-growth entrepreneurs usually find that a ripple-out effect is the better way to go. By extending their product lines, or offering additional goods and services to their same customer base, they limit their risk. James R. Cook has said, "The key to diversification is the enthusiasm which the clients greet it with. A smooth diversification offers the same customers an additional service they need."[23]

Unrelated ventures can frequently spell disaster. Most entrepreneurs learn pretty quickly to keep their nose in their own single business and try not to operate a second or third one at the same time. Gary Sutton, president of Checks-To-Go, told us, "Maintaining focus is the biggest challenge." Michael J. Collins, president of CEM Corporation, said, "Maintaining focus is key. We were beginning to stray from our basic technology and tried to do too many different things. Fortunately, we realized this and refocused strongly, which is the major reason for our current success." CEM, of Matthews, North Carolina, provides microwave instrumentation and has achieved sales of $9.3 million.

Nancy Vetrone, president of Original Copy Centers Inc., suggests that "focusing and staying with our unique niche and not spreading ourselves too thin, accepting types of work we were not geared up to do, was critical to our high-volume copy success."

All entrepreneurs face the question of what to do when their fast growth inevitably pauses and sometimes even levels out.

## PROBLEMS

John H. Zenger, president of Zenger Mill Incorporated, said, "In trying to stay ahead of rapid growth, an organization finally decides to go ahead and develop the internal systems, the physical facilities, the staff required of a constantly doubling organization. If that growth rate stumbles, you are in a vulnerable position. That happened to us in 1985. Everyone learned an important lesson about controlling growth and not building up overhead in anticipation of future sales."

Other people have run into the problem of vanishing markets. Philip F. Palmedo of International Resources Group said, "We started to exhaust the potential to market, and the physical capability of our well-known senior staff. The challenge was then to diversify into allied areas of work."

Gannett Company, the owners of *USA Today*, faces the same problem. "There are few major newspapers still for sale so growth by acquisition will be hard."[24] Chairman Alan Neuharth said recently, "This company was a growth company before and during my time and I am confident that it will be after my time. Gannett's philosophy, policy, and style are that none of us have been interested in just perserving any empire we inherited. We've been interested in expanding it, developing it, and making it grow."

Plenum Publishing, a niche publisher with soaring pretax profit margins has run into the same problem—nowhere to grow. Under President Martin Tash, it has been uniquely successful and its options seem to be to acquire other companies or to sell out.[25] Plenum publishes a technical line of books that it markets primarily by direct mail. The company has worked so hard at filling its niche that it's now a question of where to go.[26]

Thus far, Tash has used his surplus earnings from Plenum to take market (stock) positions on behalf of the company. Ironically, if the extraordinary valuation of this capital investment grows too much larger, the SEC may make Plenum apply as an investment company.[27]

Other companies have been challenged by trying to figure upswings and downturns of the economy. Stanley Acker, president of Pavion Limited, said, "Our ability to anticipate a downward trend in the economy in the late 1970s was key. It was my feeling that this trend would reflect upon consumer spendable income. Looking for a void in the cosmetic marketplace, I zeroed in on developing a budget price line of cosmetics. We developed a line called 'Wet and Wild' and in short, it worked." From a very small base, the company has grown to a volume of $40 million over the last eight years.

## The Problem of Success ▬▬▬▬▬▬▬▬▬▬

Others cite ego as the result of too much success. Thomas A. Ferrante, president of Intertech International, told us, "We handled our growth badly. We're still paying the price. The saga begins when you start to believe your own press and the symptoms abound. Bigger cars for everyone, a new facility with a gym and racquetball court, titles for some high-priced nonproducers, meetings, endless nonproductive meetings, and an owner who is distracted from the business while he admires his apparent but short-lived success."

A lot of people weather this kind of activity. In the case of Intertech, they simply stuck with it. "There is a happy ending," said Ferrante. "During the tough times we remembered Winston Churchill during the Battle of Britain, exhorting all Englishmen to 'never, never, never give up.' Like the stock market, lines on a sales chart go up and down as well. Adversity builds character and this character will be in there struggling as long as strength holds out."

Allen Stone of Taft Hamilton Merchandising Group said, "Nothing recedes like success. You tend to become cocky and expect all to come after you to represent them . . . to become noncreative, to stop running. The business world is jungle. To live in it and survive, you must work continually at it."

Other problems develop when the business outgrows the capacity of the founding owner/entrepreneur to run it. This was certainly the case at Garden Way Incorporated, where, despite the genius of Lyman Wood's founding vision, once the company began to approach $100 million in sales, outside professional management was required. Wood's inability to allow these people to come in with backing and responsibility, his inability to watch easily from the sidelines, led to the shakeup of the company in 1982, with a nasty stock takeover that resulted in Wood and his board of directors being thrown out.

## PROBLEMS

Others have experienced the same thing. Philip B. Pressler, president and CEO of Profile Systems Incorporated, said, "We were originally formed with two stockholders, each holding 50% of the business. The company grew rapidly over the first six years while the partners gradually grew apart in terms of business goals and management philosophies. This division of corporate objectives eventually led to an irreparable chasm that resulted in the unamicable severance of the partnership in early 1987."

Lawrence A. Youngblood, president of Petrocomp Systems Inc. of Houston, Texas, said, "It was very challenging to understand and work with the expectations and goals of the principal entrepreneur. Not unlike other growth companies, these differences could only be settled by spinning off a division of the company and its principals. Thus, software and consulting became two separate entities. Incidentally, had each of these entities operated separately, both would have made the *Inc.* 500 list."

Going separate ways from founders can be difficult. Ron Hume of Toronto, Canada, said, "Sometimes the business simply outgrows the ability of the early people to stay with it, even those with stock. We've had to buy stock back from several of our people and it's never easy. But I think they realize at the same time that the business has gotten to be bigger than them, me, or any of us."

Paul Hawken put a different light on it when he said, "Sooner or later businesses lull themselves into failure, and this often reflects their inability to learn what the immediate business environment is saying. Enterprises fail more often because of the sum total of seemingly inconsequential events acting upon them than because of a sudden disaster or discontinuity."[28]

Call them challenges. Call them problems. We all run into them. It's the way we deal with them in the end that counts. As Grantland Rice put it, "When the One Great Scorer comes to write against your name—he marks—not that you won or lost—but how you played the game." Vince Lombardi would have disagreed, saying, "Winning is the only thing."

In our next, and final chapter, we'll recount some memorable lessons from the hundreds of fast-growth entrepreneurs we've met so far. Some are in the Rice camp, some in Lombardi's, but all are wiser today than before their fast-growth experience occurred.

# Lessons

10

**D**avid Birch and his MIT group have studied 12 million companies since 1969! We've studied five years of *Inc., Venture, Forbes, Business Week,* and *Fortune* fast-growth lists, as well as "up and coming" fast-growth lists. We sent out detailed surveys to over 600 of America's fastest growing companies and heard back from half of them. We had hundreds of conversations—many by phone, many in person.

And while our role is that of reporter rather than scientist, there's no question but that we've learned many lessons along the way. And reached some conclusions.

One of the things we've learned is that most of our fast-growth entrepreneurs consider their business a classroom or a laboratory. They have attempted to maintain an atmosphere in which risks are seen as an inherent part of the business and are accepted when they arise, an atmosphere where mistakes are part of the normal day-to-day operating process, and where problems are very much a part of daily business life. An attitude that is universally allowed to prevail suggests that "our next biggest breakthrough is going to come from our most recent failure."

This atmosphere leads to a feeling of continuing on-the-job education and is the earmark of many fast-growth companies. They view the daily mail, daily sales receipts, daily orders, and daily complaints as the empirical evidence from which conclusions will arise, and new action be taken. A quest is constantly under way to improve the business.

Thus, any list of lessons learned is bound to be, by the very nature of the process, both incomplete and premature. For, this whole entrepreneurial fast-growth process more closely resembles a continuing motion picture than a snapshot of a point in time. "Our business is moving so quickly," said Ron Hume, "that whatever I tell you today is likely to be obsolete tomorrow."

But, at the same time, we have learned many lessons, and we'll try to share some of those with you. There is no way to rank these in importance; rather, they reflect the particular constituency with whom we spoke.

*Lesson 1: All of the people involved in growing their own businesses have a crystal clear vision as to where they want to get in the long term.* This lesson is characteristic of both entrepreneurs and of leaders in general. They are strong-minded, highly focused people. As George Gilder puts it in his *Spirit of Enterprise,* "Entrepreneurs everywhere ignored the suave voices of expertise: the economists who deny their role as the driving force of all economic growth; the psychologists who identify their work and sacrifice as an expression of greed; the sociologists who see their dreams as nostalgia for a lost frontier; the politicians who call their profits unearned, their riches pure luck."[2]

Many of the entrepreneurs that Gilder describes are criticized as having their head in the clouds, for thinking only in global terms, and not being willing to get down to the dirt-underneath-the-fingernails work. When America's premier direct response advertising agency, Wunderman, Ricotta, and Kline, was acquired by a larger general agency, Young and Rubicam, becoming Wunderman Worldwide, Lester Wunderman, founder of the company, was criticized for thinking only of the global picture. "He's not counting coupons anymore, that's for sure," said one of his long-time employees. "He's really thinking in cosmic terms."

Another view is voiced by Alfred P. Sloan in his book, *My Years with General Motors.* Sloan was a tremendous corporate success in his world of automobiles, yet looking back he felt he hadn't thought or acted "big enough. What if he had thought big from the start!"[3]

Lyman Wood's dream for Garden Way was to have everyone in the world plant their own garden. Fred Smith had a vision that everyone on the globe could have overnight mail delivery service, and then instantaneous Zap Mail, a newfound access to information from friends and business associates worldwide. Harry Patten wanted to offer recreational land globally. And Elliot Wadsworth is a "big picture man" at *Horticulture* magazine and White Flower Farm, both very successful fast-growth entities in Connecticut.

The founders' vision provides a magnetic, and visionary leadership. Natural leadership, not to be confused with pure charisma, comes, in many cases from the founding vision, in other cases from the technical expertise, or human skills that a company leader may have. Bill Gore at W. L. Gore and Associates believes that "no one holds any formal position of authority. Leadership emerges naturally when people attract followers."[4] Gore's now famous "lattice management" has produced results. Sales in the last ten years have grown at least 35% annually.[5] "Commitment, not authority, produces results," says Gore.[6]

*Lesson 2: Fast-growth entrepreneurs have an incurable sense of optimism.* Very few of the fast-growth executives we spoke with displayed cynicism, skepticism, or pessimism. As Paul Hawken put it, "Plan to be around for a hundred years. Or longer. We all say that a company must continuously strive to give the best service possible. I agree, but that is kind of an abstract idea. If you're planning to be here 10, 30, 70 years from now, you have to conduct your business as if the world around you will remember everything you've done to date. It will."[7]

This "longer view" has the added benefit of resulting in more relaxed selling. I found myself, promoting advertising space in our *Gardeners' Marketplace* publication, beginning to say "OK, if you're not ready for the Spring issue, no problem . . . keep us in mind for the Summer issue." The result was easier conversions, created by less sales pressure.

George Gilder calls this optimism, or "long view," a faith. "Entrepreneurs, though many are not church goers, emerge from a culture shaped by religious values. The optimism and trust, the commitment and faith, the discipline and altruism that their works require all can flourish only in the midst of a moral order, with religious foundations."[8]

All of our fast-growth entrepreneurs shared a sense of faith, whether secular (the majority) or religious. Albert J. Caperna, president of Century Marketing in Ohio, said, "As strange as this might sound God was the single biggest factor in our growth. We manufacture and distribute pressure sensitive labels, a small market niche. However, we were able to control distribution in this niche and grew very quickly. For any business to succeed as quickly as we have requires the favor of the Lord."

*Lesson 3: Fast-growth entrepreneurs do everything possible, despite their growth, to maintain a feeling of smallness, even one of family.* In many cases we have seen a company grow very quickly, reach a point of excessive "corporateness," and then spin off part of itself in an attempt to regain the entrepreneurial feeling that got it going in the first place, and that might, if recaptured, allow it to regain new levels of growth and employee satisfaction. This is certainly the pattern at 3M. It was certainly the formula for 15 years of incredible growth at Garden Way Incorporated, where Lyman Wood seemed to operate on the principle of "another day, another letterhead!" [Wood spun off Garden Way Research, Publishing, Catalog, Retail, Associates (Advertising), Marketplace, Sun Room, Workbench, Cider Press, and Gardens for All, a nonprofit research company—all within 10 years.]

*The 100 Best Companies to Work for in America*, the landmark study by Levering, Moskowitz, and Katz, recognized this: "The big companies on our roster have maintained many small company traits: they break down their operations into small units, they push responsibility down into the ranks, they don't mangle people. We were pleased also to find three divisions of large companies that qualified (for their best company list though their parent companies didn't): Bell Labs (American Telephone and Telegraph), Physio-Control (Eli-Lily), and Westin Hotels (United Airlines)."[9]

Most of the companies we interviewed, despite their success, do not have the trappings of large corporate entities. They don't have fleets of company cars; they don't go overboard on corporate headquarters; they don't have the kind of thick carpets you'd find on the 34th floor of the Time-Life Building; and they don't have limos, helicopters, or corporate jets. And this "democratic approach" generally translates into a better place to work.

As reported recently in a Hay Group and *Inc.* magazine research study on worker satisfaction, "Bigger doesn't always mean better—at least not in the minds of your employees."

According to the report, "The bigger the company the lower its worker satisfaction. Of the 3000 respondents, 88% of those in corporations with fewer than 30 employees expressed favorable opinions of their companies. The satisfaction rate dropped to 77% in companies with 70–100 employees and to 65% in those with more than 100."[10] An exception, and by contrast, is that virtually all of the employees at Hallmark, where 19,000 people work, feel that they are part of the Hallmark family, despite $1.5 billion in sales. The trick? Thinking of the company as hundreds of small companies, that comprise a larger entity. And universal belief in the company's product.

*Lesson 4: These fast-growth companies are market-driven. Their leaders increasingly are people with marketing orientation and background who look at the changing marketplace for clues as to what products should be developed, and what company directions should be taken.* Years ago, marketing was just another company function. Today, "nothing happens until somebody sells something." Zymark, with its robotic equipment for laboratories is a good example of this; it launched its business without products—only a sense of the market. Bean's ability to understand marketing demographics and zip codes unlocked its dramatic growth. Banana Republic and Sharper Image followed suit, years later. CML launched its operation with a very keen sense of "the active outdoors marketplace," with no products and very few employees. It grew to nearly $300 million in sales in less than 20 years.

In the same *Inc.* magazine–Hay Associates study of small business growth, it was determined that "55% of small firms say salesmanship is the most important building block in their businesses. And 41% say good customer service (increasingly a marketing function) . . . is more essential than new technology or innovations."[11] Certainly entrepreneurs with no marketing background or training are at a decided disadvantage as they bring their companies into rapidly changing marketplaces.

*Lesson 5: Each of the fast-growth companies we met believe in the highest level of quality in their products and services.* This rubs off, of course. Employees feel tremendous pride in being associated with quality products and services, and the firm's customers feel a great sense of value. Today it is the exception rather than the rule that a company develops quickly without a strong sense of product quality. L. L. Bean was a leader in this field with his boot. The Troy-Bilt Rototiller has as much quality as can possibly be packed into a machine. Land's End does a terrific job on its product quality, and explains it well. Their recent advertisement: "If anyone offers more buttondowns, in a wider variety, better quality, or at better prices, we don't know of it," is a classic piece of copywriting. Cuisinart built the world's best food processor for America's kitchens. Philip B. Crosby, author and quality control expert who spent years at ITT, says "Quality is free. It's not a gift but it is free. What costs money are all the un-quality things. All the actions that involve not doing it right the first time."[12]

*Lesson 6: All of our fast-growth companies have a strong and positive attitude about customer service that leads to repeat orders and extensive word of mouth advertising, both free.* The Nordstrom Co. of Seattle, Washington, which grew from sales of $100 million in 1972 to $600 million in 1982, believes simply that "The customer is always right. Many stores say that, but few practice it. Nordstrom does. The sales persons you meet in Nordstrom stores will knock themselves out for you. If you're in a Nordstrom and you're in a rush to catch a plane, you'd be surprised to find that the salesperson might drop everything and drive you to the airport."[13] This kind of service, which Paul Hawken has called "legendary," is increasingly the rule.

A number of fast-growth companies have even begun to compensate their employees on the basis of their contribution to customer service. Ameritech, the telephone holding company, considers its customers' satisfaction in setting compensation for employees, as does B.M.W. of North America. "Management Compensation Group, an employee benefits consultant, is so sold on the notion that it's instituting the policy for its executives and telling its clients to do the same," according to a recent *Wall Street Journal* article.[14]

In fact, some companies are going even further. "Rank Xerox Limited has informed 130 of its European executives that salary increases due in November will be based exclusively on customer satisfaction, as measured by an independent survey of client attitudes and an internal audit of repeat sales."[15]

At Carson, Pirie, Scott, the large Chicago-based retailer, commitment to the customer is celebrated annually at an evening event to which over 3000 CPS employees are invited, and the top performer of a superlative piece of customer service is recognized with ten $1000 bills from company president Peter S. Willmott. "It's an ongoing competition that everyone in the company is aware of and strives toward," said Graham S. Alcock, vice president of marketing for a CPS subsidiary company based in Phoenix, Arizona. "And this year we're going to come in number 1." That kind of positive competitiveness on behalf of the Carson, Pirie, Scott customer is the result of very effective fast-growth leadership.

*Lesson 7: Fast-growth companies have a strong sense of focus.* A clear statement of direction generally emanates from the top, and develops into a shared understanding. Says Jack Rinehart, of American Computer Professionals, Inc. of Long Beach, South Carolina, "Our toughest early decision was which marketplace might be the best for us. Once we selected it, we concentrated on it and expanded our role within it to just a few key clients. On the basis of this we were able to grow very quickly. This meant that we had to ignore opportunities outside of our highly focused market plan."

Alan Hahn, top U.S. executive of the Hume Group, reminds Ron Hume regularly of what "fits" his Toronto company's growth statement. "Great idea," Alan said to me recently when I suggested a new area of publishing, "but it doesn't fit our company's self-improvement focus."

A difficulty that entrepreneurs have once they've created their vision is knowing how to share it with the rest of their people. How to get word down the ranks has been one of David A. Nelson's difficulties. Nelson, president of the Comlinear Corporation of Fort Collins, Colorado, said, "Sharing the vision and getting, in response, the same high level of creativity and productivity we got from the group of founders was a problem. We have found that we must be willing to let go, give up some control to really be able to achieve our objectives. If management provides the right vision, communicates it effectively and then provides the tools and systems, workers will always succeed." Comlinear, which manufactures single-processing components, has reached the $5 million mark in sales.

Jeff Frankston, president of Inductor Supply Inc. of Huntington Beach, California, echoed this thought saying, "The biggest challenge we have is to continue painting the picture of the future and effectively sharing that picture with our people so that they can easily relate to our overall goals."

*Lesson 8: Many of our fast-growth companies have had an absolute lock on patents, software or technological break-throughs.* Zymark, the robotic laboratory equipment company from Hopkinton, Massachusetts, is one of those. Xerox and Polaroid, of course, continue to be dominant in their markets because of their patents. George Gilder pointed out that "the new industrial revolution is heavily based on software created by scores of entrepreneurial American companies."[16]

Not all fast-growth companies are high tech, of course. Kurt Volk, a printing supplier in Connecticut grew very rapidly during the 1970s due to an improved production process for creating single, continuous form mailing packages for the direct marketing industry. Garden Way was constantly accused of introducing low-tech, "stone age products." And where do you place a Discovery Toys, founded in 1977 with a $25,000 family loan in Concord, California, by Lane Nemith, and which grew, as an educational toy company, to $40 million in 1985 sales?[17]

*Lesson 9: The fast-growth companies have an ability to attract, and then keep talented people.* Domino's Pizza Inc., the $1.1 billion Ann Arbor, Michigan, chain, "spends about $5 million a year on performance based employee incentives to everything from cash bonuses to vacations on the company yacht to tickets to Detroit Tigers' games. . . . Then there's the Domino's distribution Olympics—with medals and prizes awarded for excellence in categories like driving, dough-making, and veggie slicing." It's this kind of attention to the specific skills and needs of the employee that leads to fast growth.[18]

At Walt Disney, another outstanding place to work, employees are called "cast members." Speaking with one of their current marketing executives recently, we heard that "Walt Disney's rule was that management should treat cast members the way cast members treat their guests. Everything at Disney is on a first-name basis only, and everybody buys into the notion of people working together. Everyone wears a name tag at the company, management included. If you forget your name tag don't go to work." According to the spokesman, Jim Poissant

"Everyone picks up paper. The day the president of Disney walks past a piece of paper on the ground is the day the doors to Disney close."

The point that companies like this consistently emphasize is that people, however independent, will join a structure if it's equal and fair. Perhaps a corollary to this is that fast-growth companies, while they understand the need for some operating structure, are increasingly working to eliminate the notion of rank. Most of them have gotten rid of management parking places, executive dining rooms, and seniority perks. The rules of the Internal Revenue Service, as they relate to profit sharing and benefit distribution, have helped to accelerate this, in that most qualified plans must be nondiscriminatory in order to be acceptable as a tax deduction. Thus Hearstian hunting lodges for senior executives are out; Rodale fitness centers for all employees are in. Bob Teufel, president of Rodale told us, "People look forward to a run or some cycling more than a coffee break." Rodale has exceeded the $100 million mark in sales.

*Lesson 10: Most of the fast-growth companies exhibit increasing amounts of flexibility.* Particularly given the return of great numbers of women to the work force, there is a newfound need for flexibility in hours and days to meet personal needs. While "flex-time" began years ago, it is being applied more and more today. For example, at Hewlett-Packard you can begin work at 6:00, 7:00, or 8:00 in the morning; at Metropolitan Life you can schedule your own hours; and at Meredith Corporation flex-time is the rule. The best example we saw, though, was at Quad Graphics, where people can work three 12-hour days per week and alternate getting three to four days off.[19]

Other companies have proven their flexibility by eliminating commuting problems through driving their employees to work. Reader's Digest and McDonald's are both examples of how company vans and busses have improved company flexibility and increased the distance from which employees will consider commuting.

*Lesson 11: Most of our fast-growth companies have shown a great willingness to share their success with employees, once positive cash flow develops.* George Gilder shared a piece of ancient wisdom with us when he recounted the following: "Lease a man a garden and in time he will leave you a patch of sand.

Make a man a full owner of a patch of sand and in time he will grow there a garden on the land."[20]

Sharing the harvest is increasingly common—unlike the old days, when only a handful of senior executives got in on such goodies as stock options, profit sharing, and hefty bonusing. Today compensation in excess of salary and defined benefits is widespread. Employee stock ownership plans are increasingly common, and companies are looking for imaginative ways for their employees to make more money. Wilson Laboratories, a $5 million computer test equipment maker in Orange, California, in an imaginative move, began to pay its key engineering employees royalties on the sales of the products that they designed.[21] Patten, located in a rural Vermont village, buys employees lunch every day. Many companies, such as Remington Razor, have short-term, productivity-based bonuses.

And then there is the question of what to do with surplus profits in extra-good years. L. L. Bean recently gave an 18% bonus to every employee that worked in the company at the end of what apparently was a great year (1987). Others give it away to nonprofits. Many fast-growth companies with whom we spoke encourage their employees to participate in local, nonprofit activities, and will support their interests with contributions to those programs. In a dramatic move, Joan Kroc, owner of McDonald's, recently gave $235,000 to the Anderson Country School System in Tennessee—"To save the job of a teacher whose only pupil is a boy exposed to the AIDS virus."[22]

*Lesson 12: Fast-growth companies offer their employees attractive quarters in which to work.* Not plush, but inviting alternatives to the sterility of the standard corporate structure. Prescott Kelly, when asked to what he attributes the fast growth of his company said simply, "Great working conditions. We own an old colonial estate here in Redding, Connecticut, and people love to get up and come to work here. In short, it's a nice place to work." Kelly and his Institute of Children's Literature business pay no bonuses. People also spoke of the outstanding working conditions at Quad Graphics, which is decorated with wonderful art, and Zymark, which is more like a doctor's office than a factory. Richard Considine's Lincoln Log Homes headquarters in Chestertown, New York, is—not surprisingly—a log structure, which his 100-plus employees love. They also enjoy the unusual benefit of purchasing one of their own at cost.

*Lesson 13: Fast-growth companies have learned how to listen, both internally and externally.* Most of these companies encourage their employees to speak out—whether their observations are good or bad. Many of them depend on the impartial outside view of a board of directors. "Unless we had gotten a strong board of directors, people like Herman E. Anstatt, Jr., we wouldn't have grown as quickly as we did," said Don Dion of the Patten Corporation.

Guy A. Hale, chairman of the Alamo Consulting Group of Walnut Creek, California, said, "While lots of things were important along the way to our fast growth—getting a key account like General Motors, getting a financial partner like the Dana Corporation—the invaluable advice from a few good friends who made up our board of directors was particularly critical."

In addition to these 13 important lessons learned by our fast-growth entrepreneurs dozens of others were cited, including the ability to measure and change direction quickly (for overall profitability as well as for the success of all the key parts of the company); the ability to weather economic storms with a product that is strong, regardless of the ups and downs of the external business cycle; the development of a broad enough base to offset crisis in one part of the company; and, not surprisingly, just plain hard work.

Roger Turner, president of Western Controls in North Salt Lake, Utah, said, "The most critical lesson for our company was the impact of simply lots of hard work. It was several years of long hours. We had the drive to excel at all costs while being dedicated to serving a customer."

Persistence certainly comes through again and again—from Federal Express, which approached insolvency more than once in the early days, to McDonald's, where Ray Kroc *finally* got his french fries right. All entrepreneurs can take satisfaction in being reminded of the following bits of business history by Michael LeBoeuf, professor of management at the University of New Orleans: (1) In the first year of operation the Coca-Cola Company sold a measly 400 Cokes. (2) Both Hewlett-Packard and Atari turned down the opportunity to buy the first Apple Micro

Computer. First year sales of the Apple were $2.5 million. (3) Twenty-three publishers rejected a children's book written by an author who called himself Dr. Seuss. The twenty-fourth publisher published it and the book sold six million copies.[23]

The leader's role becomes one of balancing, one of orchestrating, and one of walking around and listening to what employees, customers, vendors, and detached observers have to say. Francis P. Rich, Jr., president of Action Equipment of Londonderry, New Hampshire, said, "The key to our fast growth was the balancing of our money needs, our people needs and the attitudes that people brought with them to work every day." C. R. "Duke" DuClos, president of Slotline Golf Company, Huntington Beach, California, said, "My job is to balance the company's product, powerful marketing, and good operations." Pete Willmott, CEO of Carson, Pirie, Scott, is one of the best examples in corporate America of the "management by walking around" approach that Waterman and Peters (*In Search of Excellence*) first suggested as a great replacement for the more theoretic hands-off "management by objective" approach of the 1970s. Pete might be found in the mail room, in the maintenance pit with the mechanics, or out shopping in one of his stores. Walk around with him for 15 minutes and you'll hear a dozen, "Hi, Pete," greetings.

Not all of these people view positively the role of being a "pioneer." Lyman Wood used to tell us regularly, "Buy something rather than start it." Leo Bakeland, founder of Bakelite Corporation, said, "Never be a pioneer, it doesn't pay. Let the other man do the pioneering and then after he has shown what can be done, do it bigger and more quickly; but let the other man take the time and risk to show you how to do it."[24]

On the flip side, we asked various people from management, legal, and financial backgrounds what they thought leads to reduced growth or even corporate failure. Doug Rhodes, who helped lead the growth of three different fast-growth New England companies—Warren, Gorham and Lamont; Federated Litho; and Alpine Press, Inc.—gave us seven reasons for corporate slowdown: (1) rigidity and/or omnipotency on the part of the CEO, (2) an atmosphere of intimidation, (3) poor planning, (4) lack of good response to customers, (5) lack of purpose other than profits, (6) preoccupation with short-term profits, and (7) management decisions controlled exclusively by the P and L or balance sheet.

222

A business attorney, Donald Dubendorf, of Grinnell & Dubendorf, who specializes in fast-growth company lawyering, passed on the following, "Frequently, in manufacturing, one hazard is that the management outgrows the labor force. A company may also outrun its ability to deliver. Sometimes losing perspective is a problem. Companies frequently die more from management problems than undercapitalization. Ensemble management is what you ought to try to create and you do this by occasionally sitting back and 'polishing the vision.' "

Tom Neely of A. G. Edwards, who has viewed from an insider's position numerous fast-growth companies going public through initial public offerings, which he helps orchestrate, says, "Frequently the loss of momentum is due to a loss of control and inadequate systems. Stealing and featherbedding create rotten spots and also cause the company to lose its competitive edge. This is because no one is designated to do the thing that makes the company work. Control is spread too thin and no one knows what anyone else is responsible for, or actually doing."

Mistakes are made along the way. Charles M. Leighton's CML Group, one of the most spectacular growth companies that we learned about, going from nothing in 1969 to $300 million currently—ran into serious problems when its Gokey division lost control of its inventory valuation through improperly computerized data. This systems failure led to a late breaking and highly embarrassing inventory write-down after announcing income of $4.2 million for fiscal 1984. According to one report, "The company's stock sank to $6.50, 52% below its 52 week high of $13.50 per share and 19% below its book value."[25] Said Leighton, "The right questions had been asked but nobody went in and pulled out their ledgers to make sure that everything had been reconciled—bank statements, payables and receivables."[26]

To his credit, Leighton learned the "extra step" lesson from that incident and has gone on to build a tremendous corporation based on superior understanding of the market into which he is going, rather than depending on superior product development. Leighton gets serious when he talks about mission: "My personal feeling is that everybody who stands up and says 'My job is to increase the value for the shareholders' is really missing what the mission is. To me the mission is three-fold. If you don't have a product that the consumer wants, and you don't have good employees who can grow and prosper, you are not going to increase the value for the shareholders. We can do a great job for the shareholders short term and kill them long term, if we don't do a good job with our consumers and our employees."[27]

Others cite problems of a personal nature that fast-growth entrepreneurs can run into. According to Don Dion, "The darker side of the fast growth of Patten or any other high-flying corporation is that lots of people suddenly have huge amounts of money, many of them for the first time, and they don't quite know what to do with it all. All of a sudden, people can afford whatever they want. Families can become strained, alcohol can become a problem, even cocaine becomes a problem. All this money provides choices that may be tough ones for young people to deal with."

As Paul Hawken puts it, "Business tests character like no other endeavor I know, and it reveals it too."[28] Steve Neighbors, president of Eterna Line Corporation, Boise, Idaho, confirms this saying: "Our biggest challenge was in people's personal character. So many failures happened due to the erosion of integrity, marriage instability, self-aggrandizement, and so on, despite the fact that we grew 100% a year for fifteen years. It brought with it these kinds of challenges."

A more recent example of an unwinding relationship is that of the founders of the fast-growth company, Esprit de Corp., in San Francisco, California. As the pressure has built for profit performance, it has driven the two founders, Doug and Susie Tompkins, farther apart. "It's just a matter of convenience that we stay married," said Doug Tompkins,[29] co-owner of this $40 million per year clothing company, which was founded in 1972.

People have had to learn not only to deal with bad news, but to deal with bad press. The Patten Corporation has take press criticism for its successful technique of taking undeveloped land and dividing it up into smaller chunks for recreational purposes. Most recently, Robert B. Streeter, writing in the *Berkshire Eagle* of February 12, 1988 said, "There are two things that bother me about Patten Corporation and those of their ilk. They are helping to accelerate the loss of wild places in an world which cannot affort that loss. Secondly, they view land as only a commodity, something to be profited from rather than a living organism whose every part has inherent worth, regardless of its usefulness to human beings"[30] Streeter was only about half right in his critique, but the damage was done nonetheless.

Garden Way Incorporated executives spent half their time in 1982 responding to press criticism that emanated from employee leaks and to a hostile Burlington, Vermont, community after the founder was unceremoniously dismissed.

What does the future hold? Looking to the recent past, the 1970s, George Gilder reminds us, "America's entrepreneurs exploited the opportunity to create a vast array of labor intensive enterprises that used and trained the baby-boom generation. Launching a large array of new service ventures, from fast-food restaurants and health food groceries, to record vendors and head shops, from convenience stores and barter exchanges to video boutiques and national electronic networks, from law firms and medical clinics to singles bars and jogging equipment chains, from birthing homes and computer centers, to private schools and specialized book stores, from historic preservation architects and suppliers to surgicare centers and entrepreneurial consultancies, the generation created its own jobs and professions, businesses and styles."[31]

Now, with the 1980s nearly behind us, some might suggest that fast-growth entrepreneurship is flagging. Before jumping too quickly to that conclusion, however, one should consider the entire new crop of American entrepreneurs coming along: Randy Miller of Original New York Seltzer. He's 23. His Walnut, California, company did $100 million this year. Or Michael Dell, 25, of Dell Computer, in Austin, Texas, which did $159 million. Or brother and sister team Bill and Julie Brice, 30 and 29, whose I Can't Believe It's Yogurt, Inc. yogurt shops in Dallas, Texas, did $25 million last year. ("He manufactures and I franchise," says Julie.)

Certainly growth in the 1990s won't be without challenges. According to Gilder, "The entrepreneurial achievements of the 1970s and early 1980s came in the face of a hostile press, a resistant culture and a stagnant 'economy.' The most popular literature of enterprise was devoted to the contemplation of industrial crimes, the prophecy of doom, and the talismanic protection of gold and land, much of the activity of government was channeled into choking small business with new taxes and regulations."[32]

## LESSONS

We're told that, on average, business starts are down in early 1988. But as Lyman Wood would remind us, "Averages don't mean a damn thing. I knew a guy that drowned in a stream that averaged eighteen inches deep!"

The same challenges will be there in the 1990s. Together with even stiffer competition. But despite all this, based on the hundreds of people we met, the future of fast growth for this peculiar breed of American entrepreneur has never been brighter.

# Appendix

## Listing of Fast-Growth Companies Whose Contributions Were Particularly Helpful

(Sales figures gathered from *Inc.* magazine, "America's Fastest Growing Companies" listing; company information from Main Street Marketing)

**Abacus II Computers**
Gary Jacobsen
Toledo, OH
microcomputer retailers
Founded 1980
'82 sales $1.1 MM; '86 sales, $12.6 MM

**Action Equipment Company, Inc.**
Francis P. Rich, Jr.
Londonderry, NH
retails, leases construction
    equipment
Founded 1980
'81 sales $1.2 MM; '85 sales
    $11.6 MM

**Action Packets Inc.**
Judith Kaplan
Ocala, FL
distributes gift shop items
Founded 1975
'79 sales $124 M; '83 sales $2.1 MM

**ADD Electronics**
Ronald O. Himberg
East Syracuse, NY
distributes electronic components
'81 sales $196 M; '85 sales $10.2 MM

**Advanced Computer Graphics, Inc.**
Wayne Staats
Milwaukee, WI
service bureau for computer
    graphics
Founded 1978
'80 sales $343 M; '84 sales
    $2.2 MM

**Advanced Input Devices**
John Overby
Coeur d' Alene, ID
manufactures keyboards and key
    panels
Founded 1979
'80 sales $288 M; '84 sales
    $26 MM

**Aim Executive Incorporated**
Jeffery De Perro
Toledo, OH
provides executive recruiting
    and temporary help
    services
Founded 1977
'82 sales $391 M; '86 sales
    $6.0 MM

**227**

## APPENDIX

**Akal Security Incorporated**
Hari Harkaur
Albuquerque, NM
Founded 1980
'81 sales $354 M; '86 sales
  $2.5 MM

**Allenbach Industries Inc.**
Katheleen Allenbach
Carlsbad, CA
computer software duplication
  services
Founded 1978
'79 sales $199 M; '83 sales $3.8 MM

**All-Star Printing**
Michael H. Duweck
Lansing, MI
commercial printer
Founded 1961
'81 sales $206 M; '85 $2.1 MM

**All Test Incorporated**
Thomas G. Millner
Palatine, IL
manufacturer of auto diagnostic
  equipment
Founded 1974
'79 sales $480 M; '83 sales $2.7 MM

**American Computer Professionals**
  Inc.
Jack Rinehart
Columbia, SC
computer consulting services
Founded 1982
'82 sales $415 M; '86 sales $4.2 MM

**American Leisure Industries, Inc.**
Patrick J. Gorman
Lanham, MD
travel company, membership travel
  cards
Founded 1978
'79 sales $123 M; '83 sales $5.0 MM

**American List Counsel Inc.**
Donn Rappaport
Princeton, NJ
mailing-list brokerage and
  management
Founded 1978
'79 sales $255 M; '85 sales $16.2 MM

**Analog Devices, Inc.**
Ray Stata
Norwood, MA
manufactures computer components
  and systems
'72 sales $60 MM; '84 sales
$300 MM

**Applied Energy Services**
Dennis W. Bakke
Arlington, VA
operates independent power
  facilities
Founded 1981
'82 sales $736 M; '86 sales $22 MM

**Ben and Jerry's Homemade Inc.**
Ben Cohen, Jerry Greenfield
Waterbury, VT
quality ice cream
'86 sales $30 MM

**Bennett Funding Group, Inc.**
Edmund T. Bennett
North Syracuse, NY
municipal leasing-equipment
Founded 1977
'82 sales $4.8 MM; '86 sales
  $62 MM

**Blagge Enterprises**
Timothy Blagge
Rancho Cordova, CA
distributes audio and video tapes
Founded 1977
'79 sales $409 M; '86 sales
  $15.5 MM

**Broadway and Seymour**
Olin Broadway Jr.
Charlotte, NC
computer systems and services
Founded 1980
'82 sales $1.7 MM; '86 sales
  $18.5 MM

**Calibrake Incorporated**
Steve Frisbie
Independence, MO
remanufactures auto components
Founded 1979
'81 sales $293 M; '85 sales
  $1.7 MM

**CEM Corporation**
Michael J. Collins
Indian Trail, NC
microwave instrumentation
Founded 1971
'79 sales $379 M; '86 sales
    $9.3 MM

**Century Marketing Corporation**
Albert Caperna
Bowling Green, OH
manufactures custom-printed
    labels
Founded 1980
'81 sales $792 M; '85 sales $4.8 MM

**Champion Awards**
Susan W. Bowen
Memphis, TN
sells printed apparel and specialty
    awards
Founded 1979
'79 sales $126 M; '86 sales $4 MM

**Checks-To-Go, Incorporated**
Gary Sutton
El Cajon, CA
distributes business forms
Founded 1978
'80 sales $325 M; '84 sales $2.8 MM

**CIT Construction Inc. of Texas**
Gregory Paul Hilz
Stafford, TX
general contractor
Founded 1980
'82 sales $1.5 MM; '86 sales $10 MM

**Comlinear**
David Nelson
Fort Collins, CO
manufactures single-processing
    components
Founded 1980
'82 sales $380 M; '86 sales $4.7 MM

**Compact Performance Inc.**
Keith Bigelow
San Ramon, CA
distributes remanufactured auto
    engines
Founded 1977
'81 sales $195 M; '86 sales $3 MM

**Computerized Lodging Systems**
David W. Berkus
Long Beach, CA
resells computer systems
Founded 1981
'81 sales $883 M; '85 sales
    $8.7 MM

**Comstock Leasing Incorporated**
David C. Duxbury
San Mateo, CA
small-ticket leasing
Founded 1980
'80 sales $121 M; '84 sales $1.5 MM

**Condor D. C. Power Supplies Inc.**
Len Wallace
Oxnard, CA
manufactures switching equipment
Founded 1979
'79 sales $507 M; '83 sales $10.0 MM

**Consolidated Dutchwest**
Bruce McKinley
Plymouth, MA
retails wood stoves
Founded 1980
'82 sales $1.1 MM; '86 sales
    $18.5 MM

**Contract Furnishing and Systems
    Limited**
Jack F. Gold
New York, NY
office furnishings dealer
Founded 1978
'79 sales $2.9 MM; '83 sales
    $16.9 MM

**Corinthian Communications**
Larry Miller
New York, NY
media buying
Founded 1976
'81 sales $20 MM; '86 sales
    $112 MM

**CPA Services, Inc.**
Betsy Morris
Brookfield, WI
publishes CPA newsletters
Founded 1979
'81 sales $140 M; '85 sales $1.1 MM

## APPENDIX

**The Crosby Vandenburgh Group**
W. Allan Vandenburgh
Boston, MA
publishes magazines, guides, and
  directories
Founded 1980
'82 sales $934 M; '86 sales
  $13.3 MM

**DATA 3 Systems, Inc.**
Richard C. Anderson
Santa Rosa, CA
software
Founded 1980
'80 sales $113 M; '84 sales $6.2 MM

**The De Wolfe Companies, Inc.**
Richard B. De Wolfe
Lexington, MA
provides real estate, financial
  services
Founded 1949
'82 sales $1.2 MM; '86 sales $12 MM

**DDF Transportation**
John W. Hies
Tonawanda, NY
freight company
Founded 1981
'82 sales $137 M; '87 sales $6 MM

**Donnelly Corporation**
Donnelly Family
Holland, MI
manufactures auto accessory
  products
Founded 1905
'65 sales $3 MM; '84 sales
  $75 MM

**Dreyer's Grand Ice Cream Inc.**
T. Gary Rogers and William F. Crog
Oakland, CA
ice cream producers
Founded 1977
'77 sales $6 MM; '87 sales $162 MM

**Dynamark Security Centers, Inc.**
Wayne E. Alter
Hagerstown, MD
electronic protection devices
Founded 1977
'80 sales $376 M; '84 sales $5.2 MM

**Early Cloud**
Newport, RI
sells software products
Founded 1981
'82 sales $114 M; '86 sales $5.5 MM

**Eastway Delivery Service Inc.**
John Oren
Houston, TX
delivery services
Founded 1977
'79 sales $605 M; '83 sales
  $4.2 MM

**The E C Corporation**
Orlino C. Baldonado
Oak Ridge, TN
technical managerial services
Founded 1977
'82 sales $493 M; '86 sales $16 MM

**Economy Restaurant Equipment
  Co., Inc.**
B. D. Effron
Orlando, FL
restaurant equipment and supplies
Founded 1979
'79 sales $103 M; '83 sales $1.1 MM

**El Camino Resources, Limited**
David E. Harmon
Sherman Oaks, CA
computer equipment dealer and
  lessor
Founded 1979
'82 sales $7.1 MM; '86 sales
  $55 MM

**Electra Form Inc.**
Steven A. Bright
Vandalia, OH
manufactures injection tooling
Founded 1979
'80 sales $1.4 MM; '84 sales $10.2
  MM

**Elgin Syferd**
Ron Elgin, David Syferd
Seattle, WA
advertising and public relations
Founded 1981
'81 sales $223 M; '85 sales
  $3.1 MM

**230**

**Environmental Marketing Group**
John Whelchel
Boca Raton, FL
environmental services, wastewater
    treatment
Founded 1977
'79 sales $473 M; '84 sales $4.5 MM

**Fastec Industrial Corporation**
Charles R. White
Elkhart, IN
Founded 1979
'79 sales $273 M; '84 sales $13.7 MM

**The Foreign Candy Company, Inc.**
Peter W. DeYager
West Hull, IA
imports and distributes candy
    (Black Forest Gummy Bears)
Founded 1978
'82 sales $1.6 MM; '86 sales $16 MM

**Forever Living Products, Inc.**
Rex Maughan
Phoenix, AZ
manufactures and distributes Aloe
    Vera products
Founded 1978
'79 sales $8.4 MM; '83 sales $90.4
    MM

**Garden Way Inc.**
Jairo Estrada
Troy, NY
Lyman Wood, Founder 1966
gardening supplies/machinery
'76 sales $30 MM; '87 sales $200 MM

**General Alum & Chemical
    Corporation**
James A. Poure
Holland, OH
chemical producer of aluminum
    sulfate
Founded 1978
'79 sales $657 M; '86 sales $7.5 MM

**Godlick and Company**
Neil B. Godlick
Philadelphia, PA
certified public accountants
Founded 1980
'81 sales $281 M; '85 sales $1.9 MM

**Granada Systems Design**
Gulab Bhavnani
New York, NY
communication software
Founded 1979
'81 sales $222 M; '85 sales $1.6 MM

**Group Benefit Services**
Cathy and Bill Simmons
Hunt Valley, MD
health insurance and fringe benefits
    for trade and professional
    associates
Founded 1980
'82 sales $179 M; '87 sales $20 MM

**Hanley-Wood, Inc.**
Michael Hanley
Washington, DC
magazine publishing
Founded 1976
'79 sales $536 M; '86 sales $10 MM

**Hawaiian Pacific Elevator Corp.**
Len A. Ganote
Honolulu, HI
elevator installation contracting
Founded 1977
'79 sales $166 M; '84 sales
    $3.7 MM

**Hill International**
Irvin E. Richter
Willingboro, NJ
consulting firm for construction
    industry
Founded 1976
'79 sales $1.2 MM; '86 sales
    $50 MM

**Hume Financial Services**
Ron Hume
Toronto, Canada
financial publishing
Founded 1975
'86 sales $75 MM

**Inductor Supply, Inc.**
Jeff Frankston
Huntington Beach, CA
distributes electronic components
Founded 1979
'80 sales $935 M; '84 sales $5.4 MM

# APPENDIX

**Information Builders Inc.**
Gerald D. Cohen
New York, NY
manufactures proprietary computer
  software
Founded 1975
'79 sales $2.7 MM; '86 sales $72 MM

**Intertec Components, Inc.**
Thomas A. Ferrante
Longwood, FL
distributes electronic products
Founded 1976
'79 sales $426 M; '84 sales $3.4 MM

**International Resources Group**
Philip F. Palmedo
Setauket, NY
natural resource consultant
Founded 1978
'80 sales $472 M; '84 sales
  $3.1 MM

**Island Water Sports, Inc.**
Kirk G. Cottrell
Deerfield Beach, FL
surf shirts, water sporting goods
Founded 1979
'82 sales $350 M; '86 sales
  $10.4 MM

**Jewell Building Systems, Inc.**
Everett G. Jewell
Dallas, NC
manufactures metal prefab
  buildings
Founded 1977
'79 sales $441 M; '83 sales $5.0 MM

**Jiffy Lube International, Inc.**
W. J. Hindman
Baltimore, MD
car lubrication franchise
Founded 1979
'89 sales $239 M; '86 sales
  $30.4 MM

**J L Associates, Inc.**
Linda G. Watkins
Hampton, VA
management services contracting
Founded 1978
'82 sales $1.5 MM; '86 sales $12 MM

**L. L. Bean**
Leon Gorman
Freeport, ME
outdoor clothing, equipment
  cataloger
Founded 1912
'75 sales $30 MM; '87 sales
  $500 MM

**Management Consulting and
  Research Inc.**
Dr. Gerald R. McNichols
Falls Church, VA
defense consulting
Founded 1977
'79 sales $125 M; '83 sales $2.1 MM

**Mandex, Inc.**
Carl A. Brown
Springfield, VA
telecommunications engineering
Founded 1974
'81 sales $2.5 MM; '85 sales $16 MM

**MD Resources, Inc.**
Judith E. Burger
Miami, FL
health care personnel (recruits
  physicians)
Founded 1979
'79 sales $141 M; '86 sales $1 MM

**Miller Business Systems, Inc.**
James B. Miller
Arlington, TX
office supplies and equipment
Founded 1967
'81 sales $7.6 MM; '85 sales
  $43.9 MM

**Mira Flores Design Inc.**
John Hewett Chapman
San Francisco, CA
manufactures hotel amenities
Founded 1980
'80 sales $177 M; '84 sales $6.8 MM

**MMS International**
Richard C. Green
Redwood City, CA
provides on-line market analysis
Founded 1974
'82 sales $1.7 MM; '86 sales $10.9 MM

**Moss Telecommunications**
Gerard J. Schaefer
Grand Rapids, MI
telephone and data cable systems
Founded 1977
'81 sales $139 M; '85 sales $1.4 MM

**Motion Designs, Inc.**
Marilyn Hamilton, Don Helman
Fresno, CA
Quickie Wheel Chairs
Founded 1980
'81 sales $368 M; '86 sales $15 MM

**M. W. Halpern and Company**
Marty Halpern
Garland, TX
general contracting
Founded 1979
'82 sales $597 M; '86 sales
$5.1 MM

**National Decision Systems**
Mike Stansbury
Encinitas, CA
markets data base applications
Founded 1979
'82 sales $914 M; '86 sales
$10.8 MM

**National Health Care Affiliates**
Mark E. Hamister
Buffalo, NY
owns and operates health care,
residential facilities
Founded 1977
'79 sales $464 M; '86 sales $39 MM

**National Title Company**
Stephen C. Vallone
Houston, TX
real estate/insurance agency
Founded 1978
'79 sales $341 M; '83 sales $2 MM

**Network Rental**
Perry J. MacNeal
Atlanta, GA
rentals, rent-to-own household
appliances
Founded 1981
'82 sales $1.1 MM; '86 sales
$12.1 MM

**Night Caps Incorporated**
Gerald L. Kasten
Milwaukee, WI
waterbeds and waterbed products
Founded 1979
'79 sales $106 M; '83 sales $1.7 MM

**Northland Environmental**
Richard M. Henley
Burbank, CA
water purification, distillation
equipment
Founded 1975
'81 sales $727 M; '85 sales $6.4 MM

**Nor-Cote Chemical**
Norman G. Wilcott, Jr.
Crawfordsville, IN
manufactures special inks and
coatings
Founded 1976
'82 sales $375 M; '86 sales $2.8 MM

**Northwest Gears Incorporated**
V. Beecher Wallace
Everett, WA
gearing business
Founded 1979
sales $1.5 MM

**O/E Automation**
Cass T. Casucci
Troy, MI
office automation sales and
consulting
Founded 1979
'82 sales $2.2 MM; '86 sales
$52.8 MM

**Oneida Asbestos Removal**
Frank B. DuRoss
Marcy, NY
provides asbestos abatement
services
Founded 1981
'81 sales $222 M; '86 sales $4.8 MM

**The Original Lincoln Logs Limited**
Dick Considine
Chestertown, NY
log home manufacturers
Founded 1979
'87 sales $20 MM

## APPENDIX

**Original Copy Centers**
Nancy Vetrone
Cleveland, OH
provides legal and corporate copy
    services
Founded 1975
'82 sales $158 M; '86 sales $2.1 MM

**Patten Corporation**
Harry Patten
Stamford, VT
land sales, real estate development
Founded 1968
'80 sales $2 MM; '87 sales
    $120 MM

**Pavion Ltd.**
Stanley Acker
Nyack-on-Hudson, NY
cosmetics
Founded 1976
'79 sales $148 M; '83 sales $9.9 MM

**Perry Morris Corporation**
J. Jeffrey Morris
Newport Beach, CA
finances new and used leasing
    equipment
Founded 1981
'82 sales $1.1 MM; '86 sales $6 MM

**Petrocomp Systems Incorporated**
Lawrence A. Youngblood
Houston, TX
consulting personnel for oil and
    gas companies
Founded 1979
'80 sales $213 M; '84 sales $3.1 MM

**Philip Crosby Associates Inc.**
Philip B. Crosby, Jr.
Winter Park, FL
management consulting
Founded 1979
'80 sales $1.7 MM; '84 sales $20 MM

**Phoenix Advertising, Design and
    Promotion, Inc.**
Martha Sander-Smith
Elm Grove, WI
advertising and marketing services
Founded 1979
'80 sales $118 M; '84 sales $666 M

**Pioneer/Eclipse Corporation**
William H. Wilson
Sparta, NC
high-speed floor maintenance, in-
    dustrial cleaning equipment
Founded 1978
'79 sales $279 M; '86 sales $16 MM

**Plow and Hearth**
Peter Rice
Madison, VA
retails mail order gardening
    products
Founded 1980
'82 sales $279 M; '86 sales
    $3.7 MM

**PNS, Incorporated**
Arnold Johnson
Racine, WI
packing and shipping franchise
Founded 1976
'79 sales $292 M; '85 sales $3.8 MM

**Professional Bank Services, Inc.**
W. Timothy Finn III
Louisville, KY
financial consultants
Founded 1978
'79 sales $218 M; '83 sales $1.2 MM

**Pro-File Systems, Incorporated**
Philip Pressler
Conshohocken, PA
records management, color-coded
    filing systems
Founded 1979
'81 sales $196 M; '85 sales $1.9 MM

**Properties of America**
Phil Grande
Williamstown, MA
sells real estate
Founded 1974
'82 sales $1.4 MM; '86 sales
    $9.8 MM

**Publications and Communications**
Gary L. Pittman
Austin, TX
publishes computer trade journals
Founded 1979
'82 sales $764 M; '86 sales $5 MM

**Quality "S" Manufacturing**
Jimmie Dale Weir
Phoenix, AZ
trailer kitchens
Founded 1977
'82 sales $204 M; '86 sales $9 MM

**Record Exchange of Roanoke**
Donald Rosenberg
Charlotte, NC
records
Founded 1979
'80 sales $108 M; '84 sales
    $806 M

**Renovator's Supply**
Claude and Donna Jeanloz
Miller's Falls, MA
catalogers of brass decorative
    hardware
Founded 1978
'79 sales $262 M; '86 sales $25 MM

**Right Associates**
Virginia M. Lord
Philadelphia, PA
outplacement and reemployment
Founded 1980
'81 sales $2.1 MM; '85 sales
    $12 MM

**R. L. Drake Company**
Ronald E. Wysong
Miamisburg, OH
manufactures satellite communica-
    tions equipment
Founded 1942
'80 sales $9.5 MM; '84 sales
    $69 MM

**Robbins Communications**
Daniel J. Robbins
Pittsburgh, PA
installs communications cable
Founded 1978
'82 sales $572 M; '86 sales $5.5 MM

**Royal Silk**
Prakash Melwani
Clifton, NJ
silk clothing sold via catalog/retail
Founded 1978
'79 sales $651 M; '86 sales $40 MM

**San Diego Design Incorporated**
Constance Karsh
Santee, CA
manufactures home entertainment
    centers
Founded 1979
'82 sales $1.9 MM; '87 sales $25 MM

**Schreiber Corporation, Inc.**
Peter T. Worthin
Trussville, AL
wastewater treatment equipment
Founded 1979
'81 sales $1.6 MM; '85 sales $9.6 MM

**The Sharper Image**
Richard Thalheimer
San Francisco, CA
high-tech catalog
Founded 1975
'79 sales $8.2 MM; '86 sales $125 MM

**Shelter Components Incorporated**
Larry Renbarger
Elkhart, IN
supplies component parts to hous-
    ing and R.V. markets
Founded 1979
'79 sales $637 M; '83 sales $29.3 MM

**S. J. Electro Systems, Inc.**
Stephen P. Johnston
Detroit Lakes, MN
manufactures alarm systems/liquid
    level controls
Founded 1975
'79 sales $125 M; '86 sales $2.3 MM

**Slotline Golf**
Clouis R. "Duke" Duclos
Huntington Beach, CA
manufactures and sells high-tech
    golf clubs
Founded 1975
'79 sales $366 M; '86 sales $7.3 MM

**Software Results Corporation**
James R. Ebright
Columbus, OH
develops and sells software, data
    communications
Founded 1975
'79 sales $470 M; '83 sales $3.2 MM

## APPENDIX

**S.R.S. Network Incorporated**
Thomas K. Sheridan
New York, NY
provides database and communications consulting services
Founded 1978
'82 sales $688 M; '86 sales $7.9 MM

**Star Video Entertainment, Inc.**
Arthur Bach
Jersey City, NY
Founded 1979
'80 sales $2.9 MM; '84 sales
$42.6 MM

**Straub Metal Services Inc.**
Frederick W. Straub
Bear Creek, PA
stainless steel producers, warehousing and manufacturer's agency
Founded 1979
'79 sales $250 M; '86 sales $2 MM

**Super 8 Motels**
Dennis E. Bale
Aberdeen, SD
economy lodging
Founded 1973
'82 sales $1.9 MM; '86 sales
$58.5 MM

**Systems Research and Applications**
Ernst Volgenau
Arlington, VA
technical services to federal
government
Founded 1978
'79 sales $190 M; '83 sales $4.8 MM

**Techne Electronics Limited**
Joe Musolino
Palo Alto, CA
vehicle security systems
Founded 1972
'79 sales $220 M; '86 sales $2.5 MM

**Technicomp Publishing, Inc.**
Eric Berg
Cleveland, OH
technical training services
Founded 1979
'81 sales $193 MM; '85 sales
$1.4 MM

**Technology Constructors, Inc.**
Richard Lee
Arvada, CA
general contractors
Founded 1978
'79 sales $184 M; '84 sales $1.8 MM

**Tele America, Incorporated**
Larry Kaplan
Northbrook, IL
telemarketing
Founded 1980
'81 sales $236 M; '86 sales $1.6 MM

**Telco Research Corporation**
Dr. James E. Jewett
Nashville, TN
telecommunications software and
consulting
Founded 1977
'79 sales $632 M; '84 sales $5.4 MM

**Temps**
Crystal S. Ettridge
Washington, DC
temporary help
Founded 1981
'82 sales $987 M; '86 sales
$19.4 MM

**T. H. Hill Associates**
Tom H. Hill
Houston, TX
management and engineering
consultants
Founded 1980
'81 sales $754 M; '85 sales
$4.3 MM

**Toucan Business Forms Inc.**
Gerald A. Inglesby
Hyattsville, MD
manufactures business forms
Founded 1980
'80 sales $186 M; '84 sales $1.7 MM

**Transpo Electronics, Inc.**
Frank Oropeza
Orlando, FL
manufactures electronic components
to the auto aftermarket
Founded 1978
'79 sales $895 M; '83 sales $5.0 MM

**T. J. MacDermott Corporation**
T. W. MacDermott
Kingston, NH
management of dining services
Founded 1978
'79 sales $1 MM; '86 sales $10 MM

**Ugly Duckling Rent-A-Car System**
Thomas Spann Duck
Tucson, AZ
used rental-car franchising
Founded 1978
'79 sales $2.5 MM; '86 sales
$63.5 MM

**U S Signs**
Ronald Farmer
Houston, TX
electronic signs
Founded 1980
'80 sales $187 M; '84 sales $2.2 MM

**Vantage Computer Systems, Inc.**
Robert S. Maltempo
Wethersfield, CT
develops software for life insurance
industry
Founded 1970
'79 sales $1.3 MM; '83 sales
$10.6 MM

**Vocational Training Center**
Marshall Lasky
St. Louis, MO
operates vocational schools
Founded 1961
'79 sales $237 M; '86 sales $10 MM

**Waterbeds Plus Incorporated**
Bill Bohlman
Oshkosh, WI
manufactures waterbeds
Founded 1974
'80 sales $1.3 MM; '84 sales $7.9 MM

**Web Technologies**
John Jaran
Oakville, CT
manufactures laminated flexible
products
Founded 1981
'81 sales $184 M; '85 sales
$7.5 MM

**Western Controls**
Robert Turner
North Salt Lake, UT
electrical distributors
Founded 1977
'79 sales $242 M; '83 sales $1.4 MM

**Western Pacific Data Systems**
Neil T. Hadfield
San Diego, CA
industrial software
Founded 1979
'80 sales $445 M; '84 sales $4.4 MM

**Whitebirch Incorporated**
Robert B. Spizzo
Breezy Point, MN
time-shared and campground
development
Founded 1974
'81 sales $1.9 MM; '85 sales $17.8 MM

**Xscribe Corporation**
Robert F. Mawhinney
San Diego, CA
manufactures computer-aided
transcription equipment
Founded 1978
'82 sales $4.1 MM; '86 sales
$29.8 MM

**YWC**
Stephen Kellogg
Monroe, CT
environmental consulting services
Founded 1980
'81 sales $333 M; '85 sales $5.3 MM

**Zenger Miller Incorporated**
John Zenger
Cupertino, CA
market management training
systems
Founded 1977
'79 sales $760 M; '84 sales $3.1 MM

**Zymark**
Frank Zeeny, Burleigh Hutchins
Hopkinton, MA
develops and sells water
chromatography equipment
Founded 1981
'82 sales $163 M; '86 sales $12 MM

# Notes

**Chapter 1**

1. Norris and Ross McWhirter, *The Guinness Book of World Records* (New York: Bantam Books, 1973), pp. 99–103.
2. Christopher M. Byron, *The Fanciest Dive* (New York: W. W. Norton, 1986.
3. "The Class of '82," *Inc.*, December 1987, p. 17.
4. "The Class of '82," p. 17.
5. David L. Birch, *Job Creation in America* (New York: The Free Press, 1987), p. 7.
6. Mack Hanan, *Fast Growth Strategies* (New York: McGraw-Hill, 1987), pp. 11–12.
7. Hanan, *Fast Growth Strategies*, p. 32.
8. "Marketing Strategies for Maximum Growth," *Direct Marketing*, May 1987, pp. 32–39.
9. Tom Peters, Direct Marketing Association Annual Convention, Las Vegas, Nevada, October 1985.
10. Tom Peters and Robert Waterman, *In Search of Excellence* (New York: Harper & Row, 1982), pp. 13, 109.
11. Laurence Shames, *The Big Time* (New York: New American Library Books, 1986), p. 33.
12. Hanan, *Fast Growth Strategies*, p. 12.

## NOTES

13. Shames, *The Big Time*, p. 122.
14. Shames, *The Big Time*, p. 123.
15. Birch, *Job Creation*, p. 4.
16. "Direct Line," The DMA, New York, NY, December 1987, vol. 4, no. 12 (December 1987), p. 4.
17. Hanan, *Fast Growth Strategies*, p. 12.
18. M. R. Montgomery, *In Search of L. L. Bean* (New York: New American Library, 1984), p. 17.
19. Montgomery, *L. L. Bean*, p. 21.
20. Montgomery, *L. L. Bean*, p. 32.
21. Montgomery, *L. L. Bean*, p. 171.
22. Montgomery, *L. L. Bean*, p. 184.
23. Montgomery, *L. L. Bean*, p. 213.
24. Montgomery, *L. L. Bean*, p. 219.

**Chapter 2**

1. Robert Dalzell, *The Enterprising Elite* (Cambridge, MA: Harvard University Press, 1987), jacket.
2. Mack Hanan, *Fast Growth Strategies* (New York: McGraw-Hill, 1987), p. 4.
3. Earl Nightingale, *What Might Have Been* (Nightingale and Conant, audio cassette).
4. M. John Storey and Donald R. Dubendorf, *The Insider Buyout* (Pownal, VT: Storey Communications, 1985), p. 21.
5. Kevin Farrell, "There's No Stopping Now," *Venture*, February 1985, as quoted in Storey and Dubendorf, *The Insider Buyout*, p. 22.
6. Storey and Dubendorf, *The Insider Buyout*, pp. 22–23.
7. Hanan, *Fast Growth Strategies*, p. 143.
8. Hanan, *Fast Growth Strategies*, p. 143.
9. Hanan, *Fast Growth Strategies*, p. 3.
10. Stanford University Business School, Conference on Entrepreneurship, 1985, Palo Alto, California.
11. A. David Silver, *The Entrepreneurial Life* (New York: John Wiley & Sons, 1986), pp. 37, 211.

12. Storey and Dubendorf, *The Insider Buyout*, pp. 19–21.

13. William A. Delaney, *How to Run a Growing Company* (New York: AMACOM, 1981), p. 46.

14. Delaney, *A Growing Company*, p. 7.

15. Birch, p. 194.

16. David L. Birch, *Job Creation in America* (New York: The Free Press, 1987), p. 194.

17. Richard Considine, telephone interview, February 1988.

18. Delaney, *A Growing Company*, p. 45.

19. Steven C. Brandt, *Entrepreneuring: The Ten Commandments for Building a Growth Company* (New York: New American Library, 1982), p. 88.

20. Ray Kroc, *Grinding It Out* (New York: St. Martin's Press, 1977), p. 71.

21. Kroc, *Grinding It Out*, p. 59.

22. Birch, *Job Creation*, p. 31.

23. Paul Hawken, *Growing a Business* (New York: Simon and Schuster, 1987), p. 21.

24. Birch, *Job Creation*, p. 31.

25. Duane Newcomb, *Fortune Building Secrets of the Rich* (West Nyack, NY: Parker Publishing, 1983), pp. 32–33.

26. Newcomb, *Fortune Building Secrets*, p. 33.

27. Newcomb, *Fortune Building Secrets*, p. 33.

28. Newcomb, *Fortune Building Secrets*, p. 33.

29. Birch, *Job Creation*, p. 67.

30. Birch, *Job Creation*, p. 67.

31. William A. Delaney, *How to Run a Growing Company* (New York: AMACOM, 1981), p. 16.

32. Delaney, *A Growing Company*, p. 21.

33. Brandt, *Entrepreneuring*, p. 16.

34. Brandt, *Entrepreneuring*, p. 20.

35. Hawken, *Growing A Business*, p. 39.

36. Delaney, *A Growing Company*, p. 107.

37. Delaney, *A Growing Company*, p. 111.

38. Brandt, *Entrepreneuring*, p. 86.

39. Brandt, *Entrepreneuring*, p. 87.

## NOTES

40. Brandt, *Entrepreneuring*, p. 87.
41. Birch, *Job Creation*, p. 195.


**Chapter 3**

1. James R. Cook, *The Start-Up Entrepreneur: How You Can Succeed in Building Your Own Company into a Major Enterprise Starting From Scratch* (New York: Harper & Row, 1986), p. 116.
2. Jim Kobs, "Marketing Strategies for Growth," *Direct Marketing*, May 1987, p. 32.
3. Eliot Janeway, review of Robert Boyden Lamb's "Running American Business. Top CEO's Rethink Their Major Decisions," *Wall Street Journal*, June 1, 1987, p. 10.
4. Curtis Hartman, "The *Inc.* 500 Honor Roll," *Inc.*, December 1986, p. 91.
5. *Time*, August 17, 1987, p. 51.
6. *Time*, p. 51.
7. Jim Kobs, "Marketing Strategies for Growth," *Direct Marketing*, May 1987, p. 37.
8. "Home Shopping Network Annual Report," 1986.
9. "HSN Report," p. 3.
10. "HSN Report," p. 4.
11. David Birch, *Job Creation in America* (New York: The Free Press, 1987), pp. 65, 69.
12. Ray Kroc, *Grinding It Out* (New York: St. Martin's Press, 1977), p. 2.
13. Kroc, *Grinding It Out*, p. 178.
14. Horace Sutton, "Ex-Patriots with British Appetites," *The Transcript*, March 19, 1988, p. 7.
15. Stephen P. Galante, "Small Business Consultants Cash in on Quest to Create Next McDonalds," *Wall Street Journal*, June 1, 1987, p. 25.
16. Joe Joggerst, "Selling with the Wind," *Review*, October 1987, p. 83.
17. Joggerst, "Selling," p. 81.
18. M. R. Montgomery, *In Search of L. L. Bean* (New York: New American Library Books, 1984), p. 176.
19. Montgomery, *L. L. Bean*, p. 223.

20. Montgomery, *L. L. Bean*, p. 188.

21. Montgomery, *L. L. Bean*, p. 23.

22. Montgomery, *L. L. Bean*, p. 190.

23. Montgomery, *L. L. Bean*, p. 197.

24. Paul Hawken, *Growing a Business* (New York: Simon and Schuster, 1987), p. 124.

25. Hawken, *Growing a Business*, p. 124.

26. Duane Newcomb, *Fortune Building Secrets of the Rich* (West Nyack, NY: Parker Publishing, 1983), p. 114.

**Chapter 4**

1. James R. Cook, *The Start-Up Entrepreneur: How You Can Succeed in Building Your Own Company into a Major Enterprise Starting from Scratch* (New York: Harper & Row, 1986), p. 202.

2. Steven C. Brandt, *Entrepreneuring: The Ten Commandments for Building a Growth Company* (New York: New American Library Books, 1982), p. 202.

3. Robert R. Owen, Daniel S. Garner, and Dennis S. Bunder, *The Arthur Young Guide to Financing for Growth* (New York: John Wiley & Sons, 1986), p. 9.

4. M. John Storey and Donald R. Dubendorf, *The Insider Buyout* (Pownal, VT: Storey Communications, 1985), pp. 194–195.

5. Owen, Garner, and Bunder, *Financing for Growth*, p. vi.

6. Kevin Farrell, "There's No Stopping Now," *Venture*, February 1985, p. 42.

7. Farrell, "No Stopping," p. 42.

8. Farrell, "No Stopping," p. 42.

9. David Birch, *Job Creation in America* (New York: The Free Press, 1987), pp. 78–79.

10. Birch, *Job Creation*, pp. 78–79.

11. George Kozmetsky, Michael D. Gill, Jr., and Raymond W. Smilor, *Financing and Managing Fast Growth Companies: The Venture Capital Process* (Lexington, MA: D. C. Heath, 1985), p. 52.

12. Storey and Dubendorf, *The Insider Buyout*, p. 134.

13. Birch, *Job Creation*, p. 79.

## NOTES

14. Duane Newcomb, *Fortune Building Secrets of the Rich* (West Nyack, NY: Parker, 1983), p. 73.

15. Ray Kroc, *Grinding It Out* (New York: St. Martin's Press, 1977), p. 106.

16. Paul Hawken, *Growing a Business* (New York: Simon and Schuster, 1987), p. 111.

17. Kroc, *Grinding It Out*, p. 108.

18. Kroc, *Grinding It Out*, p. 109.

19. Hawken, *Growing a Business*, p. 137.

20. Owen, Garner, and Bender, *Financing for Growth*, p. 90.

21. Owen, Garner, and Bender, *Financing for Growth*, p. 90.

22. Storey and Dubendorf, *The Insider Buyout*, p. 195.

23. Low Price Stock Survey Fact Sheet, Hammond, IN: Dow Theory Forecast, 1987.

24. Kroc, *Grinding It Out*, p. 87.

25. Claudia H. Deutsch, "Overstuffed Fast Food Firms," *Berkshire Eagle* (Pittsfield, MA), March 20, 1988, p. D6.

26. Owen, Garner, and Bender, *Financing for Growth*, p. 188.

27. Montgomery Garrett, "Franchises on a Roll," *Venture*, March 1988, pp. 39–40.

28. M. R. Montgomery, *In Search of L. L. Bean* (New York: New American Library Books, 1984), p. 181.

29. Montgomery, *L. L. Bean*, p. 178.

30. *Berkshire Eagle* (Pittsfield, MA), February 20, 1988, p. C3.

31. *Berkshire Eagle*, February 20, 1988, p. C3.

### Chapter 5

1. David Birch, *Job Creation in America* (New York: The Free Press, 1987), pp. 141–142.

2. "The Truth About Startups," *Inc.*, January 1988, p. 14.

3. Mack Hanan, *Fast Growth Strategies* (New York: McGraw-Hill, 1987), p. 17.

4. Curtis Hartman, "The *Inc.* 500 Honor Roll," *Inc.*, December 1986, p. 91.

5. Hanan, *Fast Growth Strategies*, p. 10.

6. James R. Cook, *The Start-Up Entrepreneur: How You Can Succeed in Building Your Own Company into a Major Enterprise Starting from Scratch* (New York: Harper & Row, 1986), p. 82.

7. Cook, *The Start-Up Entrepreneur*, p. 6.

8. Paul Hawken, *Growing a Business* (New York: Simon and Schuster, 1987), p. 178.

9. Steven C. Brandt, *Entrepreneuring: The Ten Commandments for Building a Growth Company* (New York: New American Library Books, 1982), p. xii.

10. Birch, *Job Creation*, p. 29.

11. As quoted by Frederick W. Smith, "In the Age of Customer Service, Distribution Is Marketing Too," from speech to 35th Annual Marketing Conference of the Conference Board, 1987. Reprinted in *Federal Express* Magazine.

12. Duane Newcomb, *Fortune Building Secrets of the Rich* (West Nyack, NY: Parker, 1983), p. 77.

13. Ray Kroc, *Grinding It Out* (New York: St. Martin's Press, 1977), p. 10.

14. Kroc, *Grinding It Out*, p. 77.

15. Lucy Doggett Russell, "Original Copy Duplicates Success," *Entrepreneur*, April 1987, pp. 55–58.

16. Hawken, *Growing a Business*, p. 57.

17. Hawken, *Growing a Business*, p. 125.

18. Newcomb, *Fortune Building Secrets*, p. 162.

19. Al Cunniff, "The Rise of Group Think," *Warfield's*, March 1987, p. 108.

20. M. R. Montgomery, *In Search of L. L. Bean* (New York: American Library Books, 1984), p. 18.

21. Alex Taylor, III, "Why the Bounce at Rubbermaid?" *Fortune*, April 13, 1987, p. 7.

22. Taylor, "Rubbermaid," p. 77.

23. Taylor, "Rubbermaid," p. 77.

24. *Cleveland Plain Dealer*, September 29, 1987, p. 7D.

25. *Plain Dealer*, September 29, 1987, p. 7D.

**Chapter 6**

1. David Birch, *Job Creation in America* (New York: The Free Press, 1987), p. 1.

## NOTES

2. Birch, *Job Creation,* p. 33.

3. Paul Hawken, *Growing a Business* (New York: Simon and Schuster, 1987), p. 13.

4. Robert Levering, Milton Moskowitz, and Michael Katz, *The 100 Best Companies to Work For in America* (New York: NAL Penguin Books, 1984), p. 8.

5. Levering, Moskowitz, and Katz, *The 100 Best Companies,* p. 452.

6. Levering, Moskowitz, and Katz, *The 100 Best Companies,* pp. 215–216.

7. Levering, Moskowitz, and Katz, *The 100 Best Companies,* p. 383.

8. M. John Storey and Donald R. Dubendorf, *The Insider Buyout* (Pownal, VT: Storey Communications, 1985), p. 201.

9. Levering, Moskowitz, and Katz, *The 100 Best Companies,* p. 385.

10. Levering, Moskowitz, and Katz, *The 100 Best Companies,* p. 386.

11. Storey and Dubendorf, *The Insider Buyout,* p. 218.

12. Hawken, *Growing a Business,* p. 203.

13. Levering, Moskowitz, and Katz, *The 100 Best Companies,* pp. 99–100.

14. Levering, Moskowitz, and Katz, *The 100 Best Companies,* p. 101.

15. Levering, Moskowitz, and Katz, *The 100 Best Companies,* p. 428.

16. Levering, Moskowitz, and Katz, *The 100 Best Companies,* p. 15.

17. Levering, Moskowitz, and Katz, *The 100 Best Companies,* p. 15.

18. Joan M. O'Connell, "Dreyer's: Scooping Out a Profitable Niche," *Business Week,* May 27, 1986. Reprinted by McGraw-Hill.

19. Levering, Moskowitz, and Katz, *The 100 Best Companies,* p. 140.

20. Levering, Moskowitz, and Katz, *The 100 Best Companies,* p. 42.

21. Levering, Moskowitz, and Katz, *The 100 Best Companies,* p. 47.

22. Levering, Moskowitz, and Katz, *The 100 Best Companies,* p. 148.

23. Levering, Moskowitz, and Katz, *The 100 Best Companies,* p. 266.

24. Levering, Moskowitz, and Katz, *The 100 Best Companies,* p. 134.

25. Sharon Nelton, *In Love and in Business* (New York: John Wiley & Sons, 1986), p. 244.

26. Levering, Moskowitz, and Katz, *The 100 Best Companies,* p. 16.

27. Levering, Moskowitz, and Katz, *The Best Companies,* p. 308.

28. Levering, Moskowitz, and Katz, *The 100 Best Companies,* p. 246.

29. Levering, Moskowitz, and Katz, *The 100 Best Companies,* p. 356.

30. Levering, Moskowitz, and Katz, *The 100 Best Companies,* pp. 259–260.

31. Levering, Moskowitz, and Katz, *The 100 Best Companies*, p. 374.

32. William H. Younger, Jr., "The Management Team," speech at The Challenge of Growth, the 4th annual Conference on Entrepreneurship, May 18, 1985. Stanford Center for Entrepreneurship, Stanford, CA.

33. Levering, Moskowitz, and Katz, *The 100 Best Companies*, p. 162.

34. Levering, Moskowitz, and Katz, *The 100 Best Companies*, p. 161.

35. Levering, Moskowitz, and Katz, *The 100 Best Companies*, p. 163.

**Chapter 7**

1. Milind M. Lele, *The Customer Is Key* (New York: John Wiley & Sons, 1987), p. 70.

2. Michael LeBoeuf, *How to Win Customers and Keep Them for Life* (New York: G. P. Putnam's Sons, 1987), p. 51.

3. LeBoeuf, *How to Win Customers*, p. 156.

4. James R. Cook, *The Start-Up Entrepreneur* (New York: Harper & Row, 1986), p. 142.

5. Paul Hawken, *Growing a Business* (New York: Simon and Schuster, 1987), p. 177.

6. Philip B. Crosby, *Quality Is Free* (New York: McGraw-Hill, 1979), as quoted by Joseph M. Queenan, "Quality is Becoming Job One," *Venture*, March 1988, p. 89.

7. Tom Peters and Robert Waterman, *In Search of Excellence* (New York: Harper & Row, 1982), p. 14.

8. Peters and Waterman, *In Search of Excellence*, p. 173.

9. Peters and Waterman, *In Search of Excellence*, p. 191.

10. LeBoeuf, *How to Win Customers*, p. 163.

11. Lele, *The Customer Is Key*, p. 25.

12. Peters and Waterman, *In Search of Excellence*, p. 158.

13. Peters and Waterman, *In Search of Excellence*, p. 158.

14. Peters and Waterman, *In Search of Excellence*, p. 158.

15. Lele, *The Customer Is Key*, p. 181.

16. Constance Jones and the Philip Lief Group, *The 200 Best Franchises to Buy* (New York: Bantam Books, 1987), p. 313.

## NOTES

17. Peters and Waterman, *In Search of Excellence*, p. 185.

18. John Schneider, "Direct to the Consumer," *Nation's Business*, June 1985, p. 29.

19. Sharon Morgan, "New Designs for Maximum Mobility," *American Way*, June 1985, p. 54.

20. Joseph M. Queenan, "Quality Is Becoming Job 1," *Venture*, March 1988, p. 88.

21. Lele, *The Customer Is Key*, p. 98.

22. Robert Waterman, *The Renewal Factor* (New York: Bantam Books, 1987), p. 139.

23. Stanley J. Fenvessy, *Keep Your Customers (and Keep Them Happy)* (Homewood, IL: Dow Jones-Irwin, 1976), p. 2.

24. Fenvessy, *Keep Your Customers*, p. 2.

25. Fenvessy, *Keep Your Customers*, p. 44.

26. Fenvessy, *Keep Your Customers*, pp. 122–123.

### Chapter 8

1. Paul Hawken, *Growing a Business* (New York: Simon and Schuster, 1987), p. 154.

2. Steven C. Brandt, *Entrepreneuring: The Ten Commandments for Building a Growth Company* (New York: New American Library Books, 1982), p. 14.

3. *Herbalgram Newsletter*, Herb Research Foundation and theAmerican Herbal Products Association #14, Fall 1987, p. 1, Austin, TX.

4. Steven C. Brandt, *Entrepreneuring in Established Companies* (New York: New American Library Books, 1986), p. 313.

### Chapter 9

1. Paul Hawken, *Growing a Business* (New York: Simon and Schuster, 1987), p. 93.

2. William A. Delaney, *How to Run a Growing Company* (New York: AMACOM, 1981), p. 32.

3. Charles Kyd, "How Fast Is Too Fast?" *Inc.* (December 1986), p. 123.

4. Lawrence Shames, *The Big Time: The Harvard Business School's Most Successful Class and How It Shaped America* (New York: New American Library Books, 1986), p. 27.

5. Eileen Davis, ed., "Fatjo's Fitness Chain Snaps," *Venture*, March 1988, p. 96.

6. "Fatjo's," p. 96.

7. Joel Kotkin, "What I Do in Private Is My Own Business," *Inc.*, November 1986, p. 68.

8. Kotkin, "What I Do," p. 66.

9. Kotkin, "What I Do," p. 67.

10. Kotkin, "What I Do," p. 70.

11. Tom Richmond, "What I Do In Public Isn't So Bad Either," *Inc.*, November 1986, p. 80.

12. *New England Annual Report 1988*, New England Business, Yankee Publishing, Dublin, NH, p. 20VT.

13. *New England Report*, p. 20VT.

14. Kotkin, "What I Do," p. 79.

15. Kotkin, "What I Do," p. 70.

16. Robert R. Owen, Daniel S. Garner, Dennis S. Bunder, *The Arthur Young Guide to Financing for Growth* (New York: John Wiley & Sons, 1986), pp. 50, 51.

17. Lucien Rhodes, "The Dream Makers," *Inc.*, November 1987, p. 116.

18. Lisa McGurrin, "Down from the High and Back from the Nitty Gritty," *New England Business*, March 7, 1988, p. 84.

19. Delaney, *How to Run*, p. 117.

20. James R. Cook, *The Start-Up Entrepreneur: How You Can Suceed in Building Your Own Company into a Major Enterprise Starting From Scratch* (New York: Harper & Row, 1986), p. 65.

21. Delaney, *How to Run*, p. 3.

22. Cook, *The Start-Up Entrepreneur*, p. 237.

23. Cook, *The Start-Up Entrepreneur*, p. 223.

24. Subrata N. Chakarzarty, "The Growing Gets Tougher," *Forbes*, June 15, 1987, p. 68.

25. Flemming Meeks, "Fish or Cut Bait," *Forbes*, June 15, 1987, p. 68.

26. Meeks, "Fish," p. 60.

27. Meeks, "Fish," p. 60.

28. Hawken, *Growing a Business*, p. 89.

1. David Birch, *Job Creation in America* (New York: The Free Press, 1987), p. 3.

2. George Gilder, *The Spirit of Enterprise* (New York: Simon and Schuster, 1984), p. 258.

3. Alfred P. Sloan, *My Years With General Motors* (New York: Doubleday, 1964), quoted in Delaney, *How to Run*, p. 74.

4. John Naisbitt and Patricia Aburdene, *Re-inventing the Corporation* (New York: Warner Books, 1985), p. 44.

5. Naisbitt and Aburdene, *Re-inventing*, p. 12.

6. Naisbitt and Aburdene, *Re-inventing*, p. 12.

7. Paul Hawken, *Growing a Business* (New York: Simon and Schuster, 1987), p. 95.

8. Gilder, *The Spirit of Enterprise*, p. 255.

9. Robert Levering, Milton Moskowitz, and Michael Katz, *The 100 Best Companies to Work for in America* (New York: NAL Penguin Books, 1984), p. xvi.

10. Curtis Hartman and Steve Perlstein, "Joy of Working," Hay Associates–*Inc.* Study, November 1987, pp. 61–71.

11. Hay Associates—*Inc.* Study.

12. Philip B. Crosby, *Quality Is Free* (New York: McGraw-Hill, 1979), p. 1.

13. Levering, Moskowitz, and Katz, *The 100 Best Companies*, p. 290.

14. "Be Nice to Customers," Labor Letter, *Wall Street Journal*, March 8, 1988, p. 1.

15. "Be Nice to Customers," p. 1.

16. Gilder, *The Spirit of Enterprise*, p. 52.

17. A. David Silver, *The Entrepreneurial Life* (New York: John Wiley & Sons, 1986), p. 232.

18. *Venture*, February 1988, p. 21.

19. Naisbitt and Aburdene, *Re-inventing the Corporation*, p. 67.

20. Gilder, *The Spirit of Enterprise*, p. 23.

21. Naisbitt and Aburdene, *Re-inventing the Corporation*, p. 67.

22. "Kroc Sends Needy School $235K," *Berkshire Eagle* (Pittsfield, MA), February 12, 1988, p. 6.

23. Michael LeBoeuf, *How to Win Customers and Keep Them for Life* (New York: G. P. Putnam's Sons, 1987), p. 10.

24. James R. Cook, *The Start-Up Entrepreneur* (New York: Harper & Row, 1986), p. 230.

25. J. Lang Davison, "The CML Group Discovers Some Expensive Prices of Decentralization," *New England Business*, November 19, 1984, p. 64.

26. Davison, "CML Group," p. 65.

27. *New England Business*, March 21, 1988, p. 76.

28. Hawken, *Growing a Business*, p. 28.

29. Peter Waldman, "Esprit's Fortunes Sag as Couple at the Helm Battle over Its Image," *Wall Street Journal*, March 16, 1988, p. 1.

30. Robert B. Streeter, "Beware of Patten Corporation," *Berkshire Eagle*, February 12, 1988, p. 9.

31. Gilder, *The Spirit of Enterprise*, p. 50.

32. Gilder, *The Spirit of Enterprise*, p. 47.

# Bibliography

Birch, David. *Job Creation in America: How Our Smallest Companies Put the Most People to Work*. New York: The Free Press, 1987.

Brandt, Steven C. *Entrepreneuring: The Ten Commandments for Building a Growth Company*. New York: New American Library Books, 1982.

———. *Entrepreneuring in Established Companies*. New York: New American Library, 1986.

Byron, Christopher. *The Fanciest Dive*. New York: W. W. Norton, 1986.

Cook, James R. *The Start-Up Entrepreneur: How You Can Succeed in Building Your Own Company into a Major Enterprise Starting from Scratch*. New York: Harper & Row, 1986.

Crosby, Philip B. *Quality Is Free*. New York: McGraw-Hill, 1979.

Dalzell, Robert F., Jr. *Enterprising Elite: The Boston Associates and the World They Made*. Cambridge, MA: Harvard University Press, 1987.

Delaney, William A. *How to Run a Growing Company*. New York: AMACOM, 1981.

Dubendorf, Donald R., and Storey, M. John. *The Insider Buyout*. Pownal, VT: Storey Communications, 1985.

Fenvessy, Stanley J. *Keep Your Customers (and Keep Them Happy)*. Homewood, IL: Dow Jones-Irwin, 1976.

Gilder, George. *The Spirit of Enterprise*. New York: Simon and Schuster, 1984.

Hanan, Mack. *Fast-Growth Strategies: How to Maximize Profits from Start-up Through Maturity*. New York: McGraw-Hill, 1987.

**253**

# BIBLIOGRAPHY

Hawken, Paul. *Growing a Business*. New York: Simon and Schuster, 1987.

Hickman, Craig R., and Silva, Michael A. *The Future 500*. New York: New American Library Books, 1987.

Kozmetsky, George, Gill, Michael D., Jr., and Smilor, Raymond W. *Financing and Managing Fast-Growth Companies: The Venture Capital Process*. Lexington, MA: D. C. Heath, 1985.

Kroc, Ray. *Grinding It Out: The Making of McDonald's*. New York: St. Martin's Press, 1977.

LeBoeuf, Michael. *How to Win Customers and Keep Them for Life*. New York: G. P. Putnam's Sons, 1987.

Lele, Milind M. *The Customer Is Key*. New York: John Wiley & Sons, 1987.

Levering, Robert, Moskowitz, Milton, and Katz, Michael. *The 100 Best Companies to Work for in America*. New York: New American Library Books, 1984.

McWhirter, Norris, and McWhirter, Ross. *Guinness Book of World Records*. New York: Bantam Books, 1973.

Montgomery, M. R. *In Search of L. L. Bean*. New York: New American Library Books, 1984.

Naisbitt, John, and Aburdene, Patricia. *Re-inventing the Corporation*. New York: Warner Books, 1985.

Nelton, Sharon. *In Love and in Business: How Entrepreneurial Couples Are Changing the Rules of Business and Marriage*. New York: John Wiley & Sons, 1986.

Newcomb, Duane. *Fortune-Building Secrets of the Rich*. West Nyack, NY: Parker, 1983.

Owen, Robert R., Garner, Daniel, R., and Bunder, Dennis S. *The Arthur Young Guide to Financing for Growth: Ten Alternatives for Raising Capital*. New York: John Wiley & Sons, 1986.

Peters, Thomas J., and Waterman, Robert H., Jr. *In Search of Excellence: Lessons from America's Best-Run Companies*. New York: Harper & Row, 1982.

Peters, Tom, and Austin, Nancy. *A Passion for Excellence: The Leadership Difference*. New York: Random House, 1985.

Shames, Laurence. *The Big Time: The Harvard Business School's Most Successful Class and How It Shaped America*. New York: New American Library Books, 1986.

Silver, A. David. *The Entrepreneurial Life*. New York: John Wiley & Sons, 1986.

Sobel, Robert, and Sicilia, David B. *The Entrepreneurs: An American Adventure*. Boston, MA: Houghton Mifflin, 1986.

Storey, M. John. *Starting Your Own Business No Money Down*. New York: John Wiley & Sons, 1987.

Thurow, Lester C. *The Zero-Sum Society: Distribution and the Possibilities for Economic Change*. New York: Basic Books, 1980.

Townsend, Robert. *Up the Organization: How to Stop the Corporation from Stifling People and Strangling Profits*. Greenwich, CT: Fawcett Publications, 1970.

Waterman, Robert H., Jr. *The Renewal Factor: How the Best Get and Keep the Competitive Edge*. New York: Bantam Books, 1987.

# Index

**257**

## INDEX

## INDEX

# INDEX

## INDEX

## INDEX